D0226188

Josefina Niggli, Mexican American Writer

Josefina Niggli,
Mexican American Writer

A CRITICAL BIOGRAPHY

Elizabeth Coonrod Martínez

University of New Mexico Press ← Albuquerque

© 2007 by the University of New Mexico Press
All rights reserved. Published 2007
Printed in the United States of America

12 11 10 09 08 07   1 2 3 4 5 6 7

Library of Congress Cataloging-in-Publication Data

Martínez, Elizabeth Coonrod.
Josefina Niggli, Mexican American writer : a critical biography /
Elizabeth Coonrod Martínez.
     p. cm.
Includes bibliographical references and index.
ISBN 978-0-8263-4272-0 (pbk. : alk. paper)
1. Niggli, Josephina, 1910–1983 2. Mexican American authors—
20th century—Biography. 3. Mexican Americans in literature.
I. Title.
PS3527.I66Z78 2007
818'.5409—dc22
[B]
          2007015081

Design and composition: Melissa Tandysh

for my adored nephew, Bill Coonrod
and for Bill Fisher, a partner on the Niggli trail

⤚

Contents

Acknowledgments

Along the journey of creating a book, many people help make it possible; in the case of this book a major contributor of information was Bill Fisher of San Antonio, whose passion and dedication to uncovering traces of Josefina's journey through life were constant and relentless. We shared the marvelous experience of visiting Josefina's resting place for the first time on her birthday in 2005, only realizing later the significance of that date. She had likely summoned us, and has guided the creation of her biography.

Thanks also to John Igo in San Antonio for sharing his memories; to Paula Shirley in South Carolina, who graciously provided copies of her audiotapes from her interview with Josefina in 1980; and to Bryce Milligan for introducing me to Bill and to John. Librarians and archivists who provided essential information and access to documents include: George Frizzell in the Hunter Library at Western Carolina University; Mendell D. Morgan, Dean of Library Services, and Basil Aivaliotis, Head of Special Collections, at the Mabee Library at the University of the Incarnate Word in San Antonio; Hermann Trojanowski, historical archives at UNC–Greensboro; Jessica Tyree, historical archives at UNC–Chapel Hill; and Kathleen Ketterman at the UNC Press manuscripts office.

A special thanks to Dr. Judy Maloof at UNM for reviewing the initial manuscript, and to MFM for helping in the exploration of western North Carolina in 2004. Thanks from the bottom of my heart to Beth Hadas, for believing in this book project and the need to bring greater critical attention to a marvelous trailblazer and writer.

The following are acknowledged for their kind and gracious permission to reproduce Josefina Niggli's plays, narratives, and photographs:

Western Carolina University Foundation (to whom Niggli bequeathed copyright permission for republication of all published works and unpublished manuscripts).

Southern Historical Collection, Southern Folklife Collection, and University Archives Manuscripts Department at the University of North Carolina at Chapel Hill, Wilson Library, Chapel Hill, North Carolina, for *Cry of Dolores.*

The University of Texas Institute of Texan Cultures at San Antonio, for two photographs taken in San Antonio.

The Niggli collection in Special Collections, the Mabee Library at the University of the Incarnate Word in San Antonio, for the "Dream" excerpts.

William Fisher of San Antonio, for photographs reproduced from a Niggli family scrapbook.

John Igo, for the photo of Josefina with her dogs, from a Christmas card.

CHAPTER ONE

Introduction and Early Life

1910–1935

When I was a young kid, starting out as a writer, I had a shining goal. I was going to present Mexico and the Mexicans as they had never before been presented. Well, I did. I made the big time. I even made M.G.M. and Book of the Month. You see, I reached my goal and passed it.

—Josefina Niggli

In the early twentieth century, women artists and intellectuals who wished to create and publish had to swim against the stream. Many young women continued traditionally defined roles, while the more daring intrepidly followed their dreams and embarked on careers, carving a new path for women. They attended college and traveled alone, weaving their way between the fine-line distinctions of scandalous and respectable. The risks they took inspired future generations and rendered such notable figures and trailblazers as photographer Margaret Bourke-White, novelist Pearl Buck, and singer Josephine Baker.

1

Like them, Josefina María Niggli rose to acclaim in an era when women were neither encouraged to pursue careers nor greatly distinguished. But Niggli is an exception; she was saluted as a world-class playwright in the 1930s, and as a best-selling novelist in the 1940s. And yet, by the late twentieth century, she had been mostly forgotten. Like other great women trailblazers, Niggli was an independent woman ahead of her time. Her passion and life's work was to reveal Mexico, to create understanding of its culture through her stories. Niggli felt that *Mexican* history and its people were greatly misunderstood and even dismissed by Americans. Therefore, she decided to create her stories and plays in English, to inform and educate the U.S. public. Her primary artistic goal was to create a good *story*, with interesting and complex characters. But when publishers told her it had to include an American (U.S.) hero, with Mexicans only as villains, Niggli would not relent. "They would say, 'You don't really think anyone will read this, do you?' [she stated in 1980], but I said, if it's a really good story, I couldn't see why people wouldn't read that. I figured that if I sat down and kept writing until people were aware that there was this beautiful world south of the border, people would see there was something in the world besides their own [experience]. And, it happened. I think that it was when I started doing my thing that the door opened for [what is now called] Chicano literature" (Shirley 1980).

With the exception of a few short-story writers whose work did not see major release, Niggli is the only writer of the 1930s and 1940s who revealed Mexican life and culture from an insider's point of view, in English, and of high creative quality. She exposed the roots of Mexican culture, its myths and lore, and the lives of the *campesinos* or peasants. She also documented, for the first time in creative works in English, the changes brought on by the Mexican Revolution, from feminist ideals to the *mestizo*'s (person of mixed blood) rise in Mexican society.

From the child with a keen eye for observation in her native Monterrey, to the teenager transplanted to San Antonio, Texas, who was asked to write a play for her church theater, to the award-winning playwright and novelist, Hollywood screenwriter, theater director, and professor, Niggli relentlessly pursued her life's passion. In the process she lived a remarkable life and left behind a literary and cultural treasure, one of few women achieving this during the first half of the twentieth century.

Unlike the aforementioned women artists, Niggli grew up in a country remaking itself following the volatile political struggles of the Mexican Revolution. Her childhood experience was not that of Mexico City, which lured artists and intellectuals by the 1920s, but instead that of the Monterrey valley in northern Mexico, a land of weather extremes and breathtaking natural wonders, a land settled by immigrants whose descendants remain fiercely independent. Even before Texas launched its bid for independence from the relatively new country of Mexico in the early nineteenth century, the region to its south—now the states of Coahuila and Nuevo León—had already made moves in that direction. Once Mexico finally—after three centuries of colonial rule—obtained freedom in 1821 from Spain, the "Spanish" regions far from its capital did not feel protected by centralist politics conducted several weeks' journey away in Mexico City. Like those in other far-reaching corners of the former colony, they often made decisions on their own. Nuevo León's capital of Monterrey had more in common with the cities of Saltillo to the east and San Antonio (Texas) to the north, which together formed a triangle of trade and commerce during the late nineteenth century. With the ushering in of a new century, the Mexican Revolution was launched from northern states, and Monterrey became a hub of development and enterprise following this significant civil war. Niggli grew up in this environment.

She is of the Mexican literary generation of Mariano Azuela, Martín Luis Guzmán, Nellie Campobello, and Alfonso Reyes (he was born in Monterrey like her), but Niggli completed her formal education in the United States and embarked on a writing career in English. In terms of her literary track record, Niggli has much in common with Laura Esquivel (two generations later), whose bestseller *Malinche: A Novel* was well acclaimed, translated into several languages, and made into a film that attracted much attention. Second novels in each case were totally different from the first, with a complicated content that was not readily understood, and third novels for each received even less attention, despite the fact Niggli's was on the iconic figure of the Virgin of Guadalupe. The depiction of female cultural icons is another aspect connecting Niggli and Esquivel in terms of their later work. Esquivel's most recent novel is on the infamous Mexican Malinche figure.[1] The region of Niggli's upbringing, Northern Mexico, is connected to the rise of Mexican American or Chicano literature in the United States. Several members of the early political movement, originating from the states of Chihuahua, Sonora, and Coahuila, cited their indigenous Yaqui or Tarahumara background in their writings. Due to their great distance from the colonial seat in Mexico City, Northern Mexico and the U.S. Southwest were for centuries a connected entity. In fact, they are still connected in music: *Tejano* music in Texas, and Mexican *norteño* rhythms are related. In the literary world, however, little connection has been drawn between the characteristics of northern Mexico life and that of the U.S. Southwest.

Raymund Paredes first brought attention to Niggli's works in 1972, in an anthology published with Américo Paredes titled *Mexican-American Authors*, which included one of Niggli's plays and three chapters from her first novel. He discussed her work in a significant first essay on "The Evolution of Chicano Literature," published in the journal for the study of Multi-Ethnic Literature of the U.S. (MELUS) in 1978. He referenced Niggli again in 1980, in an article on the surfacing of a Mexican American literature, published in the *Los Angeles Times*. That same year, a book that was a first in highlighting the ethnic perspective in creative works by women, *The Third Woman: Minority Women Writers of the United States*, included Niggli in its section on Chicano writers. Niggli was interviewed that year for an extensive biographical essay published in 1981 in the *Dictionary of Literary Biography Yearbook* (authored by Paula Shirley). Critical studies since then have not been as extensive; however, contemporary Latino critics consider Niggli a landmark writer of the early twentieth century for evoking the sense of a hyphenated existence. In 1985 (two years after her death) she was lauded for her depiction of women's roles by two women scholars assessing Niggli's intrepid and successful efforts to reveal Mexican culture, as a native who innately understood Mexican life and philosophy. In 1987 Gloria Anzaldúa describes her writing as that of a consciousness caught between borders. In 1995, Tey Diana Rebolledo cites Niggli's frequent themes of alienation, "of being an outsider in Mexican as well as American culture. . . . Many of her characters are of mixed heritage, and struggle with issues that arise from this heritage, [of] being a Mestizo in racially conscious societies" (25). Rebolledo cites from Gloria Treviño's study (1985 dissertation) on three early twentieth-century Chicana or Mexican American women writers who created "a literary tradition in English [while] also consciously pursuing the creation of a 'female space' that 'articulated the concerns particular to the minority woman'" (24).

Niggli's 1936 play *Soldadera*—which features a sweet-natured, illiterate Adelita, who becomes a valiant soldier by her act of courage and sacrifice—has received the greatest critical attention. Here Niggli defines class struggle (an issue that would permeate her works) as not only the main conflict of the Mexican Revolution but also an internal struggle over gender differences, which accounts for its interest among scholars. Alicia Arrizón (1998) states that "Niggli uses the drama to explore women's heroic role in the revolution and to illustrate the personal and ideological motivations that made them active protagonists" (44). While Adelita becomes a martyr in Niggli's play, other female characters also represent the Mexican woman as strong and heroic, similar to the roles María Félix would portray on the big screen. Niggli is the first writer to bring the "Adelita" image—a symbol of struggle and freedom for the U.S. Chicana—to English-language literature. Whereas in Mexico "Adelita," along with Emiliano Zapata and Pancho Villa, symbolizes the revolutionary cause, in the United States it signifies a woman's challenge to patriarchal rules against her, and the espousing of a cause promulgating her rights and status. It was not until many years after Niggli's publications that a Mexican woman would be represented as a thinking, acting being. The fact that Niggli was a woman is significant for American as well as Mexican letters, for few women of her era attained access to the publishing world or were able to earn a living from literary publications.

Since the 1980s, Chicana writers—who now obtain publishing contracts in great numbers—portray the origins of Mexican culture in the lives of their characters, including themes of a life lived crossing borders, both literally and figuratively. For example, in *Canícula, Snapshots of a Girlhood en la Frontera* (1997), Texas writer Norma Elia Cantú depicts a female's coming-of-age experience on the Laredo, Texas, border, with occasional trips to see family in Monterrey. And Sandra Cisneros's novel *Caramelo* (2002), as well as some of her earlier stories, also portray the back-and-forth experience of many Chicanos.

Josefina Niggli blazed the trail for creative works in English with a Mexican topic. Her work is noteworthy for its innovation and lyrical style, for its revelation of Mexican philosophy and essence in an era that predates Chicano awareness in the United States, and for its superb content—village life, indigenous lore, northern Mexico climate and customs, and mestizo political consciousness. She received major awards and the attention of the New York literary scene and of Hollywood, as well as international fame. She lived in the United States most of her adult life, but her creative spirit never left Monterrey, where her life began.

Monterrey

The heart of the northeastern region of Mexico is the city of Monterrey, created in a valley mostly surrounded by mountains, where settlers discovered a natural fountain, and the flood plain of the eastward-flowing Río Santa Catarina (so named by the Spaniards in 1579). The first Spanish settlers were nearly finished off by floods and original peoples (a mix of Otomíes and Tlaxcaltecans, the latter transported to the area by Hernán Cortés as part of his army in pursuit of gold). The valley was resettled by a contingent of Sephardic-Jewish Spaniards seeking a remote location to practice their faith, and by the late seventeenth century, a stronger settlement emerged, connected to the launching of mining work in the region. The building of the city's cathedral began in 1770, and in 1782 construction commenced for the now significant landmark el Palacio del Obispado, or Bishop's Palace, on a hill overlooking Monterrey. During the nineteenth century, it is rumored that a French contingent became lost in this northern region during Maximilian's short reign, and that this accounts for the blue eyes and blonde hair often found on regiomontanos, as people from Nuevo León are called. The French did invade and reside in Monterrey during the mid-1860s, but previously, U.S. soldiers under Zachary Taylor occupied the city for a short period in 1846. By the second half of the nineteenth century, many immigrants from Europe settled in this valley.

Industrialization began in the late eighteenth century with the founding of two landmark businesses: a brewery, Cervecería Cuauhtémoc, and a foundry, Fundidora de Fierro y Acero de Monterrey. Since many of the revolutionary leaders were from northern states, this industrial hub was strategic at the inception of the Mexican Revolution. In 1914, rebel troops led by Pancho Villa overthrew federal forces and occupied the Bishop's Palace. The Mexican Revolution culminated in victory for the mestizos (those of mixed ethnic-racial heritage, with an emphasis on the Indian culture), ushering in a new era for Mexican society. Until then, the nation had been run by a minority of upper-class white Mexicans and foreigners who owned massive tracts of land, while mestizos and Indians were denied resources and the right to education. The government formed under a new constitution in 1917 exposed the need to review stark differences in class and cultural origin, emphasizing rights for all citizens, including education and landownership—privileges that had not been permitted since Spain's conquest of the Americas four centuries earlier. Such radical change provided rich opportunities for artists, writers, and photographers to document a changing era. Under the new government, Monterrey's social environment would change and its economy would surge; this is related well by Niggli in her second novel *Step Down, Elder Brother*, which will be discussed in chapter 3.

Niggli was born in Monterrey on July 13, 1910—the same year dictator Porfirio Díaz was ousted and the Mexican Revolution was launched. Her family—like many others in this region—greeted the new change, but later fled to Texas when violence erupted between the victors. The first president of the new order, Francisco I. Madero, was assassinated in 1913, and other leaders within a decade. Not unlike other families, the Nigglis led a somewhat nomadic life for several years, moving back and forth across the border, giving up their residences to seek safety. Josefina was primarily home-schooled, although she attended third grade for six months in the town of Eagle Pass, Texas (on the border across from Piedras Negras and 75 miles west of Laredo). During the 1917–18 year, her mother required hospitalization, and while she was in recovery in Eagle Pass, Josefina was boarded at Bonn Avon School in San Antonio. At some point, she also attended an American school in Mexico City for a few months.

Her father helped found a new plant in the town of San Nicolás de Hidalgo (founded in 1828 as Villa de San Nicolás de Hidalgo, but often shortened to simply "Hidalgo"). The small town is among a cluster of five villages in a valley just west of Monterrey, flanked by high-peaked mountains that cradle a beautiful canyon called El Potrero Chico. Early biographical accounts state that Josefina grew up on a *hacienda* (likely a country home) in Hidalgo. This country home, identified on a website as *Casa de la gerencia* (the manager's home), was built by Frederick Ferdinand for his new bride. This town has established monuments to the men who worked at the beginning of the cement industry founded here, as well as to two Mexican heroes, Miguel Hidalgo y Costilla and President Lázaro Cárdenas. Josefina enjoyed growing up here, but the political instability and intermittent violence of the war years forced the need for safety and departure from the area. She and her mother left to establish a new home in Texas when she was fifteen. Josefina would return regularly for visits once she was an adult.

In a desire to separate the powers of church and state, decrees under the new government led to the outlawing of priests and religious ceremonies, which was too radical a move and led to the Cristero War.[2] In addition, the revolutionary leader from the north, Pancho Villa, had been assassinated in 1923 (and Emiliano Zapata in 1919).

In San Antonio, Josefina completed high school and embarked on advanced studies. Her father continued working in Mexico (all sources show him continuing to work there until near the time of his death). It is apparent they kept two homes into the 1940s; Josefina regularly made visits to Monterrey and Mexico City, visiting family, godparents, and other friends. From 1925 her primary residence would be in the United States, but Mexican culture and a strong sense of its roots would influence and imbue her work. Josefina celebrated her fifteenth birthday—the traditional *quinceañera*—at her original home, a fact mentioned in her 1980 interview (Shirley). Such coming-out parties included a gala affair with prominent members of society invited. Niggli stated that the governor of Nuevo León was present and asked her what she would like for a present. She said, "all of Monterrey," an unusual comment in itself for a teenager. The governor's response, however, was cut off at the end of the tape.

Mexican by birth and upbringing, and American through her parents, Josefina María Niggli became one of the earliest Mexican American writers with a predominant theme in her works of life lived between two cultures and two nations. Although fully bilingual, she chose, like many other U.S. Hispanics or Latinos, to write in English. She is one of the few women writers of the early twentieth century to distinguish herself in a variety of literary genres.

Although her first name was originally spelled "Josephine," she was often called "Josephina," phonetically more appropriate to Spanish. Occasionally in the late 1930s, and by the 1940s, she made the switch to "Josefina." Print sources did not always pick it up the same way, therefore her professional name is at times spelled with an "f" and at other times with a "ph" (in fact, research on databases needs to be pursued under each spelling or some items will be overlooked). Her Texan and Mexican friends always called her Josefina, and her name appears as "Josefina Niggli" on her headstone.

Her Peers

Sister Mexican artists Anita Brenner and Frida Kahlo, born in 1905 and 1907 respectively, have in recent decades received greater attention for their artistic contributions than Niggli. They reached their heyday in the same era as she, but by the mid-1950s Brenner faded from the limelight and Kahlo had died. In that era Niggli also retreated to the quiet life of a professor in a remote corner of the U.S. South. But she did not stop writing.

Born in 1910, Niggli is more appropriately a "child" of the Mexican Revolution, as Kahlo declared herself, citing her year of birth as 1910 in solidarity with the Mexican struggle for social equality. Born in Mexico City, Kahlo is known for her unique and innovative art, created throughout a lifetime struggle with chronic pain, and for her independence of spirit despite marriage to the famous Diego Rivera. Brenner, born in Aguascalientes—the capital of a small state by the same name southwest of Nuevo León and south of Zacatecas—shared with Niggli the experience of leaving her home for Texas at various intervals when revolutionary fighting heated up. Brenner also attended high school and college in San Antonio, and then began a writing career in English as a journalist, historian, translator, and modern-art critic. Although she launched her career a few years earlier, Brenner's principal writings—on Mexican art, history, and culture, including Mexican folk tales—were published in the same two decades as Niggli's, the 1930s and 1940s.

Another Mexican artist, Dolores del Río, was born in 1904 in the northern state and city of Durango, which her family was forced to flee in 1910. While her father left to work in the United States, she and her mother settled in Mexico City with relatives. She married at age seventeen and spent the next two years traveling in Europe. Upon her return, she and her husband lived in Mexico City, which attracted many international artists during the 1920s. A silent-film director from Hollywood encouraged her move to Los Angeles, California, in 1925, which launched her film career. After more than twenty films in the United States, Del Río returned to Mexico in 1942, where she began making films in what is considered Mexico's golden era of cinema, also appearing from time to time in additional U.S. films.

Pearl Buck was born in 1892 in West Virginia, Josephine Baker in 1905 in St. Louis, Missouri, and Margaret Bourke-White in 1904 in New York City. These three and Anita Brenner died in the early 1970s. Kahlo died in 1954, leaving Niggli and Del Río to survive until 1983. While Brenner and Kahlo died in Mexico, Del Río and Niggli had been living in the United States at the time of their decease and can be categorized as both Mexican and U.S. Latina. All of these women are outstanding contributors to twentieth-century art and history, and enduring examples of talented women who pursued careers.

For each, the 1930s was a significant decade. Buck (who lived in China for most of her life) published *The Good Earth* in 1931, leading to her receiving a Pulitzer in 1935 and becoming the first woman to be awarded the Nobel Prize in Literature in 1938. Baker, who went to Paris in 1925, attempted to return to the United States and encountered strong racism, which determined that the rest of her life—and the success she achieved—would occur abroad. Bourke-White, a forerunner in the emerging field of photojournalism, was the first photographer hired by *Fortune* magazine in 1929 (during the 1930s Brenner was the Mexican correspondent for this magazine), and the principal photographer for *Life* magazine when it was launched in 1935. Kahlo, who married Diego Rivera in 1929, had begun creating her self-portraits in 1926. She traveled with Rivera to San Francisco, California, in 1930, then to Detroit, and to New York. She returned to Mexico City in 1933, after which her unique paintings took on a bolder tone. Each of these extraordinary women was in New York shortly before or during the mid-1930s, when Niggli moved to the East Coast.

Brenner attended Our Lady of the Lake College in San Antonio for one semester and then the University of Texas in Austin for one year. In

1923, she traveled to Mexico City alone, took some classes at the National University (UNAM) in Mexico City (posed in the nude for an Edward Weston creation), and embarked on a career in newspaper writing. In 1927, she moved to New York City and, after a few rejections, found a publisher for her first and excellent book *Idols Behind Altars* (1929). Her experience, and her knowledge of the Spanish language and its literature helped her test out of requirements for a bachelor's degree and gain admission to a doctoral program at Columbia University in 1927. Upon receiving her doctorate in 1930, she was awarded a Guggenheim Fellowship to study Aztec art (at museums in Europe as well as in Mexico). In 1943, she published one of the first documented texts in English on the Mexican Revolution. Like Niggli, she always considered herself Mexican. She spent the last several years of her life at her family home in Aguascalientes. Brenner and Niggli shared similar life experiences—shuttling between Mexico and the United States, and a passion for writing about Mexican culture and people. They may have crossed paths at some juncture (Brenner's friend and fellow journalist in Mexico City, Carleton Beals, wrote reviews on both women's books).

Niggli also received major fellowships in the 1930s: two Rockefellers for her playwriting studies, as well as fellowships and grants from the University of North Carolina, several New York City entities, and the Breadloaf Conference Fellowship in Vermont. Meanwhile, Del Río made numerous films in the United States between 1926 and 1942, and more than fifty in her lifetime. An excellent singer and dancer, Del Río blazed the trail for the Carmen Miranda craze of the 1940s and 1950s. Del Río's and Niggli's paths seem not to have crossed. After Del Río left Hollywood, Niggli would arrive to write television and film screenplays in the late 1940s and early 1950s.

By 1935, Niggli was living in Chapel Hill, North Carolina, which served as her launching pad to publication. Her parents had discovered in northern Mexico a rich life's experience; meanwhile, their daughter absorbed Mexican history, politics, culture, and traditions, and defined these in her creative work for an English-language audience. Niggli's eloquent novels and humorous and historic plays distinguish Mexican culture and the borderlands, long before contemporary writers would portray these.

Family History

Josefina Niggli's great-grandparents on her father's side (a great extended family), of Swiss and Alsatian heritage, immigrated to Texas in the early 1840s (after Texas proclaimed its independence from Mexico), and settled in Castroville, a brand new settlement just west of San Antonio. Biographical accounts state that later they moved to Mexico, although it was really Eagle Pass on the border. At the Niggli gravesite in San Antonio, Texas, the oldest marker is for Ferdinand (her grandfather), with the dates 1849–1885. His wife Josephine (1852–1912) is buried alongside him. Their son and Josefina's father, Frederick Ferdinand Niggli (1876–1945), rests opposite, with his wife and daughter alongside. Niggli's father's siblings (it is likely that Frederick Ferdinand had them moved to the San Antonio plot) are buried to either side of Ferdinand and Josephine: his brother Oscar L. (1880–1915), sister Ferdna (1886–1978), William J. (1873–1922, his elder brother and mentor after losing their father), and William's wife, Lucy (1880–1964). Not included are several other Niggli relatives who resided in Eagle Pass (as indicated in public records and a family scrapbook).

A raised central stone indicating "Niggli" divides the plot. All head-stones are simple gray markers laid flat against the ground. Josefina's maternal grandmother, Phoebe Morgan (1851–1945), rests next to her mother, Goldie Morgan Niggli (1883–1968). Goldie is described in early accounts as a concert violinist of Irish, French, and German descent who grew up in Missouri, excelled at music, and trained in New York City. She spent summers in residence playing in orchestras at fancy Eastern hotels. During the winter off-season she traveled as part of a string ensemble, and the group found winter-long engagements, starting in 1904, for several years at the prestigious Menger Hotel in San Antonio, Texas. This is where she met her future husband; they were married in 1909. A scrapbook discovered in 1996 in the attic of a North Carolina house included various concert and recital programs for Goldie, a telegram announcing Josefina's birth, and many photos taken in northern Mexico and San Antonio, up to Josefina's fifteenth year. One clipping indicates a private party organized by Josefina's father and held in Eagle Pass, at which Goldie provided the musical entertainment. Goldie's paternal grandparents were from Virginia, but moved to Ohio just before the Civil War; her paternal grandfather, Henry, was a gun smuggler during the Civil War, according to Josefina.

Information about her father's father, Ferdinand, is found in a recently published book documenting the violent deaths of U.S. marshals and deputies. Titled *Deadly Affrays: The Violent Deaths of U.S. Marshals*, by Robert Ernst and George Stumpf (2005), the book states that Ferdinand Niggli was born in Texas to immigrant parents, and was elected Medina County (west of San Antonio) sheriff in 1876, reelected in 1878 and again in 1880. In 1882, he was appointed deputy U.S. marshal and moved to San Antonio. He retained his home in Castroville, and in August 1885 he was attending an annual celebration (and on duty) when another sheriff (who was a German immigrant) shot him fatally. He died the following day. The book cites a year of birth that corresponds with that at the Niggli burial site, but it does not mention his family or any information prior to his election. In 1885, his son (Josefina's father) would have been nine years old. In 1890, his widow moved to Eagle Pass, where some of her husband's family already resided.[3]

Frederick Ferdinand's eldest brother, William, worked as an auditor for the Mexican and International Railroad (M&I) in Piedras Negras. In 1893 he hired Niggli's father as an office boy; within a few years Niggli had risen to the position of general agent at the important Torreón station (the location where U.S. and Mexican railroads were first connected in 1884, launching the Mexican "International" railroad). He was hired away as the general manager of Cementos Hidalgo upon its creation in 1906. He also had a stake in other Niggli businesses.[4] In time, he became comptroller of several factories in Mexico.

Goldie and Frederick Ferdinand were married in 1909, at St. Mark's Episcopal Church in old town San Antonio. Born the following year, when her parents were twenty-seven and thirty-four years old, Josefina María was their only child. When she and her mother moved to San Antonio from northern Mexico, Josefina wrote her first play for a theater group sponsored by this church. Throughout her life, Niggli's mother would be a constant companion. In San Antonio, Goldie's mother also lived with them.

In Torreón, Niggli's father—who went by the nickname of "Fritz"— had met the influential and successful businessman Juan F. Brittingham, who would soon establish Cementos Hidalgo near Monterrey (in 1906), asking Niggli to manage the plant.[5] Not satisfied with his half-ownership in the cement plant, three years later Brittingham also founded a glass factory, Vidriera Monterrey, where Niggli was manager and also had a partial ownership. Thousands of Brittingham's letters and documents are now archived at the Universidad Iberoamericana-Torreón. These include his frequent correspondence with Fritz Niggli. While research has been conducted on Brittingham, none has been pursued on Josefina Niggli's father, who is an interesting figure in terms of early twentieth-century commerce in the Monterrey, Nuevo León region.

The Cement Plant and Her Father's Work

Her father's work coincided with the rise of one of the more prominent businesses in Monterrey. Josefina always stated in biographical reports that when she was a child, he worked as the manager of a cement plant in Hidalgo, near Monterrey. Her first novel, *Mexican Village*, is based in part on his role in that plant. It is here that cement was first created from a mixture of clay with limestone particular to a nearby quarry, which, with the addition of water, formed a soft and manageable substance that set hard (later joined with other mineral substances like sand and stone to form various grades of concrete).

The institution was founded with the opening of Cementos Hidalgo in 1906. Cementos Portland Monterrey began operations in 1920, and in 1931 the two companies merged, becoming Cementos Mexicanos, known as CEMEX. "Portland Cement," as the process is now known, is an artificial mineral substance used in building and engineering construction. In the 1960s, CEMEX grew significantly with the acquisition of several more plants throughout Mexico; it went public in 1976, and by 1982 doubled its exports. During the 1990s, it acquired plants in several other countries, and is currently the worldwide leader in ready-mix concrete production.

Niggli's first novel gives eyewitness to this history, describing the characters of a small village where life revolves around the workers and the manager, and their work at a cement plant. It depicts the first stages of a factory operation that is now part of the major global economy. With the exception of some World War I years (while Goldie was in Eagle Pass), Fritz Niggli forever after worked in Monterrey.

While the city of Monterrey is Mexico's third-largest city and the wealthy industrial center of northern Mexico, the region received little if any focus in literature prior to the late twentieth century. Niggli's second novel, *Step Down, Elder Brother*, describes life in this significant city during the immediate post-Revolution, a fact that so impressed a contemporary Mexican writer from Monterrey that he embarked on translating her novel to Spanish (discussed in chapter 4), thus rescuing it for Mexican history and literary contribution in that region.

San Antonio

The home Niggli and her mother settled into in San Antonio in 1925 may have reminded them of the stately nineteenth-century mansions of Monterrey. In *Step Down, Elder Brother*, the principal character describes Escobedo Street, with its "picturesque aspect of long rows of houses with their iron barred windows, their heavy carved doors, and now and then the brass plaques that informed the passerby that here lived a doctor or a lawyer or an engineer . . . one house painted purple, one yellow, another green" (4–5). The Vázquez de Anda family resides in a "huge house with its Spanish coat-of-arms on Padre Mier, East," with further description in chapter 7 (anthologized here). Since her father spent a few years of his childhood (following his father's death and before the move to Eagle Pass) living a few miles away, it meant that he had "arrived" economically to be able to own a house on the fanciest street in the city.

Although not as ornate, nor with bars on the windows (in Spanish custom these prevented a young woman from eloping or being kidnapped from the house), the Niggli family home at 221 King William Street joins stately two-story houses shaded by huge pecan and cypress trees on a wide, impressive street. The elegant King William neighborhood was created by German immigrants, of which a large number arrived in Texas during the 1830s and 1840s, quickly making money when Texas became an independent nation. They continued to arrive throughout the century, and the street that provided entry to the neighborhood from downtown was named for Kaiser Wilhelm I, King of Prussia in the 1870s. During the 1870s about one-third of San Antonio's population spoke German.

The street's name was changed during World War I, but then

restored, in English language, a few years after the war had ended. Many of the original homeowners and their children left for newer parts of San Antonio. During the 1940s the neighborhood saw a general decline; in fact, the downtown area suffered great deterioration during and following the Second World War, and several of the former prestigious mansions were converted to apartments.

The neighborhood experienced an upsurge in the late 1950s, with interest in the preservation of historic areas, restoring its status to "fashionable." Niggli's mother sold the home in 1957, and in 1967 the neighborhood was designated the first Historic Neighborhood District in Texas, with zoning protection. The principal streets of Madison and King William are intersected by Beauregard Street, where, two blocks east at the corner of South Alamo, is a restaurant with a personality that matches the current neighborhood; MadHatters Tea House and Café, owned by René Guerrero, serves up organic meals and homemade baked goods. Since Niggli spent considerable time in England later in her adult life, she would likely have appreciated its British-inspired theme.

In recent years, several homes along King William have been renovated to new prestige, but Niggli's block remains uneven in renovation and disrepair. Running parallel to her street is the equally notable Madison Street. To the west is the San Antonio River, now known for its tourist attraction the Riverwalk. In fact, this district occupies land that was once irrigated farmland belonging to the Mission San Antonio de Valero, better known as "the Alamo." The area now known as the "historic King William district" was subdivided into lots in the 1860s and laid out with the present streets.

Niggli's former home—a large, white-brick, two-story structure with an enclosed upstairs porch—is in need of paint and repair, its siding discolored or crumbling in several places. Two overgrown (surprising for the area) palm trees to the left of the house (as entered from the street) compete for space in the driveway. Huge fruit trees in the yards on either side envelop the house in shadows and soil the ground with their messy wild fruit. Blackberry bushes currently encircle the house's front perimeter, nearly swallowing a short fence. The wide, sideless porch in front of the house holds a cluster of chairs. A former garage in back of the house appears to be an additional residence.

Running parallel to Beauregard is East Guenther where, on the other side of South Alamo Street (east of the principal historic area), Sandra Cisneros has lived for many years. She caused a commotion in 1997 when she painted her house purple with turquoise trim. Members of the city's Historic Design and Review Board wanted a more conservative color, which they declared was in keeping with original tones. Cisneros argued that her color was far older, dating back a thousand years to the colors used by Aztec royalty. After several letters to the editor and news-paper editorials, the controversy subsided, principally because Cisneros had discovered that lavender was used in the original color scheme by the German settlers. Niggli would have enjoyed the irony.

Niggli's works share several commonalities with those of the Chicago-born author who now prefers to live in San Antonio. In Cisneros's novel *Caramelo* (2002), characters recall the violence and great hunger suffered during the Mexican Revolution. One spends time working in "the north" (Chicago), where he meets several non-white artists of an earlier era, including Josephine Baker. Characters in *Caramelo* celebrate Mexican-indigenous customs, but some charac-ters disparage indigenous heritage. Niggli's plays and novels situated in the post-Revolution showed the desire to overcome racism and to celebrate Indian heritage (including a preference for rich colors) as the true essence of Mexican culture. In her writing, Niggli wove iconic female cultural symbols into her stories, such as the Mayan Ixtabai and the Virgen de Guadalupe. Cisneros focuses on la Llorona in short stories such as *Woman Hollering Creek*. While Niggli was one of the first to do so, she and Cisneros have empowered the female image in literature by identifying female symbols of Mexican culture.

When Niggli arrived in 1925, San Antonio still had a small-town feeling, although its population had just increased substantially (to more than 162,000) with the influx of new residents fleeing the Mexican Revolution. In Niggli's early adult years, poor or non-English-speaking Mexicans were segregated. When she attended church in San Antonio during the 1940s, she preferred sitting on the "Mexican side," where she could listen to commentary in Spanish (Shirley 1980). Niggli had easy access to items she was used to procuring in Mexico, whether food, leather goods, pots and pans, or even the traditional Mexican dress she wore during a high-school celebration. Sheet music for songs she adapted into her plays was purchased at La Casa de Música, at West

Houston and Santa Rosa Streets (as a child, she played violin and performed in recitals). Niggli frequented the Mexican *mercado* (which in those days was not a tourist attraction) for produce and household goods, and attended Main Avenue High School (now Fox Tech) near downtown. Population growth remained slow during the 1930s, but soared again with the wartime boom of the 1940s (and the expansion of military bases in San Antonio), when Niggli alternated residence between San Antonio and Chapel Hill, and worked on two novels. By 1960 San Antonio had become a booming city of 588,000.

As a teenager in San Antonio, Niggli may have felt torn from her place of origin, but she enjoyed the company of many other Mexicans around her. At the high school, she launched herself into representing her Monterrey roots by performing the *jarabe tapatío* on several occasions with another Mexican, Abraham Barrera. They posed for a newspaper photographer wearing traditional Mexican festive attire. Early on, she applied her learning of Mexican culture during childhood to verse and drama. She also published her first poem, "The Texas Child," in her high-school newspaper in 1925.

Niggli is described in the 1949 edition of *Current Biography* as being of medium height, with hazel eyes and brown hair. Her vivaciousness, sharp wit, and great energy are not as easily described, but they can be gleaned from a variety of sources and photographs depicting her life. The Incarnate Word college newspaper, *The Logos*, reported in 1936 that their alumna (who had received an award in North Carolina) was remembered by the faculty and the student body "not only for her scholarly work but also for her happy disposition and her readiness to help others."

College Life

In the fall of 1926, Niggli enrolled in the College of the Incarnate Word (now called the University of the Incarnate Word), which was at the time a girls' Catholic college with the nuns' dormitory central to the campus. Currently, Trinity University is located on the opposite side of Highway 281, but did not exist yet in that era. Now a coed institution, Incarnate Word is a huge complex of red brick buildings located in Alamo Heights, a few miles north of downtown San Antonio. The university now sports several new buildings, including a retirement home built for the nuns (no longer visible on campus) constructed to the north of campus. The main entrance is on the east, from Broadway, a principal thoroughfare to downtown. Currently, typical college businesses—sandwich shops and copy centers—line Broadway, and the huge diner Earl Abel's for many years occupied the opposite corner across from the college. Although it barred Mexican clientele until after the Civil Rights Movement, this restaurant was considered a historic San Antonio landmark for decades (the structure was recently demolished and the restaurant relocated).

Pursuing a major in philosophy with a minor in history, Niggli found a new writing coach in Dr. Raymond E. Roehl, head of the English Department and one of the few professors who were not nuns. As her mentor, he entered her poems and stories in various writing contests (Roehl also guided many other young writers to publication). Niggli took second place in the *Ladies' Home Journal* College Short Story Contest, for a story titled "Thunder in the Air." Meanwhile, she published poems and one short story in the college magazine and yearbook *The Logos*,[6] serving also as literary editor during the 1927–28 and 1928–29 years, and general editor for 1930–31. "The Sacrifice," published in the 1928 yearbook *The Logos*, is an interesting story set in pre-Hispanic Mexico. A youth called Maxtla rushes on foot to get to "the capital" (apparently meaning Tenochtitlan) and ask the high-priest Hualpa's aid in healing his brother Io, struck down by illness. He encounters an old man along the path, who tells him the priest has already departed. Addressing the old man as "tzin," the proper Aztec form for nobility, the youth discovers that he is talking to Quetzalcoatl. When he returns home, he finds his brother cured, released from the grip of "the lesser gods." This story demonstrates Niggli's desire to reveal Mexican myth and morality tales from indigenous culture.

According to the Incarnate Word college records, she was not enrolled during the 1929–30 year, but she returned the following year and graduated in 1931. Later, Niggli indicated in her employment record that she worked for Dr. Roehl as secretary between 1929–31, and the contributor's note to her poem published in *Interludes* states that she was "playing hooky at Columbia" University in 1929–30. Niggli's mother also took classes at Incarnate Word as a non-major student, according to Josefina's graduation yearbook. In this era Niggli also began submitting her stories and poems to national newspapers and magazines, but they have been difficult to locate. Her own record of publications years later is somewhat unreliable. Most sources indicate, however, that she published several short stories and poems during the early 1930s.

Her Early Poetry

Josefina's first small book is a collection of eight poems under the title of *Mexican Silhouettes*, which was self-published (by her father) in 1928 in Hidalgo, Nuevo León. It included "The Mexican Idler," "A Goat-Herder's Song," "False Blue," "Aztecan Fantasy," "Monterrey," "Goats at Evening," "The Tortilla Girl," and "A Mexican Night Song."

In 1930 Niggli took first place in a National Catholic College Poetry Contest, which garnered the publication of the two poems she had submitted, "The Hills of Mexico" and "The Goat-Herder's Song," in the Catholic anthology *This Light*. In each, she evokes the serenity and geographic beauty of the quiet countryside of northern Mexico. The latter captures the sound goats make, with her use of the Spanish word for goat (aaah sound), and the first is a description of northern Mexico in poetic language. Niggli also took second place in a Young Poet's Contest sponsored by the magazine *Interludes*, which published her poem "The Mexican Idler" in 1931. "A Tourist in a Mexican Town" had been published in the Denver journal *The Echo* in 1928, and "The Hills of Mexico" appeared in the *North American Review* in 1935.

Three years after its first release, *Mexican Silhouettes* was reissued (in San Antonio, the title page indicates "The Silhouette Press" at 221 King William Street), with different contents. It included five poems from the original edition—"False Blue," "The Mexican Idler," "Goats at Evening"—and two with altered titles: "The Goat-Herder's Song" (it would later appear as simply "Goat Herder's Song" in *Mexican Life* in July 1934), and "Mexican Serenade" (instead of "A Mexican Night Song"). An additional six were new poems: "A Garden at Night," "The Trumpet Call," "Discontent," "The Third Old Man," "A Tourist in a Mexican Town," and "The Hills of Mexico."

Her father, who still had his contacts from years of work with the Mexican railroad, was now the administrator/financial comptroller for a glass-producing factory in Monterrey, and traveled frequently by train.

He had the 1931 chapbook sold in the dining car of most international routes. Niggli proudly recalled during a 1980 interview that her father also walked into the largest English-language bookstore in Mexico City, across the street from the Alameda theater, and had it placed for sale there.

Her poems reveal Niggli's first attempt at interpreting Mexico to Americans, pinpointing as audience the "tourist" who does not understand Mexican culture. It launched her lifetime goal to capture the genuine Mexico she knew and relate this to an English-language public. She published additional poems in such magazines as *Mexican Life* and *American Poetry Journal* during the early 1930s, and in an anthology of prize-winning poems from San Antonio, *Young Pegasus*, in 1928. These were never collected in a book. None, however, demonstrates the innovation or artistic quality of her drama and narrative.

The poems anthologized here depict her personal biography and her creative stance. Two are from the original publication of *Mexican Silhouettes*, "Monterrey" and "The Goat-herder's Song," and two are new poems from the second edition of *Mexican Silhouettes*, "A Tourist in a Mexican Town" and "The Hills of Mexico."

Plays and Her Future

Niggli became a legendary figure after her departure from the College of the Incarnate Word. She kept in frequent contact, and during the late 1930s and 1940s, newcomers would frequently hear the nuns chirping about what Josefina had produced or published. Teachers and staff were often spectators at Niggli's first performances (as well as skits directed by her) for the St. Mark's Players, a nonprofessional theater group connected to St. Mark's Episcopal Church, and then the San Antonio Little Theater (SALT). Niggli had already gained popularity writing and producing shows (mostly serial thrillers) for KTSA Radio, and after college participated in a theater workshop for budding playwrights and actors. She studied with Coates Gwynne, director of the new SALT (the original Little Theater had merged with another community theater group), which opened a playhouse in 1929. Under Gwynne's guidance, she began to create skits and brief one-act plays, producing some herself. Several were prepared for an audience of disabled World War I veterans, staged at the Fort Sam Houston Hospital Barracks. The skits were typed and mimeographed at the Niggli family home, where rehearsals occurred. The actors were often former classmates. Her semiprofessional premiere was as an actress in Oscar Wilde's *Lady Windermere's Fan* during the 1931–32 SALT season. During the following season, her mother was director of a musical program featuring "The Niggli String Ensemble." For the 1934–35 season, Josefina is cited in SALT programs as one of the theater directors, and her "original scripts" are being read in the workshop. She sat on the SALT board and had at least one play produced, *Sorella.*[7]

During the early 1930s, Niggli and her mother divided their time between San Antonio and Monterrey, and with her father, they made frequent trips to Mexico City. The new glass-producing factory her father managed was prospering, the cement plant continued to prosper, and they enjoyed the fruits of a booming economy now that revolutionary struggles had subsided. He would continue to work as comptroller of both businesses. Due to this prosperity, the Niggli family likely enjoyed life the way it is described in *Step Down, Elder Brother.* Josefina could travel to Mexico City and to San Antonio regularly and spend time with close friends. She was especially close to the Larralde family, and particularly the children: "Elsita," to whom she dedicates *Step*, and her brother Rómulo, who had become an actor in the United States, using the name Romney Brent. Although friends in this era traveled to Europe, Niggli was not frivolous; she possessed a strong urge to write and accomplish something (this contrast is portrayed in *Singing Valley* between the siblings). She also contemplated doing further advanced studies.

Niggli stated in passing during a 1980 interview (Shirley) that she was engaged to an army colonel who had served with the rebels during the Revolution (when he was a captain), whose family had a long military history (similar to a character in the play *The Ring of General Macías*). He shared with her several eyewitness accounts of personalities and actions during the struggle, including anecdotes about Pancho Villa and about the women *soldaderas*; Niggli told Paula Shirley he provided specifics she would include in her plays *Soldadera* (1936) and *This is Villa!* (1938). However, she said she got the "argument" between the main characters in the latter play from Venustiano Carranza's memoirs; she also relates that she wrote this play around a particular red hat that an actor wanted to use (see chapter 2). Niggli has further stated that she was an expert on the subject: "I knew the Mexican Revolution; I'd read all the great novels, Mariano Azuela, etc." (Shirley). During the interview, Niggli did not explain why she never married. In the case of the military officer fiancé, he was assigned to diplomatic posts in Paris and London during the 1920s, and at some point returned to Monterrey and died young (according to Shirley). Niggli provided no further information about this or other possible relationships.

Instead, after college she set her sights on professional playwriting. Her mother had read an article in a New York magazine about a cutting-edge playmaking company getting its start in North Carolina, and she suggested it to her talented daughter as her next step. Josefina wrote to three universities renowned for their playwriting programs, the University of Iowa, Yale University, and the University of North Carolina at Chapel Hill, and—perhaps concerned about whether she could endure a different type of climate—she asked each "the same question: Does it snow and how cold does it get?" (Shirley 1980). Niggli said she could not remember what Iowa said, while an extensive reply from Yale provided information on variability and duration of snowfall. It was North Carolina's response that most impressed her. She chuckled that Frederick H. Koch, director and founder of the Carolina Playmakers, wrote: "Who cares if it snows? we're in the theater!"

Surely Niggli's early writing experience, her success with radio plays, and her work with the Little Theater in San Antonio, all made her a candidate of interest to each of the program directors. But she so enjoyed Koch's retort that she immediately chose his program. Koch additionally possessed the interesting coincidence of sharing her father's first name. As it turned out, Koch's program was a perfect fit for Niggli's goals: his emphasis on down-home "folk" drama suited her purposes of adapting small-town Mexican life to dramatic presentations. Furthermore, the Carolina Playmakers was a cutting-edge theatrical company, with East Coast prominence and a close connection to New York City and the publishing world.

Unbeknownst to Niggli, when she traded the hot, dry terrain of northern Mexico and southern Texas for the lush terrain and colder climate of North Carolina in 1935, it would become her home for practically the rest of her adult life, as well as the cradle of her future publishing activity. Her aspirations were greatly served by this university's prestige and the contacts she would make with important and luminary personalities.

The Goat-Herder's Song

Come down from the mountains,
Go down to the sea;
For Ana is there
Waiting for me.
Cabra—Cabra.

The sunset's a crown
I shall bend for her hair;
The mountain's an emerald
For Ana so fair.
Cabra—Cabra.

The morning is done,
The afternoon too;
The night sings in silver,
"I'm coming to you."
Cabra—Cabra.

The Hills of Mexico

Hills of Chinese purple,
Like amethysts afloat
Upon a sea of emeralds,
'Midst opalescent boats.

Higher than the breath of man,
Lower than his soul:
Jewel studded, military
Hills of Mexico.

They stand like silent sentinels,
With pikes of cactus thorns
Fashioned from Chinese jade.
Cactus crowned with tuna,
Flaming, too sweet tuna,
And the thorns
Slide along the fingers, slip between the fingers,
Like tiny heathen idols made of stone.
Like white, subtle idols made of stone.
And lower down the hill slopes,
Hidden by the green shrubs,
Hidden by the green shrubs,
Are slender, tall, palm trees,
Clad in olive drab.
A company of soldiers,
With here and there a captain,
Tall against the sky.
Their laughing young companion—
Singing eternally—
White armed, lightly dancing brook,
Teasing men and captains by the hour.
Daring to steal a stone . . .
A fairy-tinted flower heart . . .
Even a spike from the
Sea-green cactus.

A Tourist in a Mexican Town

It was so hot the road curled into
a spiral
Beyond the silent house
Standing pink against the sun.
The silence came down like the sword
of Michael
In the path of the devil.

"What's the cross for, over the door?
Is it a holy place?
The home of a priest?
Or is it consecrated in death?"

That house? Why, that's the *molino*
where the sugar's made."

"But the cross?"
"Oh, that's to keep the lightning off."

Monterrey

Mexico, my beloved,
is not the clashing of cymbals
nor the curving
of vermilion sails
over the heart
of the wind;
it is not
a vivid slash
across the mouth
of the world

But, when the moon touches the silken waves
of the Lerma
and the carnations
breathe their scents
into the souls of a thousand birds
forcing them to sing
of something
they but dimly understand—
this, my beloved,
is Mexico.

CHAPTER TWO

Playmaking in North Carolina

1935–1942

The Carolina Playmakers—a company that rose to national prominence by the early 1930s—was founded in 1918 at the University
of North Carolina, Chapel Hill, with the hiring of an inspiring leader
and professor of dramatic literature, Frederick H. Koch. Modeled on
the community-theater idea, its specific purpose was to produce student
plays, and to provide theatrical events for an audience not necessarily
knowledgeable about high theater.[1] Playmaker performances were often
staged outdoors in the Forest Theatre, designed by Koch and opened
in the summer of 1919. The university had had no formal program in
drama until Koch's arrival, only a few courses taught in the English
Department. In fact, a separate Department of Dramatic Art was not
established until 1936. In 1928, the first issue of *The Carolina Play-Book*
appeared, a type of magazine-newsletter that would continue for sixteen
years until Koch's death in 1944, providing scripts of new plays, articles
on drama by local and national figures, and notes about the work of this
company. Koch, who was forty-one years old when he arrived at UNC,

had completed his studies at Harvard and served as a faculty member at the University of North Dakota. His great magic was that he believed in his students, which led them to believe in themselves. His students fondly called him "Proff."

The sole male student in the founding class (at the close of World War I) was, according to Koch, a "tall mountain lad with burning eyes" named Thomas Wolfe. (Later, the world-famous Wolfe would show up from time to time at Chapel Hill; Niggli seemed to have a distaste for him.) Paul Green had arrived at UNC in 1916, attended for one year, then served for two years overseas during World War I. He returned in 1919 and studied under Koch, producing his first play in 1920. He became one of the most prolific of the earliest Playmakers and was known for his symphonic dramas, attracting large audiences each summer. Green's plays often combined music, serious dialogue, burlesque skits, songs, and poetry, similar to some of Niggli's folk plays. Sixteen years her senior, he would exert a great influence on her and others in the company. He and his wife Elizabeth became lifelong friends of Niggli's. Green received a Pulitzer in 1927 and was a faculty member and adviser to the Carolina Playmakers during the 1930s and 1940s. A particular play, *The Field God* (which opened in 1927 at the Greenwich Village Theatre), is a folk drama, with a title interestingly similar to Niggli's *The Fair God*. Green's early plays often had an epic format with serious topics, the most prominent being *Jeremy Johnson* (1936) about the struggle of the individual against war and violence. His later work is more characterized by musical dramas. He was also especially interested in the film medium, finding the motion-picture camera one of the greatest instruments for storytelling; his play about the Old and New South, *The House of Connelly* (staged in 1931), was converted to a movie in 1934 by 20th Century Fox, with the title *Carolina*. Green spent several years in Hollywood on various occasions, and may have been instrumental in getting Niggli work in Hollywood. They composed a musical drama together in 1953, *Serenata*, for a summer festival in California.

By the time Niggli joined the Carolina Playmakers in 1935, men outnumbered women. She dove energetically into the responsibilities of writing, producing, and acting. She even participated in the statewide Dramatic Association conference in Chapel Hill that fall by giving a talk on Mexican folk theater. A member of that season's theatrical group, she joined others on a bus tour, performing plays in various cities in North Carolina and surrounding states. She also wrote an article for the December 1935 issue of *The Carolina Play-Book*, where she describes the troupe's thirty-third tour (November 13–26), stating that at each juncture "Little Theatre folks" were very excited to receive them.[2] Youthful exuberance and a playful tone are evident in her report on their experiences. The first stop for the group was the town of Charlotte, followed by a performance in Red Springs, then a return to "the Hill" (Chapel Hill) for clean clothes and a night's sleep. Niggli jokes that everyone was trying to doze on the "Show-Bus, but the stage manager had a talkative streak, and *managed* (no pun intended) to keep everyone awake until we reached home. Our beds never looked so good." On Monday they departed for Smithfield, where classrooms became their dressing rooms, and she remarks that their observations of posters on the walls around them elicited chants of "two plus two equals four, etc." as they changed costumes. Niggli cites a few "disasters" and accidental dramatic turns during their performances, as well as their amazement upon viewing historical sites in the next town, Nashville. They stopped for lunch in the "ancient village inn of stage-coach days. In the dining room, one hundred and seventy-five years old, we wondered if Lafayette, and Washington, and perhaps General Lee had eaten there." She adds that Jefferson Davis "surely had" done so, for they noticed a Confederate flag hanging in the school auditorium.

Niggli describes their stop in Morehead City and enjoyment of an oyster roast, a ride to the sand dunes, and the learning of a "sea chantey." Other stops included "Little" Washington, Kinston, Salisbury, Greensboro, and Guilford in North Carolina, and Hampton in northern Virginia. Here they performed at the Hampton Institute, "one of the largest Negro schools in the United States," where the second play—which had a different title—was changed and "printed on the Hampton playbill as *Big John* out of consideration for the Negro feeling about the word 'Nigger.' Naturally, this play held great interest here since it presented the struggle of a Negro share-cropper [a play written by Fred Howard]." Since it is a play with twists and ironic tension, Niggli states that "racial feeling was running high, and they felt it. . . . However, as the play progressed and the audience understood, the disturbance ceased and at the reception tendered us by the Hampton Players afterwards, there was much generous praise for the author and his play."

Tooth or Shave

One of the three plays being performed on the tour was Niggli's own first play for the company, *Tooth or Shave*. A comedy with only four characters, it is situated in the quaint village of Santa Catarina, at the foothills of the western mountains on the outskirts of Monterrey—a village that would continue to appear in nearly all of her writings. The main character of *Tooth or Shave* is based on the real-life barber, who was also the village dentist when an emergency arose, of Niggli's childhood village, San Nicolás de Hidalgo (according to a 4 June 1939 article in *The San Antonio Express-News*). This farce was so popular that two productions were staged that year.

The Cry of Dolores

During 1935 Niggli also wrote and produced *The Cry of Dolores*, a one-act play based on the story of Mexico's historic shout or "cry"—effected by the priest Miguel Hidalgo y Costilla—that symbolically launched the struggle for independence. At that moment, however, it was a rally for independence from France, which had invaded Spain in 1808 and now occupied the throne. Niggli's goal is to reenact the very historic moment, with the appropriate characters. She makes this point in her foreword:

> This is the story of a miracle . . . a miracle that aided a small band of patriots to free Mexico from the bondage, not of Spain, but of Napoleon Bonaparte.
>
> The situation, the characters, the scene, and even the speeches have been lifted directly from the pages of history. In this instance, at least, history is stranger than fiction.

The "cry" goes out from Father Hidalgo's pulpit, after he rings the church bells at close to midnight, in the small village of Dolores. This occurs on September 15, 1810—a date hastily pushed up by the rebels once their plan was discovered, so that they would not be arrested and killed. Several rebel leaders, including Ignacio Allende, were in the city of Querétaro when word was leaked to the authorities that they had hidden a cache of arms. The military began a search from house to house, but Allende had already left for Dolores (in the nearby state of Guanajuato) to alert

Hidalgo. Allende was a trained military officer, while the priest possessed a great talent for inspiring and leading the masses.[3] The elite *criollos* were interested principally in preserving their connection to Spain, and later in setting up their own monarchy. But the mestizo and Indian masses, most of whom had no access to education or work except as servants and slaves, wanted freedom. They were inspired by the priest Hidalgo, who created schools for artisans, workshops for carpentry and blacksmithing, and cultivated vineyards and olive groves, all of which meant they could work independently. While Niggli does not cite these specifics, she features Hidalgo as the older, respected figure (he was, in fact, fifty-seven), and mestizo freedom the primary motivation for the rebellion.

In the latter decades of the eighteenth century, Spanish authorities tightened their grip on the colonies in the Americas, often jailing or severely punishing those who would instigate the idea of freedom (inspired by such philosophers as Voltaire, Rousseau, and Descartes, whose books were outlawed by the Spanish crown). Those in high society, however, had created literary societies where they were able to sneak in books or discussions, and in time these societies became political hotbeds for underground leaders. Niggli appropriately cites their existence and how the "literary" groups helped foment the action about to unfold.

She also does not shrink from portraying the heroic woman's role in the insurrection. Niggli makes her principal character Josefa Ortiz de Domínguez (played by Niggli in the Carolina Playmakers production), the person who gets word to the rebel leaders that they are about to be caught. While true to Mexican history, the use of this strong female character also represents a feminist move, perhaps as a result of the rich 1920s era when women became involved in politics and won the right to vote (in the United States), an activity that was then squelched in most nations following the worldwide depression. In fact, her lead female character stands out more than any of the other characters, including the famous priest. In real life, Josefa paid dearly for her patriotic deed. She was betrayed and then jailed (in a convent) in 1811, put on trial in Mexico City, and found guilty; for her tirades against Spanish colonial authorities, she was again jailed in a stricter convent and not released until the Independence War ended in 1821.

The Cry of Dolores opens with Josefa's daughter, Lolita, crying and pouting because she fears for the safety of her fiancé, the captain Ignacio Allende, whom she tries to convince to desist from rebellious actions. He tries to console her by announcing that he has brought with him a distinguished guest, Don Miguel Hidalgo. Niggli uses this arrival to depict the polite phraseology and formal greetings of a Spanish household: "Our house is your house," and "your servant." The man who accompanies the priest Hidalgo, Don Carlos, is said to be the warden of the city prison; Doña Josefa will get his help after her husband leaves. (In real life the person who helped Doña Josefa was the city mayor, Ignacio Pérez.)

Father Hidalgo tells them the time is near for the "cry of freedom"; he then repeats the traditional saying "Long live our sacred Mother of Guadalupe" (Guadalupe as spiritual guide would figure in nearly all of Niggli's plays). Doña Josefa expresses her desire for the release of more than one hundred political prisoners in jail. Hidalgo responds, "Señora, you are our mast of courage." She is a crucial character; it is she who will encourage and convince both her daughter and, later, Don Carlos that it is an important historic moment. She says, "Now is the time to free our country! I dedicate myself to the revolution although it may cost all of us our lives." Doña Josefa forthrightly supports the underground movement. In the play as in real life, Josefa's husband Miguel is aware of his wife's leanings and subversive work, but he is bound first to perform his duties as magistrate (royal official) for the city of Querétaro. Therefore, he must make the arrests when the order arrives. As truly occurred in history, he locks his wife in so that she will not warn the rebels. It is the evening of September 15, which Niggli has Doña Josefa pinpoint to indicate exactly when the "cry" to battle occurs. With Mexico's cry to arms, the future has begun, says Josefa Domínguez, concluding the play with: "Up with the true religion, down with false government. The sixteenth of September! What a glorious day for all of us."

Thus Niggli instructs her English-language public on how Mexican independence was finally achieved, in an era much later than that of the United States. Here, in one of her first one-act plays performed by the Carolina Playmakers, Niggli also launches her "cry" or *raison d'être*. Prominent contemporary Mexican writer Elena Poniatowska defines literature by Mexican writers as "un largo grito," a long, or ongoing shout (quoted in Chevigny). By representation of the originating moment of Mexican history, with its shout for independence, in one of her initial works, Niggli surely defines her own personal yell or *grito*, in typical Mexican fashion. She makes her stand: her writing career would espouse her Mexican heritage. The name "Hidalgo" was also of great significance to Niggli (as it is throughout Mexico). It graced the village where she grew up, and provided the setting for her first novel; it is also a frequent name on monuments throughout Mexico. Thus the powerful symbols of Hidalgo as national father, and "the cry" recognized and espoused by all patriotic Mexicans launched Niggli's literary career.

The passionate political message of this play was likely little understood by U.S. society, which probably accounts for it not being published. But Niggli also achieved a subversive tactic in terms of Mexican tradition. She not only recreated a significant historical moment in drama, she substantiated the quick resolve and intelligence of a Mexican woman, making her actions evident in official history. Critical sources have pointed out that Niggli's women characters are independent, free-thinking, and free-acting creatures, ahead of their time. They display the political concerns of the early twentieth century, when women in several countries were finally seeing the fruition of their decades-long political struggle to have the right to vote. In Mexico, the Women's Movement was constant and strong during the 1920s and 1930s, then abruptly cut off. Despite some high-level political support, the ratification of women's right to vote was buried, and women did not receive that privilege until 1947. As the new political system solidified in the years following the Revolution, women's roles were unfortunately again subsumed, culturally reverting to the practice of the past.

The Cry of Dolores has a feminist touch similar to that employed by contemporary dramatist Cherríe Moraga in *Heart of the Earth: A Popul Vuh Story* (2000), based on the origin of human life in the Americas. In Moraga's play, the grandmother figure is the one who comes up with the idea of creating human beings from corn, in contrast to the foiled attempts (from mud and wood) of her husband and another male god. While feminist roles occur in many of Niggli's works, her early display of consciousness is equal to many examples in later Mexican American literature. Niggli may have been far from Mexico, but she demonstrates a connection to her roots, her childhood experience, and Mexican history, as well as a desire to reveal Mexican culture to an English-language public and to bring attention to women's accomplishments. These would become lifelong themes in her body of work. These first two plays launched her practice of alternating comedies and historical dramas (the latter also often contained an exaggerated comedic element).

As Niggli entered into her second year at Chapel Hill, she wrote and produced two new comedies set in Mexican village life, which would become the two plays that made her famous: *The Red Velvet Goat* and *Sunday Costs Five Pesos*. She also created two additional historic dramas (also one-act), *Azteca* and *Soldadera*. The first is based on life for young women in the indigenous era before Spanish arrival, with a surprise twist. Two sisters are in love with the same man; one's jealousy drives her to orchestrate the sacrifice of her sister at a sacred women's temple, but the male hero changes the outcome by choosing to sacrifice himself with her. Each of the four plays were first staged during 1936, with additional productions the following year.

Soldadera

Soldadera: A Play of the Mexican Revolution—featuring a significant Mexican female symbol, the soldier-woman or "Adelita"—is about heroic women during the Mexican Revolution. It is the first written work in either Mexico or the United States—after Niggli's *The Cry of Dolores*—that commemorates women soldiers. It has continued to be staged for decades (most recently in San Francisco in 2006). *Soldadera* was also immortalized by being selected for publication in *The Best One-Act Plays of 1937.* This is the principal play by Niggli that is cited and studied in contemporary academic articles, most likely because of its portrayal of women figures in early twentieth-century culture. Only this play (with the exception of some minor discussion on *This is Villa!*) and Niggli's novel *Mexican Village* have actually been discussed in contemporary criticism. In fact, Niggli's entire literary reputation in the United States rests on *Soldadera*, and on the novel *Mexican Village*.

Alicia Arrizón's book *Latina Performance: Traversing the Stage* (1999) devotes considerable attention to *Soldadera* in one of its chapters. Arrizón notes Niggli's dual placement of the Adelita figure as the female object of male desire and martyr for the patriarchal revolutionary cause, as well as a symbol—along with her companions—of women's involvement in the Mexican Revolution. Her older characters demonstrate women forced to leave their homes after losing everything, including sons, and who were—quoting from Niggli's synopsis—"dragged along after their men, cooking for them, tending their wounds, guarding their ammunition, fighting when necessary." Thus Niggli's drama is one of the earliest representations of the heroic role of women in war.[4]

The scene for *Soldadera* is a campsite high in the Sierra Madre mountains, near the city of Saltillo (most of Niggli's body of work would depict the geographic region between Monterrey, the Santa Catarina river valley to its west, and the nearest large city, Saltillo). The date is indicated as 1914. The women, with the exception of the group leader, are illiterate, much as the majority of Mexico's Indian and mestizo population at that time. Thus, they can easily be duped by an intellectual from Mexico City—Niggli's character "The Rich One"—who is a federal soldier held as a captive at the campsite. As this representative of Porfirio Díaz's society scoffs at the women, their leader, Concha, states flat out that she will stop the *federales*. Niggli also uses the term "Grandfather Devil" here, which will appear again and again in her works to refer to Indian lore for the place in hell that awaits those who do wrong.

Niggli likely picked up her lead character's name, Adelita, from a Casasola photo caption (either in his first *Álbum gráfico* published in 1921 or from newspapers) for the likeness of a woman soldier—so dubbed because of the popularity of the Mexican *corrido* (ballad) titled "Adelita."[5] In fact, verses of this song, composed during the Revolution, are sung and discussed in her play. In the corrido, Adelita is the woman either left behind or desired by a soldier, who wants to share his stories with her and have her accompany him on the Revolutionary march. The traditional corrido did not evoke the woman's own heroics in combat, however. As Arrizón declares, Niggli's play was the first theatrical representation, north or south of the border, of women's participation in the Revolution. Historically, soldaderas have been viewed romantically and nostalgically, but in the current era the word has come to denote an ideological consciousness toward the formation of women's identity. The Mexican woman had been visualized in song as an inspiring force backing, and serving, the men, but not in active combat. Niggli's play is the earliest depiction of an "Adelita" as a thinking and acting human being, portraying this symbolic woman as valiant participant in a struggle against oppressive forces.

Thus Niggli put into words, in 1936, the story not only of the Revolution—which she would continue to do with subsequent plays—but also the crucial fact of women's involvement in social change. Niggli had her finger on the pulse of a significant new development in social and feminist consciousness that only decades later would be explored as a turning point for women. The Adelita figure is to contemporary literature the symbol of women's rebellion, one who resists powers that limit and control her. In fact, for contemporary Chicana writers, "Adelita" equals "Chicana."

Arrizón compares Niggli's *Soldadera* to a 1936 narrative, *Francisco Villa y La Adelita*, by Mexican Baltasar Dromundo in which the "Adelita" is represented as a woman soldier who gives a speech at a victory dinner. The revolutionary General Villa is immediately fascinated and soon makes a pass at her, whereupon her companion becomes jealous, wants to kill Villa but refrains because he is the general, and instead kills himself. Up to this point, Dromundo's story is more similar to Niggli's 1938 play *This is Villa!*. Dromundo's story goes on, however, to have Adelita banished from camp by the general, whereupon she rejoins soldiers in fighting and is killed on the battlefield. Niggli's play, on the other hand, demonstrates active and conscious forethought on the part of the soldaderas. Niggli is ahead of her time in creating a significant female cultural symbol (her play was written before or simultaneously with Dromundo's book) that also fits the early twentieth century's success of the suffrage movement.

Arrizón sees weakness in Niggli's depiction of the Adelita character as naïve and unknowing, tying into a romantic interpretation. I don't agree. This character can be better understood if we bear in mind that Niggli's discourse consistently involved portraying Mexican history and the people's makeup, why they act and react the way they do (Niggli's dramas were always directed to an English-language audience). A majority of Mexicans (mestizos) had been kept illiterate and without access to the goods of modern society by the controlling elite, decades after gaining independence from Spain. Therefore, young mestizos were going to be illiterate.

The heroic sacrifice of Niggli's Adelita plays logically into the hands of dominant narratives on the Mexican Revolution, as noted by Arrizón and Tabea Alexa Linhard, but Linhard shows that there is resistance as well as accommodation to patriarchal tradition in the Niggli character's free choice to die. She personifies the steps taken by many other women, even if it is only a set of footprints. As Linhard states, "the symbol Adelita and the character Adelita clash in Josephina Niggli's play." Adelita in Niggli's play is a symbol of change (a subtle message for her public), as well as of mestizo victory. On the other hand, Adelita is indeed a young, poor woman who will never have the chance to tell her own story.

It is understandable that *Soldadera* has been considered critically more than Niggli's other plays. It shines forth in an era when master narratives were only those created by male writers, little attention was given to Mexican women's participation in history, and in the United States, little attention to Mexican culture. While Adelita is sacrificed for the Revolution and thus cannot enter Mexico City victoriously on horseback like Villa or Zapata (as the famous photographs and posters would forever inform us), the other women in the play—especially the intellectual leader Concha—resist women's erasure in history, and by their participation, their beliefs, and their antagonism toward the elite in power, mark their own revolutionary stance. With *Soldadera*, Niggli more solidly launches two primary themes: women as contributors to society, and the mestizo consciousness or philosophy of the Mexican people.

On the seventieth anniversary of its initial production, *Soldadera* was staged in San Francisco, California, in 2006 by a professional company called Multi Ethnic Theater, founded in 1993. *Soldadera* was selected for a month-long run as part of a festival titled *Celebrating Latina Courage & Culture*, performed at Next Stage Theater on Gough Street. The actors and reviewers found in it reflections that connected to their own families' personal stories and were true to history. In their promotional material, MET stated that *Soldadera* represents "the strong mestiza women who disregarded European rules for female behavior," and called Adelita "a revolutionary figure who resists powers that limit and control her." The director, fifty-three-year-old Douglas Marshall, said he first discovered the play (having found Niggli's book of plays in the library) in 1981. Once he was established with the San Francisco theater scene, he wanted to do more plays with "historical value," and as he got to know two particular actresses, he felt they were indeed the characters Concha and María. Current-day politics around immigrant issues motivated Marshall to select a Mexican-themed play to stage in

September—the era of Mexican cultural awareness. Initially the final show would have occurred on November 20, the anniversary of the Mexican Revolution, but the season was shortened. When the actresses were cast, "they were immediately struck by how much information Niggli gave her characters," Marshall said, as actors often have to spend considerable time researching their characters in order to prepare for a role. He continues: "As a play with seven strong female roles, it wasn't too difficult to see what this play would mean not only to people of Mexican origin, but to women in general, being a play written by a woman, a Latina, about women who, save for her play, have little mention and recognition for their role in Mexico's freedom." The San Francisco opening program included a ten-minute slideshow of vintage photos of Mexican revolutionary figures including soldaderas, and at the end, a photo of Niggli herself in the 1960s. Marshall concludes: "I think I could make a career doing her plays, one acts and three acts, and would be very keen about doing a movie about her. She holds such an interest from so many points of view. Here is someone that anyone would benefit from knowing more about."

The Red Velvet Goat

Niggli's comedies (staged the same year as *Soldadera*), *The Red Velvet Goat* and *Sunday Costs Five Pesos*, have become the two most frequently performed of all her plays. While each play was registered with Samuel French as soon as it was first produced, making the plays easily accessible, Niggli's own anthology published in 1938 additionally helped promote these comedies. *The Red Velvet Goat* was first published in the prominent *One Act Play Magazine* in July 1937, and was also selected by her coach, Proff Koch, for his *American Folk Plays*, a book published in 1939.[6] It is curious to find her play under this title, although perhaps Koch intended to broadly indicate the continent. Ten years later, this play was selected once again by another of Niggli's professors, Samuel Selden, for a more appropriate collection, *International Folk Plays* (1949).

This play-within-a-play, subtitled "A tragedy of laughter and a comedy of tears," involves a man who mounts a play in the patio of his house—with himself, his wife, and son as actors—in order to accrue some extra cash to buy a goat. He makes the mistake, however, of cutting cloth from his wife's old red velvet dress for one of the props. She is infuriated by what he has done, and by the end of the play, turns the tables on him by using his profits from the performance to purchase a new dress. With Niggli's typical theatrical sparring between the genders, unusual twists, and comedic revenge, this play became immediately popular and moved to a New York City venue. Selected by the One-Act Repertory Theater for their opening season, which was then delayed for a year, it was performed in a short run—together with other short plays, including one by Jean Giraudoux—beginning on January 16, 1938, at the Hudson Theater. The season included only five performances.

An editorial the following year (January 1939) in *One Act Play Magazine* calls the One-Act Repertory company's first season disappointing. The editor observes, however, that *The Red Velvet Goat* was a highlight, although it could have been better "had the actors succeeded in conveying the Latin temperament, and if the play had been compressed into a shorter interval and supplied with fewer pyrotechnics." He does not mention Niggli, and these comments only criticize this specific presentation of the play.

In summer of that year, a newspaper article in the *San Antonio Express-News* by critic Amy Freeman Lee states that *The Red Velvet Goat* was performed on Broadway "with great success" (June 4, 1939), adding that *Sunday Costs Five Pesos* has been a favorite in England, where "one performance of it is presented to an English audience somewhere every night." This article assesses Niggli's career, including the publication of her anthology of plays, and calls *The Red Velvet Goat* "the most interesting of the group." Freeman Lee quotes Niggli directly: "It is a comedy written in poetic dialogue with a romantic flavor" [then she compares the fact that her characters create a homemade play to the San Antonio practice of *Los pastores* presentations during the Christmas season]. "If there is a moral to be found in this play, I think it is this: that we may thank God that there are still grown people who retain the hearts of children." Only twenty-nine years old at this time, Niggli's success demonstrates her lifelong goal to portray *what* people do and *how* they do it, rather than analyzing *why* they do it.

In London, during World War II, *The Red Velvet Goat* was in fact performed at various locations during each night of the Blitz in May 1940 (according to several newspaper sources), and frequently during the entire war period. An interview years later, in 1978, quotes Niggli remembering hearing of her play's success even before she had traveled abroad: "During World War II soldiers who had been at Chapel Hill when she was there told her that when their transport ship put in at Ireland, they walked down the street and saw her name on a marquee advertising her plays" (Wolcott). It is a play that has remained popular through the years, both in the United States and in England.[7] In fact, in 1965—twenty-six years after its first debut in New York City—*The Red Velvet Goat* was performed as street theater by the Mobilization For Youth (M.F.Y.) Summer Theater Project, as reported in the *New York Times*. The following year, it was performed at Questors Theatre in London by another group of students. It is a play that often appeals to young people; it is fun, as well as short enough to deliver together with other activities.

Sunday Costs Five Pesos

The title of this comedy derives from a pre-Revolution Mexican law that fines or punishes citizens for causing an altercation on the day of rest. The female roles are principal in this play and include a petulant female who becomes jealous of another young woman who moves in on her man. Her friends remind her not to cause a fight on Sunday. The dénouement brings all members of the small village together to see that several misunderstandings, and an accident, caused the great tumult. All is resolved.

Sunday Costs Five Pesos first saw publication in *One Act Play Magazine* in 1938 (as well as in Niggli's own anthology). It was performed as an opera in 1950, by a composer in the town of Charlotte, North Carolina. The play is timeless in terms of interest for educational purposes. It was published in *Invitation to Drama: One Act Plays for Secondary Schools* in 1956, and again selected for the book *15 International One-Act Plays* in 1969. *Sunday Costs Five Pesos* and selections from *Mexican Village* appeared in the very first anthology of *Mexican American Authors* in 1972.

Both *The Red Velvet Goat* and *Sunday Costs Five Pesos* continue to this day to attract British audiences; in fact, as recently as 2002 each was staged at the Tain Royal Academy in Scotland. (During the early 1950s,

Niggli taught in Bristol at the Old Vic Theatre School, which may retain an archive of her works).

Sunday Costs Five Pesos is also frequently staged in the United States. In Southern California in 1974 it was performed by students in the Arcadia High School drama department, as well as by the Players Theater in the town of Burbank. In 1986, it was staged by the Las Vegas (New Mexico) High School Players, and in 1999 it was revived in Fort Worth, Texas, by a newly formed theater group, Teatro Main Street, trying to launch a "Hispanic theater" tradition. Its season opened with *Soldadera*; later, *Sunday* was staged, together with a few scenes from *Tooth or Shave*.

In her two years in the program, Niggli had become a key member of the Carolina Playmakers. She was fully involved in directing, acting, designing costumes and sets (even doing much of the sewing herself), and her work was appreciated and well received by the public and the press for its uniqueness for the era. She offered a new angle to the company's commitment to regional, folk-oriented plays—the only member who portrayed and explained Mexican culture.

Niggli also created two full-length dramas: *The Fair God* (based on Maximilian's short reign in Mexico), and *Singing Valley*, which served as her thesis. *The Cry of Dolores* and *The Fair God* were never published. No copies were found in her manuscripts at Western Carolina University, but they are preserved in the Carolina Playmaker's manuscript archives at Chapel Hill. *The Fair God* was produced in 1936 by the Carolina Playmakers, and has received no attention since then. (Niggli included an excerpt of it in her *Pointers on Playwriting* text.)

Singing Valley

The three-act play *Singing Valley: A Comedy of Mexican Village Life* was written in partial fulfillment of requirements for the awarding of her M.A. in Dramatic Art in 1937. It portrays the west-of-Monterrey valley of Niggli's childhood. An unattributed epigraph, following a dedication to her coach and professor Samuel Selden, states: "He on whose heart the dust of Mexico has lain, will find no rest in any other land," a tribute to the land of her birth that sounds like a Mexican *dicho*, or saying. Although labeled a "comedy," it is more a descriptive history of the valley, with both dramatic tension and comedy. In a critical book describing the advent of the "new" novel in contemporary Mexico, Carlos Fuentes stated in 1969 that humor was an essential tool of twentieth-century Mexican creative works. Narrative as well as dramatic works comprising parody, picaresque improvisation, or sentimental irony were judged by Fuentes as markers of true Mexican literature (30). Evidently, Niggli had her pulse on new literary strategies and tendencies in Mexico; this play is a straightforward story with comedic elements that help open its political and historical discourse.

Singing Valley is also a demonstration of popular culture—in fact, part of the narrative tradition from which Mexican telenovelas were later created (in the 1960s). In other words, it is a classic example of the Mexican way of relating a story, rendered in contemporary televised culture as a telenovela. While this genre is translated simply as "soap opera" in English, that is an erroneous definition. Telenovelas are actually short-running televised serials where principal characters interpret drama and history, and minor characters provide a comedic element.[8] They frequently describe and give emphasis to the cultural practices in a particular region of Mexico. Before television, there were *radionovelas*, and there have always been *fotonovelas*, small pocket books sold at newspaper stands, with comic-book-style portrayals of historic and contemporary issues. "Novela" is the word in Spanish for novel or story, hence its ubiquitous use. These traditional stories for everyday life always depict a "lord of the manor" bad guy who does harm to those who oppose him (the antithesis to the good principal character), and a priest to provide counsel to the good people and mediate conflicts between the two. The bad guy in *Singing Valley* is Don Rufino, who rules over the valley's residents (in the past, he has even had his rival's son kidnapped, and later released only after the man desisted from opposing him). Don Rufino is said to be the "step-son of *Grandfather Devil*," a character from peasant lore that Niggli cites continuously in her works (she also created a one-act play based on this figure, which was never published).

The new hero's arrival brings hope to the community. Don Antonio is the good character who returns to the land of his youth and wants to help his people. He is wealthy and powerful enough to defy Don Rufino. *Singing Valley* unveils the classic conflict of Spanish colonial tradition between *patrón* (land boss) and peasant, and the play takes place in an era that reveals tensions of "progress" against retaining old structures of power, a clash between old and new orders in Mexico.[9]

Niggli's play is set in the year 1935, the moment of Don Antonio's return. He has been in exile for thirty years, during which time he made his fortune. He now wants to help his community by building a hydro-electric plant—here called a "power-house"—to pump water for irrigation and bring farming to the valley. Don Rufino is a godfather of sorts; the only rich man in the valley, he owns the goats that provide its economy. Other men, even if they have their own herd, must work for him. He controls pricing and commerce. One young man has found a way to escape his clutches; he is a candy maker and the mail carrier, as well as a singer of ballads as he rides his donkey up the hill. Don Antonio is welcomed with open arms by members of the community, and they become overjoyed by the prospects of independent livelihood. They are tired of the wicked Don Rufino's control. Don Antonio is accompanied by his young adult children, Abel and Lupita, who plan to leave and return to the big city (New York) as soon as they can. As the story ensues, however, Abel falls in love the valley, while his sister haughtily longs for the finer things of life. He is also a singer and yearns to learn the songs of this valley, which Lupita disdains, preferring modern music.

Singing Valley includes love interests (as in telenovelas) for both of the young people, and a matronly woman, Doña Beca, who barks orders and keeps the young women from disobeying traditional rules. Early in the play, Abel's impression of the valley evokes Mexican love of region or *patria*, as often related in Mexican music and telenovelas. For him, "the air shimmers like an opal." He says: "Look at this view, Lupita. Those mountains across the valley are so close I believe I could touch them with my hands. I've seen a lot of things, but I never saw purple mountains before. Look! Look, some goats are coming down it. They appeared, just out of nowhere. Tiny little white things."

A cornerstone cultural element in this play is its description of Mexico's patron saint, the Virgin of Guadalupe. When Don Antonio arrives to reoccupy his former home, he immediately reacts to the empty niche in the wall and asks where the icon is. The village priest replies that he took her to the church for safekeeping and will now return the Blessed Lady. Later in the play, the icon is displayed prominently, and characters say their prayers before her (as done frequently in contemporary telenovelas). A selection from Act I is included here, with dialogue between Abel and Lupita, and then Ester, relating some of the history of the village and the goat-herder tradition.

The Holy Virgin's namesake is, of course, Lupita, and the final act takes place on her saint's day, December 12. The worldly Lupita is little aware of this and is surprised as villagers arrive and congratulate her, wishing her well. They plan a surprise party in the afternoon with a piñata. When her newspaper friend arrives—whom she had hoped would whisk her away to New York—he is reminded by Doña Beca that it is her day, to which he replies it is "a childish institution" or custom. Doña Beca is miffed, states that he has no manners, and quickly shoos him out of the house. Lupita finally realizes that she is now "home again, among your friends," as other characters state to her. The priest says, "This house stands in the shadow of Our Blessed Lady who has worked miracles," and Lupita feels blessed as the bearer of her name. Thus the play is a classic example of Mexican popular culture—a telenovela ahead of its time, or simply a classic traditional story.

Mexican traditions are continuously reflected by Niggli, including that of celebrating saint's days (they are more significant than birthdays). In her novel *Step Down, Elder Brother*, characters plan events around their saint's days. Niggli left behind an well-developed but unpublished short story (in her Western Carolina University's [WCU] manuscripts) of unknown date that bears the title "Saint's Day." The action takes place in the chapel of a deserted hacienda, stated to have been destroyed by Indians long before, "when Texas was still part of Mexico." Now it is 1863, and a small group of soldiers holed up in the chapel appear to be engaged in the U.S. Civil War. The main characters have last names of Avila and Williams; the former is from Laredo and remembers that today is his daughter Cecilia's saint's day—he is now "far to the East" of Laredo. It is June, and he recalls when three months earlier the "Yanks" swarmed into Yellow River and took the town. The troops were greatly reduced in number before their arrival at the hacienda, due to an attack by Comanches. Thus Niggli's story is unusual for discussing a "southern" perspective, and for capturing Indian-Anglo clashes during the nineteenth century. When the men are besieged by "federal" troops, who appear to be U.S. Yankees, Avila offers up a prayer to Saint Cecilia, and in fact most of them are able to escape.

Niggli's works are frequently imbued with the Mexican popular belief in the possibility of a miracle, a *milagro*. This cultural attitude toward life makes plays like *Singing Valley* timeless; it could easily be presented as a telenovela today.

Singing Valley is very well constructed and an excellent depiction of Mexican regional life; its story rivals contemporary productions that focus on a specific region and big changes that mark its history. While the full-length play was not initially published, it would later be included (with some revisions) in a commemorative edition published by the University of North Carolina Press in 1968, titled *Adventures in Playmaking: Four Plays by Carolina Playmakers*. The selections provided here are from Niggli's original master's thesis.

It is also significant to point out that in her university thesis, Niggli applied accent marks and tildes (for example, the "~" over the "n" in Doña), which was not necessary for an English-language document. She took care to provide an accurate portrait, linguistically and dramatically, of her native Mexico. In a short acknowledgement, Niggli thanks J. Frank Dobie (the quintessential early twentieth-century writer of Texas lore) for the "collection of *dichos* which he sent me, from which were drawn many of the folk expressions used in this play."

Singing Valley and other plays (as well as her novels) demonstrate Niggli's habitual propensity to translate culturally as she writes in English. While "in just a minute" would be the English-language equivalent of *en un momentito*, her characters regularly say, "in a little moment" (stated frequently in *Singing Valley*). Her early plays and narratives consistently make typical use of the diminutive, common in Spanish usage in Mexico (while it would not be common in Spain). Niggli also frequently makes literal translations of the phrases of polite Mexican custom, such as "My house is your house" and "With your permission." Characters are always respectful and formal in Niggli's plays, using the titles Don and Doña (as was the practice by Mexican society until just recently in metropolitan areas), and "your servant," as one responds to an introduction. Another trait was to include pronouns and prepositions that are unnecessary or different in English—for example, *the* and a person's name, such as "the Doña Beca," or "I will be *in* the cantina," rather than "at," as would be used in English. This could have been Niggli's own bilingual error, but probably was more purposeful to provide a sense of the original language and culture.

First Book Published

At about the same time she completed her master's degree, the University of North Carolina Press decided to publish a book of her plays. *Mexican Folk Plays* was released in 1938 (dedicated to her mother and Samuel Selden). Niggli chose to balance her three comedies, *Tooth or Shave*, *The Red Velvet Goat*, and *Sunday Costs Five Pesos*, with two serious dramas, *Azteca* and *Soldadera*, thus depicting Mexican Indian heritage and the Revolution as well as contemporary village life. The introduction to her text was provided by Koch, and a foreword by Rodolfo Usigli, Mexican playwright and theater director at the National University of Mexico (he was only five years older than Niggli, but had been prolific in writing plays during the 1930s). Usigli may have been in New York City at the time Niggli's book was being prepared; he had received a Rockefeller Fellowship to study drama direction and composition at Yale University in 1935, and made subsequent trips between Mexico City and New York. Usigli was good friends with Niggli's childhood friends the Larraldes (Rómulo Larralde was an actor in the United States as well as Mexico), and he also knew Koch. After completion of her master's, Niggli worked for him as stage manager on a Villaurrutia play.[10]

In Usigli's eloquent foreword, he expresses regret that Niggli does not write in Spanish, stating that no other Mexicans are writing with such humor and sensitive appreciation for folk life. In fact, referring to a "four-centuries old theatrical wasteland," he considers her one of only three dramatists who are essentially Mexican, and her status unique among peers: "Mexican folk drama does not really exist. . . . In fact drama does not seem to be, up to now, the most adequate literary expression for Mexico." While calling her a forerunner, Usigli determines however, that Niggli's plays would not work if translated to Spanish, as the excessive descriptions used to educate an English-language audience unfamiliar with Mexican culture would be unnecessary in Mexico.

Years later in an interview, Paula Shirley (1980) asked Niggli about Usigli's statements, and she responded facetiously that "he had a Rockefeller from Yale, so he knew everything." Shirley said, "Well, he had some very good comments about your theater," to which Niggli responded, "He better!" Then Niggli added that she "would have written it exactly the way it was written" had she created her drama in Spanish.

"Yes, Mexico needed playwrights, but I figured the U.S. needed it more."
Niggli also suggested that Usigli did not understand the experience of
the common people, as he "grew up on the myth of the Revolution."
He was raised in Mexico City, and would not have known the experiences of northern Mexico and the country folk as she did. In the 1930s,
because of his position in Mexico, he was the bigger name. That would
soon change, however.

The arrival of her first book brought Niggli into the limelight in San
Antonio, and also in northern Mexico. She is saluted in an article published in a Spanish-language newspaper in San Antonio, *Diario de la
tarde*, which quotes from Usigli's foreword and contemplates Niggli's
"triunfos." The article further states that she is currently studying
radio production at a university in New York. She is often identified as
"Mexican" in newspaper articles (in fact, Shirley's obituary in the journal *Hispania* calls her a Mexican novelist).

The publication of her collection of plays announced to both the
English and Spanish-speaking world that her creative work represented
Mexico. While she would write several more plays after the release of
the book, Niggli would become recognized for her dramatic contribution by means of this book. Its reissue by Arno Press in 1976, the year
after she retired from full-time teaching, was likely because of continued interest in performing the plays (although the book quickly went
out of print).

From the time of her arrival in North Carolina, Niggli had embarked
on a mission of teaching Mexican cultural history to an English-language
audience. As early as June 1935, her comments in a letter to the editor in
Theatre Arts Monthly, published in New York, reflect her resolve (as well
as her characteristic humor). She first agrees with a writer in an earlier
issue that language needs to be carefully selected when doing translations. Then Niggli remarks that "It has long been a wonder to me that
the Spanish drama, unlike the Russian, Italian and French, has never
been successfully adapted in English. Surely all the world knows that
the Spanish theatre has produced *the* great dramas" (emphasis hers).
She feels that what is missing is "an understanding of what I will call,
a different passion." Niggli then begs readership indulgence while she
recounts "a brief incident that occurred in a small town of about 500
people some thirty-five kilometres from Monterrey":

A traveling stock company arrived there, and presented *Madame X*. Their stage was a few wooden planks supported on saw-horses, their costumes ranging from Stuart England to a very modern French maid. But Mexicans love the theatre, and when the great night arrived, the little square was packed. The play proceeded in a most magnificent manner until the fatal speech of the young lawyer in defense of his mother. The public was so still that the gnawing of a rat would have seemed a thunderclap. The young actor had been speaking for almost two minutes, the tears raining down his face, his arms flailing the air, and then— he stamped his foot. The stage began to rock slowly from side to side, Madame X gave a most undignified scream, and wooden planks, saw-horses, furniture and actors collapsed.

The audience picked them up, put them all back in their proper places, there was a general handshaking all around—then the public returned to rocking chairs and benches, the young actor went on with his speech from the exact place where he had left off, and the play was considered the grand success of the repertoire. That is the true spirit of the Spanish theatre. Do you wonder that it cannot be reproduced successfully in English?

She signed it, "Josefina Niggli."

What Niggli perhaps did not realize at that time was that she was describing the inherent Mexican indigenous people's propensity for outdoor theater, a tradition that dates back long before "Spanish" arrival in Mesoamerica. Indigenous theater often includes jokesters and humor to balance a serious plot.

Academic Reaction to Her Book of Plays

Years later, Niggli's first book began to receive considerable attention from academics. In October 1942, *The English Journal* recommends *Mexican Folk Plays* in an annotated bibliography on "Latin American Literature for the English Classroom." Clustered among mainly translations of Mexican and Spanish literary texts into English, the citation states: "One [play] concerns the Revolution of 1910, another ancient Aztec days, and the other three are hilarious comedies of village life."

In May 1945, in a column on "Latin America Through Drama in English" in the academic journal *Hispania*, Niggli's book is cited, as well as two other plays collected in anthologies in 1938 and 1939. By 1950, the *Educational Theatre Journal*, in a review of a new anthology that included *The Red Velvet Goat*, calls Niggli's play "a delightful farce about a Mexican family involved in some homemade theatricals." The review enthusiastically commends Niggli for her talent in creating a *sainete* (so described by Niggli in her introduction to the play), also dubbed *commedia dell'arte*. Of the nine plays in the anthology under review, the expert considers Niggli's and three others "powerful," with the rest "less successful." In September 1959, *Hispania* would again cite Niggli's *Mexican Folk Plays* in a column tabulating "materials for teaching Spanish in elementary and junior high schools." Niggli's book is described as "five one-act delightful Mexican folk plays written in English by a young Mexican woman."

This Bull Ate Nutmeg

Shortly after completing her master's degree, Niggli created a new comedy based in a small village. *This Bull Ate Nutmeg* is as clever as the earlier comedies but has not received nearly as much attention. Produced by the Carolina Playmakers in 1938, it was immediately collected for publication in *Contemporary One-Act Plays*, and selected again in 1945 for the book *Plays without Footlights*. This play has been performed frequently in recent years in community theater. Again a drama within a drama, two male characters act out the roles of bull and bullfighter for a Sunday performance in a small village. Each of the young male characters seeks the attention of the beautiful daughter of the man who owns the corral where they will perform. Unlike many of Niggli's other plays, with several female characters, this play has only one. As the characters worry nervously about the upcoming performance, a new character, a peddler, arrives in the village selling his wares, among which is what he calls a "love potion," which is actually nutmeg.

This is Villa!

That same year Niggli created another play with a theme of the Mexican Revolution, *This is Villa!*, also staged by the Carolina Playmakers in 1938.

Selected as one of *The Best One-Act Plays of 1938*, it marked the second year in a row that Niggli was distinguished for a best one-act play. The university itself awarded Niggli the Roland Holt Cup for best play in 1938 (although she produced three plays that year). Niggli's is the first creative work written in English on Villa.

This is Villa! offers the iconic revolutionary figure in the classic negative role, as a selfish and petulant man who is at times even a bully.[11] The play does, however, try to demonstrate a three-dimensional figure, discussing the famous general's background and experience to show why he has become the man he is. Other characters are Villa's right-hand man, a heartless killer named Fierro (also his name in real life); a traitor called the "Professor"; a sweet-natured young man who is loyal to Villa but "has no place in the chaos of the Revolution"; and his betrothed, a young woman whom Villa becomes interested in.

Niggli depicts Villa as an uneducated peasant with a talent for setting traps, and contrasts him with the Professor from Mexico City, who is much more cunning. He feigns devotion to the general when in fact he is planning to kill him. By the end, the Professor is outfoxed by Villa. Above all, the play demonstrates why Villa is a leader. In her foreword to the play, Niggli calls it a "portrait of a general, or, if you like, [a] portrait of a sentimental man." She admits he was a murderer as well as a military genius, but that people forget "the facet to his character" that shaped the course of his life. "The most important thing about Villa was that he came from the people, the Mexican peasant," and was connected to the land and a simplicity of life that gave him an "essential child-likeness, not childishness, that people forget." She concludes that no other man in Mexican history so represents "both the best and the worst qualities of the race."

Thus explained, Niggli's play is more about the juncture of history that the Mexican Revolution represents. In addition to the snapshot she creates of a major northern leader, she gives special attention—as with the soldaderas—to minor personalities exemplifying the men who fought and lost lives but who go without recognition. The sweet, young Antonio (who sports a red hat that Villa desires) prefers to shoot himself rather than bring harm to his leader. The Professor is wrong; the Revolution itself is not the great passion, but the people for whom it is being fought. This play received great attention in this era when the United States was on the threshold of world war.

For Niggli, this was a heady time. The year following completion of her master's, she produced three plays with the Carolina Playmakers: *This Bull Ate Nutmeg*, *This is Villa!*, and *The Ring of General Macías*. Early the following year, *This is Villa!* was published in *One Act Play Magazine* (which had published her plays for three years in a row). This issue is devoted to only three plays, principally Niggli's somewhat long one-act drama. The magazine sold for fifty cents an issue in the late 1930s (in comparison, Niggli's book *Mexican Folk Plays* is listed as costing $2.50 in 1942 and 1959), published the plays of up-and-coming dramatists such as Niggli and Langston Hughes, and issued editorial commentary on contemporary drama.[12]

In the previous year it was *Soldadera*, and now *This is Villa!* had been selected as a "best" play of the year. Such an anthology is published the year following the play's production; therefore *The Best One-Act Plays of 1937* was published in the same year as Niggli's *Mexican Folk Plays*. *The Best One-Act Plays of 1938* was published in 1939, when *One Act Play Magazine* devoted attention to her for the third year in a row and Proff Koch's *American Folk Plays* was released (which includes *The Red Velvet Goat*). The University of North Carolina had given Niggli their prestigious Roland Holt Cup, and several of her plays were being produced in Great Britain. In April 1940, when the Carolina Playmakers celebrated its twenty-first birthday, its founder used the opportunity to salute a dozen of his former playwright students with "five-star awards for distinguished achievement" (Spearman 78). These included eight men (principal Paul Green) and four women, the principal being Niggli, who was not yet thirty years old. (Later Niggli would be considered one of UNC Press's stars; she was named in 1947 as a prominent author in a brief *New York Times* mention of the university press's twenty-fifth anniversary.)

Niggli was garnering extensive publicity, but it was an era when politics would soon put restrictions on creative activity. She often made it clear she did not get involved in politics; therefore, in the case of *This is Villa!* Niggli was surprised—as related in a 1980 interview (Shirley)—by what the editor of *The Best One-Act Plays of 1938* said to her. "She asked me to lunch, and said, 'You're very young to write a play like this.' [After conversation, she added], 'Well, I have been listening to you and you don't sound as though you belong to the Communist party.'" After a guffaw, Niggli stated that Chapel Hill in those days was "rated as the

Communist school." She continued to quote the editor: "She said, 'I chose this play for its social protest,' and I said I was Catholic, I wasn't protesting anything. Then she said, 'Well why did you write it?'" Niggli laughed again and said she told the woman why, which was not at all pleasing to her. Someone had given Niggli a remarkable red hat; she kept it as a prop in the Carolina Playmakers costume shop. There had been some talk in the company about her writing a play about Pancho Villa, and then a peer or colleague (Bob Nachtmann, to whom she dedicated the play, and who became well known under the stage name Robert Dale Palmer) asked her to write a role for him wearing the red hat. "So I wrote that play just so that he could wear that hat!"

During this interview she explained how she obtained in-depth knowledge about the Revolution. "At the time I was engaged to a man who had been a captain in the Revolution, he was a colonel when I knew him, in Monterrey. He was the one who told me about the *soldaderas* and what kind of life they led, so that play was absolutely the way it really was." He also recommended books (Niggli was an avid reader) that helped inform *This is Villa!* For example, "I got that argument between Fierro and the Professor out of the Carranza memoir" (Shirley 1980).

The Early 1940s

In North Carolina, Niggli was playing an active role in other creative ventures. A short note in the March 1941 issue of Incarnate Word's *The Logos* states that she writes "all script for the radio programs of the University of North Carolina and is the official photographer. One of her poems, 'The Goat-herder's Song' has recently been set to music by Ralph Baldwin and arranged for four voices."

The very next issue of *The Logos* states that "her play *Death and Pancho Villa* has been chosen as one of the series of eight American folk plays to be given by the Carolina Playmakers of the Air in a coast to coast broadcast." Niggli, or someone else, slightly altered the title for its radio release.

A quick study, Niggli often connected her childhood memories and observations of Mexican life to an idea, and only had to conduct research for historical precision. Her talent for writing had developed early, hence her immediate success in the Carolina Playmakers company; she could quickly convert a prop (as evidenced by the red hat), an overheard comment, or a specific request into a play. (Sources have stated that a large bolt of red cloth was the inspiration to write *The Red Velvet Goat*.)

This early talent and experience led to opportunities to document her strategies in written form, to guide others, even before Niggli would begin teaching.

In Chapel Hill, Niggli developed close friendships with people who helped her, and whom she helped in return—people like Paul Green and Betty Smith. Although a little older, Smith was a fellow Playmaker in classes with Niggli and produced her first play, *Folk Stuff*, in 1935, the same year as Niggli's *Tooth or Shave*. Smith was quite prolific, however, writing more than twenty-five plays by 1940, and also editing and creating anthologies of recent plays. Smith achieved overnight fame in 1943 with her first novel, *A Tree Grows in Brooklyn*.

Smith and Niggli were working on their first novels during the same time period, based on the places where they each grew up. According to an article in a North Carolina newspaper by Lois Cranford (in 1946), Niggli sent her first two chapters to the UNC Press during several months she spent in Texas, and since she did not hear back from them, assumed it was not of interest. It was only upon her return to North Carolina that she was told they thought it marvelous and wanted more. When Niggli showed her work to Smith, her friend responded, "You'd be a darn fool if you don't finish it."

Later Smith asked Niggli for help, according to an article by Mary Ellen Wolcott: "'She had been working all night on a title, so she called me up,' Miss Niggli remembers. 'I was soundly dead to the world, and she said, "I need a title for my book." I had read every page as it came out of the typewriter, and so I said, "Oh, A Tree Grows in Brooklyn," and fell over and went to sleep.'" Smith's book would become a best seller in 1943; it would be converted to a musical in 1951, and then to a movie. Niggli's book, *Mexican Village*, would be published two years after Smith's. But in 1943, as Smith was overloaded with requests, she encouraged Niggli to do a book she did not have time for, which had been requested by *The Writer* in Boston. Niggli now took on a new role as writing coach and published *Pointers on Playwriting* in 1946. She would publish a second professional writing book, *Pointers on Radio Writing*, in 1947, and articles in *The Writer* monthly magazine during the 1940s and 1950s.

Smith included Niggli's plays in her books *25 Non-Royalty One-Act Plays for All-Girl Casts* in 1942, and *20 Prize-Winning Non-Royalty One-Act Plays* in 1943. With the first, Smith's goal was to fill a vacuum apparent in the early 1940s, the fact that no collections of plays for all-female casts existed. The introduction to Smith's book was written by her former professor at the University of Michigan, Kenneth T. Rowe, who exudes enthusiasm because of the need for such a book. As a professor and director of drama productions, Rowe makes note that "the largest single demand" he receives is for all-women plays, which he has cited through the years on a set of index cards. He welcomes such a cutting-edge collection of new plays, noting that the only similar type of text, *Treasury of Plays for Women*, was published in 1922 and "cannot last forever." In Smith's book, two of the twenty-five plays (including one by Tennessee Williams) were created by Niggli just for the book; her name prominently opens the volume with the play *Miracle at Blaise*. The other play authored by Niggli does not bear her real name, and a search for other plays under this pseudonym was fruitless. It seems that Niggli's sole intention was to help provide another option for an all-female cast, but the anonymity made it possible for her to go in a new, experimental direction. *The Faces of Deka* is authored by "Michael Morgan" and displays Niggli's interest in science fiction, which she read as a hobby.[13] (Later, Niggli wrote episodes for the television program *Twilight Zone*.) Also, Morgan was Niggli's mother's maiden name.

Miracle at Blaise

Miracle at Blaise is one of Niggli's few plays without a Mexican setting, and yet its theme is somewhat similar to that of her Mexico-based plays—that miracles occur when humans least expect them. Set in occupied France, women in a small village spy on and suspect each other, with the setting a farmhouse where an American woman participates in the French Resistance. The plot occurs on Christmas Eve. The apparition of a woman whom only the lead character sees instigates a miracle, which impacts on each of the characters and gives the play a certain magical or spiritual quality. This play was frequently produced during the war era. (A San Francisco, California, director for the Multi Ethnic Theater group is planning to stage this play in 2007.)

The Faces of Deka

The Faces of Deka is a fantastically unique representation of women as the rulers of the world, going to battle against other forces and negotiating demands. It completely turns the tables on male-female relations, showing the husband of the principal leader as more preoccupied with his attire than affairs of state. The play creates a futuristic ambience where the dynamics are similar to those of the world war era: a sense of victory for one side, while desire surges on the losers' side to then create new wars.

Niggli's wit and dramatic twists are recognizable, but what is different from her other plays is an openly feminist stance as well as the science-fiction twist. It is a talented demonstration of irony—the complete switching of one gender with the other, in terms of traditional roles and actions. Smith provided Niggli with an opportunity to vary from her usual work, and to be published—anonymously—in a significant anthology without hindering her reputation. Shortly after this, Niggli was writing *Pointers on Playwriting*, and seems to comment on this experience in a short section titled "The Use of a Pseudonym": "This is purely personal, depending on your own desires. Sometimes, of course, you are forced into using a pseudonym. I have to use one on plays that deal with non-Mexican characters, as most editors write back and say, 'We liked your play very much but what we really want is another *Sunday Costs Five Pesos*.' But if I use a pseudonym, they're happy, I'm happy, they send me a check, and that's all there is to it" (96). Niggli may have published other plays with pseudonyms, but no records have been left behind to help trace these.

The Ring of General Macías

Although written and produced in 1938, around the time Niggli also developed the play about Pancho Villa and a new comedy, *The Ring of General Macías* was not published until 1943. After creating her book for all-girl casts, Smith asked Niggli again for a contribution for her book

Twenty Prize-Winning Non-Royalty One-Act Plays.[14] Its original title was *The Ring of General Macías, A Drama of the Mexican Revolution*, and the play represents one of Niggli's most complicated dramatic plots. She had carved a path for themes on the Mexican Revolution, from the martyrdom of the "Adelita" soldier to the ambiguous nature of the revolutionary general Pancho Villa. All of her hero-characters had been rebels. With this play Niggli examines the other side, through the thoughts and reactions of a woman who is a federal general's wife.

The setting for *The Ring of General Macías* is on the outskirts of Mexico City. Raquel Macías is a member of high society in the decadent era of Porfirio Díaz, and her husband of ten years belongs to a family with a long history of military service (not unlike Niggli's fiancé). The living room of the Macías home is "luxuriously furnished in the gold and ornate style of Louis XVI," and the two female characters are attired in negligées in the "latest Parisian style." However, Niggli historically centers her plot with the date of April 1912, obviously after Díaz's overthrow but before the success of the Revolution.[15] Although Francisco I. Madero had been elected president and installed in office on November 2, 1911, he made the mistake of permitting Díaz's top general, Victoriano Huerta, to continue commanding the federal army. Madero thought the various leaders would be able to enact changes collectively. Instead, they made new demands. Emiliano Zapata's *Plan de Ayala* for land reform was drawn up on November 28. With rebel activity continuing in several regions, Huerta began to tighten the reins, and he became the new federal force—in effect, a new dictator (he would have Madero shot early in 1913). By April 1, 1912, Huerta had achieved absolute control of the central government. All federal soldiers reported to him.

General Macías is a high-ranking federal officer now in the clutches of revolutionary soldiers, two of whom surreptitiously enter his home one evening. The officer of the two (the other is a young man, barely twenty), one Captain Andrés de la O,[16] whose reputation precedes him, reveals to Raquel that her husband said she would offer them sanctuary if they showed Raquel his wedding ring. She is shocked, stating that in ten years he had never removed the wedding band (but it is his, proven by the engraving). While the captain helps himself to wine and explains this, her demeanor is calm, unafraid, and later resolved and calculating. The captain has obtained key information on the *federales* and now needs to hide until he can return to his camp. Raquel soon understands that her husband is not as brave as other military men in his family, that he made the offer simply to save himself from being shot. She must now choose whether or not to save his life by complying with the rebels, hiding them from federal officers, and then letting them depart before daybreak, so that her husband will be freed. Instead, she chooses to protect his honor and let him be shot by the firing squad, so that he does not become known in history as a coward. In the process, she kills the rebels.

Raquel Macías is a pivotal figure, a strong woman whose heroics are greater than those of her general-husband. It is easy to identify with her, but not as easy to understand what she accomplishes. The younger revolutionary, Cleto, admits he thinks her husband a coward, "because he has a duty to his own cause, [but] you are a woman. You have a duty to your husband. It is right that you should try to save him. It is not right that he should try to save himself." Once Raquel makes the decision to poison the two spies in order to save her husband's honor, she admits to Captain de la O that she realizes his side will be victorious. She is glad, she says, that he hanged the judge who gave him a five-year sentence for stealing five oranges when he was still a child, while his mother was left to die in poverty. In Niggli's *Villa* play, the Professor does not understand the motive for the Revolution. In this play, General Macías does not understand. Raquel develops an understanding of people's lives and sees why the Revolution needs to succeed. "Yes, you'll win. I know that now," she says to the captain. In this play, Niggli demonstrates both sides of the cause and why the rebels' cause is stronger. They have suffered indignities and poverty for far too long. The younger rebel tells her, "I am a poor peasant, that's true. But still I have a right to live like a man, with my own ground, and my own family, and my own future." Raquel also sees that these men are braver than her husband.

The Ring of General Macías is a very astute play. With good technical detail, intricate political revelations, and subtle intrigue, the one-act play represents high drama. Niggli also demonstrates the terrible effects of a civil war, where citizen fights citizen and no act of love or nobility can save anyone. The dramatic skill in this and the *Villa* play surpasses that of her earlier folk comedies. If this was the last play she created for the Carolina Playmakers, she concluded with her finest. She did write more plays—in fact, *A Crime in Granada* is also a strong drama about civil war and a divided people—but *The Ring* excels in terms of representing history and human psychology. This likely accounts for its inclusion in scholastic texts. A complicated plot requires critical thinking on the part of students.

In 1970, *The Ring of General Macías* was published in *Close-up: A Collection of Short Plays*, a text that studies eight plays (two of the twentieth-century playwrights are female) of conflict and human drama, following each with extensive questions and thinking points for analysis. This the only play of Niggli's known to have been translated into Spanish, and in fact of interest to instructors of Spanish classes in the United States. The translation was released at some point in the 1980s by Holt, Rinehart, with the title *El anillo del General Macías*; however, its original source no longer exists, and it is only available in online lesson plans. An Internet search shows that an instructor by the last name of Manríquez required it for a senior-level Spanish class at Memorial High School in San Diego in 1998. Also, the University of Chile Theater School published the play in mimeograph form as part of an anthology of Latin American drama, and a Web search pulls up a Paraguayan author, Josefina Plá, as translator of the play—but there is no indication as to whether it is the same version.

Critical Attention

The English version of the play is a part of the McGraw-Hill Education enterprise, in textbooks for world literature classes, at senior-level honors or AP classes. A scan of the Web will also show its inclusion in curricula for classes in Idaho, Arizona, California, Pennsylvania, South Carolina, Texas, Canada, and the United Kingdom. Several of these access the play as a Web resource under the Glencoe Online (McGraw-Hill) High School Literature series, where it forms part of Course 5 "Genre" Studies. Interestingly, a historical essay, with footnote sources on women's involvement in the Mexican Revolution, accompanies it as required reading. Niggli's play can be widely accessed in the current day due to the Internet and worldwide sales of educational materials. During 2005, *The Ring* was performed at a drama festival in Tehran, Iran, and also by high-school students in Alberta, Canada.

In one of the earliest critical analyses published on Niggli's plays,

Carmen Salazar Parr and Genevieve M. Ramírez (1985) assess both *Soldadera* and *The Ring of General Macías* with a unique exploration of her characters as "portraits of women in struggle," or Chicana figures as heroes. The authors note that there are *two* heroes in the first play—not just the iconic Adelita who sacrifices her life for the success of the Revolution, but also Concha, who is "admired by the women she leads and even by the enemy and because she exhibits traits not generally associated with or expected of women" (49). They also point out that Concha is portrayed as a three-dimensional figure, a human being no different than a man, capable of leadership as well as being both tough and warm and healing.

Salazar Parr and Ramírez also point out that Niggli's *Soldadera* is strikingly similar to Mariano Azuela's novel *Los de abajo* (1916), recognized as the "first" novel of the Revolution: "Niggli dramatizes the same events as Azuela and does so utilizing some of the same stylistic devices in naming and characterizing fictional creations" (49). The Blond One and Cricket mirror Azuela's el Güero and la Pintada, and The Rich One is similarly an intellectual provoking insurgent leadership, just as Azuela's character Luis Cervantes did. Niggli likely found copies of *Los de abajo* prominently displayed when she visited Monterrey after her relocation to Texas. Her San Antonio friend John Igo asserts that she worked on her own translation of his novel because she did not like the English translation that had been published; "she felt it didn't convey the real Mexico." With Niggli's close attention to Azuela's novel, it is evident that upon her move to North Carolina she was trying not only to relate the story of the Mexican Revolution, but to also reinstate women in the official record.

In *The Ring of General Macías*, women are three-dimensional beings of thought and action who, as Salazar Parr and Ramírez state, can be "torn between love for country and love for an individual" (50). While this is a play about honor and love, it is Raquel who sustains the honor, because her husband turns out to be a coward. She preserves both her husband's honor and that of the federal cause, while in the end acknowledging that the Revolution will succeed. As with Concha in *Soldadera*, the male-female roles are inverted: the woman is the one who makes decisions and controls the outcome as well as the lives of others. Salazar Parr and Ramírez demonstrate that Niggli's female heroes in these two plays "take their stands not for personal self-aggrandizement but as actors in a collective effort for the common good" (52). In such measure, Niggli joins Mexican novelists who represent the value of the collective community above that of the individual, as well as feminist Chicana writers, who additionally portray women's heroics.

Niggli reached her pinnacle in playwriting with *The Ring of General Macías*. Turning thirty marked a turning point on her creative path. Her elaboration of Mexican thought and culture would from here on out take the form of novels, and later movie and television scenes. In 1955 this very play was converted to a television episode (bearing the same title) as part of a weekly ABC television series, *Star Tonight*. Niggli wrote the screenplay version shortly after creating a movie screenplay from her first novel. The television series was canceled after one season. This is the only evidence of the adaptation of one of her own plays to screen, although Niggli wrote for several other series during her years in Hollywood.

The Ring of General Macías was also converted to an opera, with a performance in San Francisco during the early 1950s, according to several sources, but no reviews have been found. *Sunday Costs Five Pesos* was produced as an opera in North Carolina in 1950 (discussed further in chapter 3).

An Earlier Version of *The Ring*

The Ring of General Macías also provides an excellent example for studying a work in progress. An earlier draft left behind in Niggli's manuscripts (an excerpt provided here) demonstrates the considerable changes she made as she developed a play (even after decades had passed, as in the case of *Singing Valley*). Her manuscripts now in a special collection at Western Carolina University show that Niggli habitually went through various drafts before finalizing a work. One of her earlier versions of this particular play can be viewed on an academic database, *Latino Literature* (2005), published by the Alexander Street Press in collaboration with the University of Chicago. While this is an innovative technological attempt to collect unpublished primary sources and preserve the literary record of U.S. Latino writers, such a system can contain some errors when research is not adequately completed.

A search by "author" on this database reveals Niggli's name, a short biography, and full-text items in the categories of Poetry, Prose, Published Plays, and Unpublished Plays. The plays indicated as "published" consist of the five in Niggli's book, plus *This is Villa!*. The "unpublished" items, however, include *Singing Valley*, *This Bull Ate Nutmeg*, *The Ring of General Macías*, and *Miracle at Blaise*, which, in fact, have been published in at least one book each, and more than one in some cases.[17] Such a mistake indicates that the examples were most likely scanned from the WCU manuscripts. Further evidence of this is obvious upon comparing the database's version of *The Ring of General Macías* (which indicates several pages missing) with the published play, where characters and the plot are substantially altered. In Niggli's early draft, the ending is more abrupt, without any comments by the revolutionary captain. Raquel's decision is also less subtle. In her first draft, Niggli states the year as 1915, which doesn't work for indicating government control by "federals."

Niggli's writing process (demonstrated by various drafts in the WCU collection) was to do extensive research after first creating a work. She made copious notes (substantial records, in the case of her novels in progress), often from Spanish-language texts, which served as authorities for her creative work (research texts left behind will be discussed in chapter 4). Therefore, she likely wrote the first version of *The Ring of General Macías*, then proceeded to complete her research and make several changes. Selections from the early draft currently found on the *Latino Literature* database are included here in order to demonstrate her work-in-process. Most striking are the changes in the characters' names: the earlier version uses an older servant, Cuca, as a secondary character instead of Raquel's sister-in-law, Marica. Raquel is called Eva, and the soldiers have different names as well as ranks. The rebels are called Captain Juvencio Martínez, and his younger companion, Nicanor. "De la O" fits much better, since it was the name of a prominent revolutionary. The federal soldier was called "Colonel Chapa" in the early draft; in the final version he is also a captain, but with the name of Basilio Flores. Niggli also added a comedic element in the final version that is not evident in the early draft. Instead, the young insurgent goes out to the kitchen to find food, rather than worrying about a noise that turns out to be a rabbit.

In another example from the *Latino Literature* database, its version of *Miracle at Blaise* reads the same as the published version, with the same characters and plot, but toward the end it abruptly drops off, with the final three pages missing. Thus, the interesting ending to this play cannot be ascertained unless one consults the published play. The Alexander Street Press publishes other companion databases; in *North American Theatre Online*,[18] a search under Niggli's name provides eighteen entries (the five plays in her book, six others published, and eight unpublished items) of "plays by this playwright." These are the same as those on the *Latino Literature* database, with full-text (although in some cases incomplete fragments) with the exception of two items: *The Girl Across the Mountains*, with a date of 1950, and *Singing Valley*—neither of which includes the text itself, as in the other cases. The other plays that truly are unpublished include two that appear to be episodes for the television Westerns *Retreat from Maclellan* (1944) and *Paladin* (no date); three religious plays, *Mr. Mephistopheles* (no date, a three-act play), *Land of Promise* (1944), and *The Silver Road* (no date); *Script for May Day Pageant* (1943), which introduces a college president; and *The Defeat of Grandfather Devil* (no date), based on a myth. Thus, one can peruse more of Niggli's earlier writing on this database, but it is not reliable. A careful study needs to be conducted to document the plays that were published.

New Professional Writing

Niggli did write a few more theatrical plays during the next two decades, although principally to celebrate special events. The period of 1935–42 would comprise her outstanding contribution to English-language theater as a folk and historical dramatist. During this period, she also explored new avenues for her writing. She sought professional training in New York City:—classes at the New School for television, short story, and photography, and at Columbia University for journalism and film. She was awarded several fellowships that helped fund her training: two Rockefellers (principally for her master's studies), followed by a fellowship from New York City's Bureau of New Plays in 1938, which permitted her to live in the Big Apple and frequent the theater. Before or after her sessions in New York, she studied poetic form at the National University of Mexico (UNAM), and at El Teatro Pequeño in Mexico City.

In the summer of 1938, she enjoyed a fellowship at the Breadloaf

Conference in Vermont, where she received strategic direction toward the writing of narrative. At this point, Niggli was preparing to write her first novel, although at the time it was conceived as a work of nonfiction. The University of North Carolina Press wanted to publish a new book to follow Niggli's book of plays, and asked her to write about the people of northern Mexico whom she knew so well. That is how the assignment was known, and the first review in the *New York Times* (following numerous ads in that newspaper announcing the arrival of her novel *Mexican Village*), with the title "People of Nuevo León," described her book as nonfiction. The work was first referred to as "Farewell to My Village" in *The Logos* (1938), information that Niggli would have supplied. This alumni newsletter/magazine regularly published news on her accomplishments and kept up with her whereabouts. The previous year, *The Logos* mentioned that Niggli is "returning for the holidays from the University of North Carolina to her home in Monterrey." As the 1930s ended, she began spending more time in San Antonio.

Although the university press had asked Niggli for a new book, she had needed to flesh out her ideas. By the summer of 1939, Niggli is described as residing at 221 King William Street in a newspaper article by Amy Freeman Lee, who calls her "Mexican." Published in the *San Antonio Express-News* (June 1939), the article quotes Niggli on her goals as she developed her characters: "'I believe that a person is made up of a number of emotions, and that the people in turn make up the place in which they live, so only through knowing the people who inhabit a place does one get to know the place itself.'"

Freeman Lee (possibly a former classmate from Incarnate Word) describes the work-in-progress as the biography of a village, created through a series of character sketches. Upon the publication of *Mexican Village*, Niggli would state that it was based largely on fact, but that she had to omit certain incidents because they were too melodramatic.[19] The journalist also observes that with the exception of a book by Texan J. Frank Dobie on life in Chihuahua, no books have been published in English on life in northern Mexico. Niggli is described as a highly successful playwright, having achieved "the position of the foremost contemporary dramatist in the field of folk drama. Though she concentrates on the field of folk culture, whose appeal is topical or local, she achieves a genuine social effect. With great discrimination she selects the most significant customs of the Mexican people in order to picture this culture. . . . She complies with the fundamental principle of the drama which demands that the pictured trouble have its origin in a genuine human conflict, for while a play may develop its action from physical involvement, a drama must develop its action from moral conflict . . . that arise[s] in the mental and spiritual life of human beings."

At the time of this article, Niggli was only twenty-nine years old. The experience she had garnered and the level of success she had already achieved are truly remarkable. However, she had not decided on a permanent residence. Although her mother continued to reside in the home on King William Street even after her father's death in 1945, Niggli regularly divided her time between San Antonio and Chapel Hill, with occasional jaunts to Mexico. The family home was not sold until 1957, to a family by the name of Cabrera (with a lien paid in full and released by 1964). Ten years after completion of her graduate studies, in the 1949 edition of *Current Biography*, she would refer to her lifestyle as nomadic, stating that she had "lived in a suitcase all my life [*sic*]."

It is surprising that her record and reputation have not been more prominently displayed and recorded in San Antonio, although in 1978 the public library would bestow on her its annual Letters Award. (According to Niggli's 1980 interview, the public library had a "Niggli collection," but at some point it was eliminated.) Her alma mater, Incarnate Word University, has named her a distinguished alumna, and plans are underway by Bill Fisher for a centennial celebration in San Antonio in 2010. However, no markers announce her residence or participation in events, and information on her is scant in public-library or city historical records.

The imminent war likely opened job possibilities for Niggli in the East (more so than in Texas), where she found the Durham–Chapel Hill environment more stimulating. Therefore, she was again living on "the Hill" by fall of 1939, soon starting a full-time job as a script editor for the radio division, which was part of the university's Department of Dramatic Art. With many of the male instructors at UNC-Chapel Hill away at war during the next few years, and Paul Green in Hollywood, Niggli found several avenues open to her that normally were not open to women. She was first hired as a clerk in the business office, then worked as script director in the radio division during 1940–42, as instructor for radio courses during 1942–43, and additionally, as a member of the English Department faculty from 1942 to 1944. Upon her return to the East, Niggli completed more classes at New York University and CBS professional courses in radio writing and production, and these, together with her journalistic training at Columbia University, prepared her for jobs producing radio propaganda scripts in Spanish (to air in Latin America) for NBC International in New York, and working as a translator. With men away at war, this exceptional woman's knowledge of Spanish and experience in professional writing was recognized and rewarded.

During this period, Niggli not only reworked her script about Pancho Villa for a radio play, she also reworked Paul Green's pageant drama, the *Lost Colony*, for its successful radio presentation. Green thought it could not be done (Niggli says in an extensive piece, under the title "Letter from an Alumna," published in *The Logos* in early 1942) since it had previously aired as a radio play (and was only understood by those who had previously seen a staged production), and as a movie starring Loretta Young, which had also failed. Niggli says: "I took Paul's original script—not the printed copy—and went over it very carefully, copying all the speeches which had to do with Paul's theme, which was, of course, that in America, for the first time, a man was recognized by his innate qualities and not by the station to which he is born. I then wrote the script, using these speeches as the basis, and the result was a good radio show (as I had always known it would be). Since its production we have had letters from both the Columbia and National Broadcasting Systems, congratulating us on it."

A humorous anecdote follows, as Niggli explains that they had not been able to find an adequate actress to play the part of Queen Elizabeth. When they were trying one final time, the actress's voice did not come in well "over the microphone, which does some peculiar tricks to the voice. . . . [T]he director suggested I go in to the studio and talk to her about the part as I had imagined the Queen when I was writing it. We talked for a few minutes, and then she read it again, but it was still terrible. 'No,' I said, 'Don't you understand? Elizabeth would read the line like this.' And then I read it. Right afterwards the director came in and told her that he was sorry, she just wouldn't do, and after she left, I was bewailing the fact that no Elizabeth could be found, when everyone in the studio burst out laughing. I couldn't figure out where the joke was until Earl (the director) explained that they wasted all that time hunting for an Elizabeth and here I was in the studio all the time.... And that is why I played Queen Elizabeth."

The Creation of a Radio Series

Niggli's name (and title as script director) appears on the letterhead stationery for the radio division in this era, together with Earl Wynn as director, Robert Bowers as production manager, and Paul Green as literary consultant. The content of official letters written by her, however (as well as her personal letters to Paul Green), show her to be managing affairs, making decisions, and consulting on academic department matters. She is also the person responsible for launching a major radio series with a war-era theme.

In a letter dated January 15, 1942, to William Saroyan in San Francisco, she sounds authoritative and businesslike, explaining their new project and asking him to contribute a play. She calls the radio series the endeavor of an "experimental group" producing plays that meet "the challenge of the writer as to new ways in radio," with the script itself the star rather than the actors. Niggli informs Saroyan that the opening play for the "Men in Action" series, which would air nationally, is *The Lost Colony*. She states: "In adapting the play, I opened it with a speaker and chorus who connected the courage and dreaming of freedom of those early colonists with the courage and dreaming of freedom in the present war." She then describes other plays planned for the series.

In a letter to Green dated the following day, Niggli asks if he heard the first broadcast; she reports to be very proud of "Earl" (Wynn) for his excellent job directing.[20] She states that she received a response from William Saroyan, accepting the invitation to submit a radio script. Niggli also attaches a copy of the series schedule, January through February, which indicates a play by her with the title "1809." In the letter to Saroyan, she described it as "based on the idea that there are years of action and years of sleep—years such as 1941 when the world is making history—but also the quiet years such as 1809 when nothing happened. And yet 1809 is probably the most important year in the history of man, since more makers of destiny were born in that year than in any other." As with the reference to 1941—the year before the United States became involved in the Second World War—Niggli is obviously contemplating the year before the struggle for Mexican independence from Spain broke out. No records exist that Niggli completed such a play or that it aired. However, she substituted a different radio play written by her, the only one she would ever create based in Spain, and it became part of the series. Titled *Crime in Granada*, it was based on the murder of the renowned Spanish poet Federico García Lorca (who was killed in Spain in 1936, at the beginning of the Spanish Civil War). Niggli likely chose this theme because of the poet's prominence and death at an early age, as well as her possible interest in his drama.

A Radio Play Based in Spain

Spain's Civil War seems an excellent subject for the "Men in Action" wartime series, as it served as a precursor to the Second World War. The Spanish army, led by General Franco (who later united with the dictators Mussolini and Hitler), had overthrown the second Spanish Republic in 1936 (this civil war did not end until 1939, with Franco's victory). Federico García Lorca makes for a poetic example of a hero who sought freedom, yet did not seek exile from Spain in order to save his own life. His martyrdom, as it was considered then, had received worldwide attention. Due to Niggli's ability to read Spanish, she could access information and various points of view about his death in either language. She could also have read newspaper accounts from various countries. Her research is evident in the tightly constructed play, with emotional and dark undertones. Titled *Crime in Granada*, Niggli's radio play is the first known play to celebrate the passionate poet and playwright. It aired on February 7, 1942, with live music and an all-Anglo cast (a copy of the play is in Niggli's manuscript collection at Western Carolina University).

Crime in Granada depicts Lorca's affinity for bullfights, and demonstrates the reaction of people who comment on his poetry at a time when the Spanish Republic was under attack (before it was overthrown). Although she does not cite Franco by name, Niggli's powerful drama reveals not only Franco's ruthlessness but also how the masses can swing ideologically from one viewpoint to another—in this case, from Franco's ultraconservative stance to support of a free republic. The "Republicans" in the play manipulate and use Lorca's poetry to support their views. Niggli's Lorca character insists that his poem, quoted within the play (indicated as Niggli's translation), only celebrates a fallen bullfighter. But the characters state that the words of his poems show that he is "against the Royalist cause" (and Franco's army). Other characters later state that his poetry shows that he stands solidly "with the people." Niggli's radio play demonstrates how easily the masses determine who is right or wrong in society, and even who is permitted to speak for "God." Her discourse seems to dialogue with philosopher José Ortega y Gasset's landmark text *La revolución de las masas*.

As the tension mounts in her play, the military men determine that Lorca is a bad influence on others and that he must be stopped. A commander called "General" covertly orders his death. The character Lorca has a premonition about his own death, and a priest advises him to travel to Mexico because he is in danger (a true fact). Lorca ignores both admonitions because he is excited about an innovative traveling theater he has developed. (The similarities between Niggli and Lorca are impressive; both are playwrights, and revolution impacts both lives.) Later, the characters who represent the public will debate his fate, some making repetitive statements that Lorca is "the voice of the people, the voice of Spain," while others say he is sacrilegious.

The play concludes with the military general seeking the old priest to ask "forgiveness for those who killed him," but the priest (now blind from the effects of the war) says Lorca is "not the voice of Spain dead but of Spain alive." This poetic ending allows for hope, which the poet represents, but is also an effective technique for the theme of the radio series. The phrase "they killed Federico when the light appeared" (at dawn) evokes Lorca's own poetry; thus Niggli represents him in a dual manner—his eternal art, and that which incited political fear and marked him for assassination. Voices echo repeatedly, "The crime was in Granada. In Granada. In his Granada." The priest says, "He died in Granada, but in Spain he lives." Niggli effectively never uses the word "Communist," but she espouses in Lorca the loss of freedom.

There was no further mention in Niggli's correspondence with Green on radio plays, or the experimental group and the radio series. She would soon return to Texas and put playwriting aside.

The Cry of Dolores

FOREWORD

This is the story of a miracle . . . a miracle that aided a small band of patriots to free Mexico from the bondage, not of Spain, but of Napoleon Bonaparte. The situation, the characters, the scene, and even the speeches have been lifted directly from the pages of history. In this instance, at least, history is stranger than fiction.

SYNOPSIS

Lolita can not understand the patriotic feeling governing not only her family, but her fiancé as well. To her, revolution means only death and destruction, so she demands that Allende choose between herself and Revolution. To her horror, he chooses the Revolution. When she turns to her mother for help, Doña Josefa tells her that there are times when a man puts his duty to his country above everything else. As proof of this, Lolita's father, feeling the strength of his duty to Spain, orders the arrest of Allende.

By some miracle, a Mexican patriot is within reach of Doña Josefa's voice, and with his aid, tragedy is averted.

CHARACTERS

LOLITA DOMINGUEZ, engaged to,

IGNACIO ALLENDE, a captain in Her Majesty's dragoons.

DOÑA JOSEFA DOMINGUEZ, mother of LOLITA.

DON MIGUEL DOMINGUEZ, husband of JOSEFA, and mayor of Querétaro.

FATHER MIGUEL HIDALGO Y CASTILLA, the father of Mexican Independence.

DON CARLOS VARA, warden of the city prison.

NIMFO, servant.

The Scene: The living room of the house of the mayor of Querétaro, DON MIGUEL DOMINGUEZ, on the evening of Saturday, September 15, 1810.

It is a pleasant room, a bit stiff, a bit unhomelike, but one has the feeling that people of character and individuality live here.

There is a large barred window in the wall back center, and a door in the right wall. For furniture, there is a sofa down left with a chair near, and a table right, flanked by three chairs.

When the curtains open we see LOLITA DOMINGUEZ sitting by the window embroidering. She is a sweet, pretty girl, about 20, dressed in a soft pink gown of the period. She would be beautiful if it were not for the stubborn line of her chin.

In a moment the servant enters. He is quite a young boy, dressed all in white with a red sash about his waist, and is pure Indian in type.

NIMFO. Captain Allende asks your permission to enter, señorita.

LOLITA. (*Standing excitedly*) Admit him, immediately. And tell my mother and father that he is here.

(*Nimfo bows and goes out. Lolita runs to the mirror to pat her curls into place, and while she is doing so this IGNACIO ALLENDE enters. History calls him a "proud young captain, very handsome, in the uniform of Her Majesty's dragoons," which consists of a short red coat held in by a gold sash, white trousers, tall black cavalry boots, a cocked hat, and, hanging from his shoulders a sky-blue cape. At this time he was 31 years old with a certain charming boyish enthusiasm, and was only lately-engaged to LOLITA.*

He flings his cape and hat on a chair and stands beaming at her.)

ALLENDE. Lolita!

LOLITA. (*Starts toward him, then pauses shyly and extends her hand*). Good evening, Captain Allende. (*He goes to her and kisses her hand.*)

ALLENDE. (*With an effort at poise*) I hope that you have passed a pleasant day.

LOLITA. (*Sits on the sofa*) Very pleasant, thank you, captain. Will you be seated? My mother and father will be here in a moment.

ALLENDE. (*Gazes at her in admiration, then sits beside her . . . which rather startles her, as she had naturally expected him to sit as far across the room from her as possible . . . and takes her hand in his*). Lolita. I have a surprise for you.

LOLITA. (*Shyly pulling her hand away*) Have you?

ALLENDE. I brought a very dear friend of mine to meet you this evening. For many months now I have been anxious for him to know the girl who is so soon to be my wife.

(*At his words a strange change comes over her. She turns her face from him, touching her mouth with her handkerchief in agitation. Unable to control her feelings, she rises suddenly and crosses to the table where she stands gazing down at it. He stares at her in amazement, then goes to her.*)

Lolita! What is wrong?

LOLITA. (*Gives him a trembling smile*) Nothing . . . I . . . (*She puts her hand on his arm*) Captain Allende . . . Ignacio . . . (*Then she shakes her head and turns her back to the table.*) I am afraid that I am a very foolish creature. I beg of you, do not concern yourself with me.

ALLENDE. (*Turns her to face him*) You are my promised wife, Lolita. When you are with me, you should fear nothing. (*He kisses her*) Now tell me what is troubling you.

LOLITA. (*Clinging to his hands*) You're so changed, Ignacio. For over a year now . . . Ever since that day when it was feared that we were to fight the English . . . It is as though you were another man. And all these new friends of yours. . . . They frighten me. And then these meetings here, at night. This strange Literary Society, with the members coming so late after I am in bed. And finally this dream that I have had night after night . . . Oh Ignacio, it is more than I can bear.

(*She sits down on a chair and he kneels beside her.*)

ALLENDE. Tell me about your dream.

LOLITA. I dreamed that there was a battle. and that men were killing you . . . men in uniform, . . . Men in . . . (*She touches his shoulder*) . . . in this uniform. Please, Ignacio, tell me what it all means.

ALLENDE. (*Stands and walks to the window. Abruptly he comes back to her and draws her to her feet.*) If I were a superstitious man . . . But, no. They say dreams always mean the opposite, don't they?

LOLITA. (*Helplessly*) I don't know . . . ! Don't know anything. That is the trouble.

ALLENDE. I suppose the time has come to tell you the truth. (*He leads her to the sofa and they sit down.*) We will start with a year ago, after the mobilization of the troops when we feared war with the English. I was riding toward the barracks, when I realized that I had no idea of the military strength which we possess. Never had we seen so many soldiers united at a single instance under the command of one general. In reality we were strong, but this strength belonged to Spain. Now here is the great question. If all Mexican soldiers were united by a single thought the strength would be ours . . . We could overthrow the Spaniards.

LOLITA. (*Horrified*) You mean . . . Revolution?

ALLENDE. (*Firmly*) Revolution. Freedom at last. Freedom from oppression, from slavery.

LOLITA. And, this Literary Society?

ALLENDE. Is really a meeting of the friends of liberty, the leaders of our cause . . .

LOLITA. No! No, Ignacio. Don't you realize what this means? Death and disgrace for all of us. My dream, my horrible nightmare of a dream, was no dream at all but the truth. They are going to capture you . . . They are going to kill you.

ALLENDE. Let them . . . Let them kill all of us. What is the difference if Mexico is freed from the chains of bondage that have bound her for over two centuries.

LOLITA. (*Pleadingly*) Ignacio, does my love mean so little to you?

ALLENDE. It means everything, Lolita.

LOLITA. Then for my sake, I beg of you, give this up. These are idle hopes. Spain is all powerful. It will crush you down, and Mexico will be more pitiful than ever.

ALLENDE. Spain no longer exists. Napoleon has driven Fernando from his throne. To be bound to Spain is misery. But to be bound to France would be disgrace. We have gone too far, Lolita. We can't turn back now.

LOLITA. (*Frantically*) You must turn back, Ignacio, for my sake. I love you. If you were dead . . . If they killed you . . . Life would end for me. Ignacio, Ignacio, have pity on me.

ALLENDE. (*Putting his arms about her*) Poor child. Poor frightened child.

(*The door opens and DON MIGUEL DOMINGUEZ, MAYOR OF QUERETARO enters. He is a nice little man, with a large nose, a weak mouth, and a tendency to be foppish in his dress. He is at the time about fifty-years old. Preceding him is his wife, DOÑA JOSEFA. She is a matronly, kindly woman of forty-five. The portraits of her made at this period, show an aggressive nose, a firm chin, a stern but gentle mouth. In her neatly plaited hair is a low Spanish comb. Her dress is simple and modest with a white fichu for relief.*)

DOÑA JOSEFA. (*Startled at the tableau in front of her*) Ignacio! Lolita! What is the meaning of this?

LOLITA. (*Running to her and throwing both arms about her neck.*) Mother! Don't let him do it. Don't let him do it!

DOÑA JOSEFA. (*Puzzled*) Don't let him do what?

ALLENDE. (*Quietly*) Good evening, Doña Josefa. . . . Don Miguel.

DON MIGUEL. (*Gives Ignacio the traditional embrace, and then shakes hands*) Good evening, my boy. What miniature tempest is this?

ALLENDE. I have been telling Lolita about our plans.

DOÑA JOSEFA. (*Disapprovingly*) Telling our plans to this child.

LOLITA. (*Draws back from her*) I am not a child. After all, I'm old enough to be married, and I have a right to know what my . . . (*she draws a deep breath, sets her chin*) . . . my husband's plans are.

DOÑA JOSEFA. (*Laughs and goes to sofa. She holds out her hand to Allende who goes and kisses it.*) That is right. I forget she is no longer a child.

DON MIGUEL. (*Teasingly*) Then why does she weep like a baby?

ALLENDE. She dreamed that I was captured and executed.

DOÑA JOSEFA. To die a martyr to our cause? Who could wish for a more beautiful death?

LOLITA. I could. (*Scornfully*) To die a martyr? I don't want him to die at all. Mother, how can you be so cold? If it were father you would feel differently about it.

DON MIGUEL. Lolita! I will not have you speak so to your mother.

ALLENDE. Lolita, calm yourself.

LOLITA. Lolita this! Lolita that! (*Covers her ears with her hands*) I won't listen to anything you have to say. You can make your choice between me and this absurd idea of Mexican Independence. I will not marry a martyr. (*She flings herself on her knees beside her mother, and buries her face in Doña Josefa's lap. As Allende and Don Miguel start to speak, Doña Josefa smiles gently and places her finger against her lips, then strokes her daughter's hair.*)

DOÑA JOSEFA. You are perfectly right, Lolita. I think we have forgotten about human beings in the rhythm of our beautiful fine words.

ALLENDE. (*Horrified at Doña Josefa's about face*) I protest, Doña Josefa . . .

DOÑA JOSEFA. (*Stopping him with a frown and a quick gesture of her hand.*) In the days that are coming you will not be the only young girl to weep as she sees the man she loves marching off to battle.

LOLITA. (*Wailing*) Why does there have to be a battle or a war?

DOÑA JOSEFA. (*Gaining her point*) Ah! Now you see? You don't really understand what this is all about, do you?

LOLITA. I don't want to know.

ALLENDE. There is one person who can make you understand. I am going down to get Father Hidalgo.

DON MIGUEL. (*Startled*) But where is he? Why didn't you tell me that?

ALLENDE. He is down in the room of Don Carlos Bravo.

DON MIGUEL. (*Laughing*) What a magnificent jest on the Spaniards. The great revolutionary leader in the room of the warden of the city prison.

DOÑA JOSEFA. Fetch him immediately, Ignacio.

ALLENDE. Lolita, he will explain.

DOÑA JOSEFA. Don't bother about Lolita now. Go and bring this sainted patriot . . .

ALLENDE. Yes, yes, of course . . . (*He goes to the door where he pauses*) I . . . (*He sees Doña Josefa looking at him.*) Yes, immediately. (*he goes out*)

DON MIGUEL. What a great man Hidalgo is. I remember the first night I met him. He . . .

DOÑA JOSEFA. No reminiscences, please, Miguel. Stand up, Lolita.

(*Lolita, still pouting, stands.*) In a few moments, you will see the greatest man in Mexico today.

LOLITA. I don't want to meet him . . . All I want . . .

DOÑA JOSEFA. (*Sternly*) You said yourself, that you are a woman now, and not a child. Try to act like a woman. Now, go and wash your face. Your eyes look as though you had been crying for days. And when he comes try to behave with proper dignity. You don't want Ignacio to be ashamed of you, do you?

LOLITA. (*Slowly*) No.

DOÑA JOSEFA. (*Rises and kisses her on the cheek.*) That's a sweet daughter. Run along now, and hurry. We mustn't keep Father Hidalgo waiting.

LOLITA. (*Turns and goes out of the room, and then sticks her head back in.*) But I still don't want to marry a martyr. (*With a final jerk of her head she disappears.*)

DOÑA JOSEFA. (*Looks at Don Miguel and sighs.*) It is in moments like these that I realize that she is your daughter.

DON MIGUEL. (*Smiles*) On the contrary, my love. No one could ever call me a stubborn man.

DOÑA JOSEFA. (*Laughs softly and takes his hand in hers*) You are a kind soul, Miguel. I know that my impulsive spirit has often caused you much sorrow. Spain has given you so many honors. And now you are mayor of Querétaro, with an ardent revolutionist for a wife. Believe me, I realize what a difficult situation I have made for you.

DON MIGUEL. Do you remember that first day I saw you standing among your friends at the convent? I thought at the time, "There stands the rose I shall wear in my heart." A man can not be angry at a rose, Josefa.

DOÑA JOSEFA. (*Nods wisely*) But he can be angry at the thorns.
(*Nimfo enters.*)

NIMFO. His reverence, Father Miguel Hidalgo y Castillo. His Excellency, Don Carlos Bravo and Captain Allende.

DOÑA JOSEFA. (*Moving forward*) Ask them to enter.
(*Nimfo bows and goes out. She turns to Miguel.*) If only your conscience would allow you to be really one of us.

DON MIGUEL. (*Flings out his hand*) I am mayor of Querétaro. As long as I hold that office, my duty binds me to Spain.
(*The three men now enter. Father Hidalgo is a delicate, slender man, not very tall, with beautiful white hands. His nose is prominent, and his soft white hair falls in silky profusion to his shoulders from the*

sides of his head, as he is quite bald on top. He wears a long black coat, belted with a red sash. At this time he is 57 years of age, and he possesses to a marked degree that personality of leadership which made men follow him and his ideals long after the man, himself, was dead. The man next to him is Don Carlos Bravo, warden of the city prison. A large, red-faced, hearty man, he walks with a limp from an old wound. Doña Josefa kisses the priest's hand.)

DOÑA JOSEFA. Our house is yours, Father; and yours, Don Carlos.

HIDALGO. (*Makes the sign of the cross.*) A blessing on this house. Don Miguel, we meet again.

DON MIGUEL. (*Bows*) Our house is always open to you, Father. Don Carlos, your servant.

DON CARLOS. (*Kisses Doña Josefa's hand.*) Your servant, Doña Josefa. And yours, Don Miguel.

DOÑA JOSEFA. Please be seated.

HIDALGO. (*Peering about him near-sightedly as he sits down near the table.*) And where is the little Lolita? Has she run away from shyness at seeing this big captain of ours? (*Allende gives a forced laugh which ceases as Doña Josefa looks sternly at him.*)

DOÑA JOSEFA. Young girls are often shy, Father. She will be here presently. Miguel, perhaps the gentlemen would care for a little wine.

DON MIGUEL. Of course, of course. A glass of sherry, Father. For you, Don Carlos, a drop of good Spanish muscatel?

DON CARLOS. As a servant of Spain, I should drink her wines, but as a revolutionist, I prefer good Mexican Mescal. (*They all laugh.*)

HIDALGO. For me, a little wine. I am very tired. This business of revolution is a weary work.

DON MIGUEL. And you, Ignacio?

ALLENDE. (*Who has been watching the door for Lolita is jerked back to consciousness.*) Wine, sir.

DOÑA JOSEFA. (*As Don Miguel serves the drinks.*) We have missed you at our Literary meetings, Father.

HIDALGO. I have been baptizing converts. Ay, we have gathered about us a fine large army. Soon we shall be ready to strike.

DON MIGUEL. (*Jesting*) As mayor of Querétaro, I should report this to the Viceroy.

DOÑA JOSEFA. (*With mock sternness.*) And as my husband, you will do nothing of the sort. (*She sees Lolita enter.*) There you are, Lolita. Come and ask Father's blessing.

HIDALGO. (*As Lolita comes up to him*). So this is Lolita. (*She kisses his hand.*) Blessings on you child. Ignacio, she is even prettier than you said, and I have always learned to discount a lover's word.

ALLENDE. Father, Lolita says that she won't . . .

DOÑA JOSEFA. (*Interrupting.*) What manners are these, Lolita? Have you no word of greeting for your Godfather?

LOLITA. (*Goes to Don Carlos*) Good evening, Godfather . . .

DON CARLOS. Good evening, child. You should have been with UB [*sic*] this afternoon. Father Hidalgo staged a rodeo for us out at Dolores. Our young captain here proved himself the hero of the hour.

LOLITA. (*Without enthusiasm*) Did he?

HIDALGO. It was a fine sight. As easily as though the bull were a stuffed doll, he forced its shoulders to the ground. If all Mexicans were like him, there would be no Spaniards left in New Spain.

LOLITA. (*Turns to Allende*) Have you forgotten that your father is a Spaniard?

ALLENDE. My mother is a Mexican. I was born and reared here. I owe my allegiance to Mexico.

HIDALGO. (*Peering at Lolita*) What is this? Have we a loyalist in the camp?

LOLITA. (*Goes to Hidalgo*) Father, this would mean war. I am afraid. If Ignacio should be killed . . . and he will be killed . . . I know it, I had, a dream . . . a terrible dream. (*She starts to cry*)

ALLENDE. I told you about her dream as we were coming up the stairs. Father.

HIDALGO. Yes, yes . . . Listen to me, my child. Would you rather be married to a loyal patriot or to a coward? His country needs Allende. You must let him go.

LOLITA. I am a woman. I would rather be married to a live husband than to a dead patriot.

DOÑA JOSEFA. (*Sternly*) Then you are no daughter of mine! I only wish that I were a man, but since I am a woman, then with my blood I shall mold a patrimony for my sons.

ALLENDE. (*Pleadingly*) If you would only listen to me, Lolita. You are thinking of the old days, when a man could be proud to call himself a subject of Spain, but the old days are gone. Napoleon Bonaparte rules, instead of Fernando.

HIDALGO. The native Mexicans will not permit New Spain to fall into the hands of the French.

ALLENDE. By no means. And if the Spaniards have such an intention, it is the duty of every good Mexican to disillusion them.

DON MIGUEL. (*Anxiously*) It appears to me that if the Mexicans could assume control of the colony, then it would be returned to Fernando VII when he comes again to the throne.

HIDALGO. No. The independence of New Spain must be bought at any price.

ALLENDE. Mexicans must be aroused? And how easy it is, since the Spaniards see us only as degenerates, imbeciles, incapable of exerting the smallest sign of volition.

DON CARLOS. You are right. Only today, Don Diego de la Cerda was put into my charge with orders to place him in my most desolate cell because he refused to pay the Viceroy the gold demanded of him. Don Diego has broad lands, but he is really very poor. To pay what was demanded of him was impossible, and so he has to rot in prison.

ALLENDE. If we could only convoke a Mexican Congress to give just laws to our country, to use its vast resources for good instead of lining the pockets of dissolute men.

DOÑA JOSEFA. Yes! Yes! Now is the time to free our country: I dedicate myself to the revolution although it may cost all of us our lives.

DON MIGUEL. (*With a worried frown*) My dear, you are an impulsive woman. You must remember that I . . . (*He breaks off as the door opens and Nimfo enters.*) Well, what do you want?

NIMFO. There is a messenger here from the superintendent of Guanajuato. He says his business is urgent.

DON MIGUEL. Tell him I will be with him immediately. (*Nimfo bows and goes out*) Gentlemen, your servant. Josefa, I beg of you . . . Don't be too impressionable. (*He bows to all of them and leaves the room*)

DON CARLOS. (*Sighs*) If only Don Miguel could be made to see our side of the question. He is a wealthy man, and revolutions need money.

HIDALGO. (*Shaking his head*) At least our good Don Carlos does not pride himself on being a man of tact.

DOÑA JOSEFA. But he is right. If only we had money to help the cause. It is bad enough for us, but it is really the poor who need the freedom. There are nights when I cannot sleep for weeping over their sorrows. No one who has not seen them can ever understand how much they need our help.

HIDALGO. (*Gently*) A coin of gold weighs less than a tear from the heart.

CARLOS. Unfortunately tears won't buy ammunition.

HIDALGO. No, but the poor are used to helping one another. In Dolores, in all the small towns of my parish, it is amazing how many guns are hidden under piles of hay; how many swords are being beaten out on blacksmiths' anvils.

JOSEFA. It is this waiting . . . This waiting for the moment to strike that I cannot bear. We have waited so long, so very long.

ALLENDE. (*Anxiously*) May I tell her, Father?

HIDALGO. (*Indulgently*) Tell her.

ALLENDE. The time is almost here. The cry of freedom has been set for the second of October.

LOLITA. So soon?

DOÑA JOSEFA. (*Triumphantly*) So soon! At last? You have the plan, the names of the leaders, everything?

HIDALGO. Think of it. On the second of October, the cry of Dolores: Long Live the true religion . . . Long live our sacred Mother of Guadalupe . . . Long live America and death to false government.

CARLOS. (*Standing*) And speaking of false government, I must get back to the prison. Poor Don Diego has to be fed, along with a hundred other prisoners.

DOÑA JOSEFA. You can take him a message of hope. After October the second, no more dark cell, no more misery, for any of them.

HIDALGO. (*Rises*) Señora, you are our mast of courage. Do not fail us. Good night, my daughter. (*Turns to Lolita*) And you, my child. You have heard great news tonight. Remember, one slip of your tongue, and we are all lost.

LOLITA. I will remember. Good night, Father. (*She kisses his hand. He, Doña Josefa, and Don Carlos go out into the hall. Allende goes up to Lolita who turns away from him.*)

ALLENDE. Can't you understand, Lola?

LOLITA. You are the one who doesn't understand, Ignacio.

ALLENDE. You are right. I can't understand this loyalty of yours to Spain. If you had ever been there, or if your family were Spaniards . . . But they are not. They are Mexicans, and so are you, and so am I. Do you think that I don't want to have a hand in freeing Mexico from the power that has oppressed us for so long? You know Don Diego. Do you think it's right that he should be in prison because a Viceroy wants more gold than he has to give?

LOLITA. What do I care about Don Diego? Or Spain, or Mexico, or anything else? I am a girl engaged to a man. I want to be married, to have children, to grow old with the man I love. All I can see in this is the fact that you might be killed. That means something to me . . . Your living. I thought you loved me as I love you . . .

ALLENDE. (*Interrupting*) But I do love you.

LOLITA. No you don't. I found that out. I gave you your chance tonight, and you chose . . . Mexico instead of me. Well, that seems to be all there is to it.

ALLENDE. (*Irritated*) But it's not the same thing. There are times when a man has to put his duty to his country above everything else, and this is one of those times.

LOLITA. (*In a dead voice*) Very well then, there is nothing more for us to talk about, is there? Goodnight.

ALLENDE. (*Pleadingly*) Lolita . . .

LOLITA. (*Almost at the end of her strength*) Goodnight! (*He turns dejectedly, and as he reaches the door, Doña Josefa enters. She looks curiously from him to Lolita, and he shakes his head. She pats his cheek, he catches her hand and kisses it and then goes out. She walks thoughtfully over to her daughter.*)

LOLITA. (*Turns and looks at her*) Mother, his cape when he went out. It looked like a shroud.

DOÑA JOSEFA. My child, you must get over these morbid notions.

LOLITA. I can't help it. If only just one of you could understand how I feel.

DOÑA JOSEFA. I do. I remember when your father was first appointed mayor of Querétaro. I begged him on my knees not to accept it.

LOLITA. (*Surprised*) You did? Why?

DOÑA JOSEFA. Your father was a Mexican, and these Spanish viceroys are not in the habit of honoring Mexicans through pure goodness of heart. I was afraid they wanted to use him and his transparent honesty as a tool. Every morning I have awakened with the same thought, "Today will be the day." So far it hasn't come, but it will come. I know it will, and when it does his cape will look like a shroud, too.

LOLITA. Then why have you let him do it all these years? Why have you let him do it?

DOÑA JOSEFA. Because he felt it was his duty to his country, and when a man feels patriotic there is nothing a woman can do about it. So, if I were you, I would sit down and write Ignacio a little note and tell him that you understand at last.

LOLITA. If only I hadn't had that dream.

JOSEFA. (*Nods*) Unfortunately we can't rule our lives by . . . (*Don Miguel enters, a very worried man.*)

DON MIGUEL. (*Curtly*) Josefa! How long have our guests been gone?

DOÑA JOSEFA. I really don't know, my dear. Why? You look worried. What is the matter?

DON MIGUEL. I have just received a message from Riano, Superintendent of Guanajuato. A sergeant from Ignacio's regiment, by the name of . . . (*He consults the paper in his hand.*) . . . of Gariedo, has betrayed the revolutionary plans to the Viceroy, along with the names of the leaders. I have them here on this paper.

LOLITA. What made him do a thing like that?

DON MIGUEL. Fear of being caught himself, I suppose.

DOÑA JOSEFA. Miguel, is my name on that paper?

DON MIGUEL. No. Luckily this Gariedo seemed to know only men's names.

LOLITA. What . . . What does this mean?

DON MIGUEL. It means imprisonment, disgrace . . . Perhaps exile . . . perhaps even death . . .

LOLITA. (*Afraid to ask the question in her mind*) Father . . . The names . . . Is Father Hidalgo's there?

DON MIGUEL. It leads all of them.

LOLITA. Is . . . Don Carlos . . . ?

DON MIGUEL. No, not his . . . Luckily.

LOLITA. (*Frantically*) Father, I can't . . . Oh, why don't you tell me? Is . . .

DON MIGUEL. Yes, Ignacio's is here too. They are all here . . . Abasolo, Balleza, Aldama . . . They are all here save yours, Josefa, and our good friend, the warden downstairs.

DOÑA JOSEFA. How does it involve you, Miguel?

DON MIGUEL. Naturally, I must order their arrest at once.

LOLITA. (*Flings her arms about her father's neck*) No, no . . . Father, please . . . Ignacio means everything to me. You can't do it.

DON MIGUEL. My child, do you think I want to do it? I must. It's my duty.

LOLITA. Duty! Duty! I shall hate that word all of my life.

DON MIGUEL. (*Beckons to Josefa to draw Lolita away.*) What I do now is the hardest thing that I have ever done.

DOÑA JOSEFA. Miguel, I have asked so little of you during all our years together. Will you this once . . .

DON MIGUEL. (*Holds up his hand*) Do not put it into words, please, Josefa. If I had been a loyal subject I would have revealed the truth to the Viceroy long ago. Instead, I allowed myself to be swayed by you. But this is a direct order. If I refuse to carry it out, it would only put us under suspicion and would not help them.

DOÑA JOSEFA. I see, I understand.

DON MIGUEL. Of course I must take our servant with me to make certain that you send them no word, and Josefa, forgive me, but I am going to have to lock the door. I know your impulsive nature.

DOÑA JOSEFA. Yes, Miguel.

DON MIGUEL. (*Takes her hand.*) My dear, if there were anything I could do . . . But you can see for yourself. I have no other alternative.

DOÑA JOSEFA. I know.

DON MIGUEL. Goodbye, my . . . (*He forces a smile*) My children. (*He goes out and the door closes securely behind him. Lolita is crumpled upon the floor, weeping.*)

DOÑA JOSEFA. (*More to herself than to Lolita*) This is the hour for which I have been waiting so long. What a magnificent joke it must be for the Viceroy to send a Mexican to capture loyal Mexicans.

LOLITA. (*Sobbing*) Ignacio! Ignacio!

JOSEFA. (*Closes her eyes in pain and then goes to the door and tries it.*) He did lock it. (*For a moment her old sense of humor flashes clear.*) Your father is a very thorough man, Lolita.

LOLITA. We must do something. We must.

DOÑA JOSEFA. (*Thoughtfully*) If there were only some way by which I could get a message to them. (*She goes to the window and peers out.*) There is no one in the street I can trust. (*Impatiently*) Stop weeping, Lolita, and pray. If ever we needed a miracle, we need it now.

LOLITA. (*Who has been lying prone on the floor, now stiffens and listens acutely to sounds below her.*) Mother? Mother!

DOÑA JOSEFA. (*Goes to her*) What is it?

LOLITA. I hear someone moving around downstairs in Don Carlos's room. Do you think he is still home . . . that he hasn't gone to the prison?

DOÑA JOSEFA. (*Efficiently*) We shall soon find out. (*She beats a brisk tattoo on the floor with her heel*) Lolita, if he really is there, I will believe in miracles all the rest of my life.

LOLITA. Do you think he can reach Dolores ahead of Father? After all, Father has had a few minutes' start. Don Carlos is so slow with that limp of his. And if he gets there, what can he tell them? Oh, it's no use, it's no use. My dream is coming true. (*Her voice rises hysterically*) It's coming true! Ignacio will be killed, I know it!

DOÑA JOSEFA. (*Giving her a resounding slap*) Time enough to weep afterwards.

(*There is a knock at the door*)

DON CARLOS. (*In the hall*) Doña Josefa, what is it? What is the matter?

DOÑA JOSEFA. (*Runs to the door*) Are you alone?

DON CARLOS. But naturally. I had to return to my room for some documents. Señora, I am in a hurry. If you will open the door . . .

DOÑA JOSEFA. I can't . . . I am locked in.

CARLOS. (*Startled*) What?

DOÑA JOSEFA. Listen to me, and ask no questions. Just do as I tell you. A traitor has revealed everything to the Viceroy and Miguel has gone to arrest our leaders.

DON CARLOS. Saints in Heaven!

DOÑA JOSEFA. You must send someone to Dolores to warn them.

DON CARLOS. I will go myself.

DOÑA JOSEFA. That is better still. On the way tell the villagers to stop Miguel and his soldiers some way, any way, but stop them. When you reach Hidalgo, tell him not to wait until October 2nd. Tell him to give the cry now, tonight! The period of waiting is ended.

DON CARLOS. But we dare not strike now.

LOLITA. We must take that chance. Tell Ignacio that it is better to die fighting, than to die without a shot fired. Tell him that all my love goes with him to the battle.

DOÑA JOSEFA. Hurry, Don Carlos. Hurry!

DON CARLOS. Don't worry, Doña Josefa. By daylight Mexico will be fighting her first battle for freedom. (*His voice grows fainter as he leaves the door; Lolita and her mother stare at each other, both run to the window.*)

LOLITA. There he goes! Oh, do you think he will reach them in time?

DOÑA JOSEFA. He must reach them. (*She catches the girl's arm.*) What is the date, Lolita?

LOLITA. I think it's . . . It's the fifteenth of September.

DOÑA JOSEFA. Then by midnight Don Carlos will be with Hidalgo. Think of it. Sometime between midnight and dawn of September sixteenth, Hidalgo will give the cry that will bring Mexico to arms. Up with the true religion, down with false government. The sixteenth of September! What a glorious day for all of us.

QUICK CURTAIN

Singing Valley, A Comedy of Mexican Village Life

A thesis submitted to the Faculty of the University of North Carolina in partial fulfillment of the requirements for the degree of Master of Arts in the Department of Dramatic Art.

Chapel Hill, 1937

(from Act I)

LUPITA. (*She has been examining the niche, now turns her head*). What is this thing for?

ESTER. (*Going to her*). That's for Our Blessed Lady. She's a miracle virgin.

ABEL. What does she do? Cure people?

ESTER. No. She saved the valley from the French. That was in my great-grandmother's time.

LUPITA. (*Cooly*). Marvelous.

ESTER. Everyone in the village is so glad you've come. There's going to be a banquet with speeches!

LUPITA. It sounds too enchanting.

ABEL. (*Frowning at her*). What do you do here in the village? To entertain yourself, I mean?

ESTER. Oh, lots of things. We have picnics, and dances, and walk around the plaza, and we go to church.

LUPITA. You must be worn down from the excitement.

ESTER. We had a wedding last year. I was in it. (*With awe*) And the bride had *wax* orange blossoms.

ABEL. Couldn't she get real ones?

ESTER. Any beggar could have real ones. The guests gave enough money for the couple to go all the way to Saltillo. And all the world knows that is eighty kilometers from here.

LUPITA. How much is that?

ABEL. About fifty miles.

LUPITA. This Saltillo seems so far away to you. Haven't you ever been out of this valley?

ESTER. Once, when my father was living, I went to Monterrey.

ABEL. Did you like it?

ESTER. It was too noisy. And everybody moved so fast. I had to run to keep up with them. I like it better here.

LUPITA. (*Mocking her*) You should. It must keep you busy watching the sun rise. And you look out for the chickens, don't you?

ESTER. Oh, yes. I own a chicken. I named him Solomon, he has so many wives.

LUPITA. What a clever and original name.

ABEL. (*Angrily, to Lupita*) That will do.

(*The thrust strikes Lupita and she turns angrily away.*)

ESTER. (*Who has been perfectly unconscious of sarcasm, smiles up at Abel*) Would you like to own a chicken? I think I could get you one.

LUPITA. He'd love it. It would keep him company all day. He should have a duck, too.

ESTER. I don't think I could find a duck. Don Rufino is the only one who has any, and one doesn't ask Don Rufino for anything.

ABEL. What's wrong with Don Rufino?

ESTER. He is not a good Christian. My grandmother says he is Grandfather Devil's stepson.

LUPITA. Why should the devil love him so much?

ESTER. Because he owns so many goats. All the world knows that before men were born, God herded the sheep, and Grandfather Devil the goats. That's why goat-herders must be very pious, and be buried with their heads toward the east, or the devil will get them surely.

ABEL. I should think a man would be afraid to be a goat-herder, then.

ESTER. There is no danger if he says a prayer every morning, lights a candle to Saint Anthony every month, and washes his ears on Friday.

LUPITA. Perhaps Don Rufino forgot to wash his ears.

ESTER. That's what my grandmother says. He and his goats. He can't think of anything else. He's always talking about them.

(*They hear voices inside the house. Don Antonio's voice swells out for a moment.*)

DON ANTONIO. (*Off left*) But what would I do with a flock of goats?

ESTER. You see! What did I tell you? That Rufino. Already he wants to sell some to your father.

(*She turns with interest toward the house. Everyone now flows into the patio, Don Antonio and Don Rufino in the lead. Don Rufino is busy arguing.*)

RUFINO. But this is goat country! Farms aren't any good here. There isn't enough water. Join with me in buying goats. We can send to Torreón for fine merinos. It'll make money. Lots of money.

ANTONIO. (*In high good humor*) I have money.

RUFINO. No matter how fat the rooster, he can always eat more corn.

ANTONIO. (*With a twinkle in his eye*) Do you think I would be a success as a goat-herder?

RUFINO. (*Impatiently*) No, no, not as a herder, as an owner. All the young men in the village are herders . . . all save Carlos there. He makes candy.

DOÑA BECA. And a very honorable profession it is.

RUFINO. I said nothing against the making of candy, Doña Beca. It is all very well in its place. But there's no money in it. Now goats, goats are different. One sells the milk, one sells the cheese, one sells the meat, one even sells the skins to the shoe factory in Monterrey.

ANTONIO. I don't like goats. They smell.

(*Concha gives a high shrill giggle which she instantly quells as Doña Beca glares at her.*)

RUFINO. (*Who has glared at the interruption*) Kept in the house they protect the family from consumption.

ANTONIO. (*Looking at Lupita and Abel and smiling*) I don't think this family needs such protection.

RUFINO. Suppose you don't like goats, suppose you hate goats, suppose goats are no more than a snap of the fingers to you. What else is there to do in this valley?

ANTONIO. (*Holding up his hand*) Ah . . . What else is there to do! You ask me that, and I have the answer for you. (*He turns and walks to the gate*) An answer that I used to dream about when I was a boy, standing in this spot where I am standing now, and looking over this valley to the mountains beyond.

DOÑA BECA. (*Suspiciously*) Antonio, you're not going to try to change things again, are you?

ANTONIO. (*Staring down at the valley*) My valley. When I first left here it was my courage, my hope, the one thing that led me on. For thirty years I've remembered standing here in this spot, looking down on that village, that little toy village below me. For thirty years I've seen this valley (*He presses his hand against his forehead*) here, and now I can see it, really see it, down there.

RUFINO. It's the same as any other valley.

ANTONIO. Not to me. Never to me. You don't understand what I'm talking about because you're seeing what's there now . . . nothing but a sandy waste studded with cactus and yucas and flowering thorn. But I'm seeing what is to come. What I have dreamed of bringing here.

DOÑA BECA. So you are going to change things.

ANTONIO. Change? No. I'm going to build something new, something that has never been here. I am going to put a power-house at the bend of that river, pump water into a spider's web of irrigation ditches, plant fields of barley, groves of orange and lemon trees, make this the finest fruit region in the north. Why don't you see it, can't you see it? In two years . . . in a year we'll be looking down on gold, green gold, God's gold.

FATHER LACAYA. (*Slowly*) This valley will be a miniature California.

ANTONIO. The ground is richer than California's. The climate is even better for fruit. All we need is water, and I'm going to bring that here.

RUFINO. That's all very fine, but what about my goats?

ANTONIO. (*Shrugging*) I'm sorry. They'll have to go. There are other valleys nearby. (*On a sudden thought*) You can take them to the other side of the mountains.

RUFINO. (*Excitedly*) But this is the finest goat pasture around here. And the men in the village . . . what about them?

ANTONIO. (*Puzzled*) Well, what about them? They'll change from goat-herders to farmers, that's all.

RUFINO. That isn't all. Those men own goats in my flocks. They won't be willing to exchange a goat for an orange tree.

DON PABLO. They'll do anything to keep from working for you. . . .

(from Act II)
(The scene is now three months later . . . 5:30 of an afternoon in June. The patio has changed considerably. There is a new gate in the patio wall, and a table at the right with two chairs on either side. The bench is near the center and the stool is by the house wall. Flower pots have appeared. They stand along the right and rear walls, and there is a basket of cut flowers hanging from a long rain trough projecting from the wall at the left. When the curtains part we find ABEL sitting astride one of the chairs, his arms resting on its back. He is talking to ESTER, who is sitting on the bench with a pan in her lap peeling potatoes, and to CONCHA who is in the window-seat crocheting.)

ABEL. Why won't you teach me the words to that song?
    (*Ester and Concha look at each other and laugh*).
    All right, you needn't. I'll learn it from some other girl.
CONCHA. (*Triumphantly*) No other girl would teach it to you.
ABEL. I'll ask Carlos, then, when he brings up the mail.
ESTER. It wouldn't do you any good to know it. Would it, Concha?
CONCHA. Not that song. It's only used for singing the rooster.
ABEL. And perhaps you think I can't sing the rooster?
ESTER. (*Pointing her finger at him*) Whom would you sing it to?
ABEL. I know a lot of girls who would be glad to have me sing it to them.
    Lola, or Carmen, or Rosa . . .
ESTER. To them? Bah!
ABEL. And why "bah" to them?
CONCHA. (*Gaily*) Because Alfonso Tóma walked three times around the plaza with Lola. He'd put a knife in your back.
ABEL. I'll walk three times around the plaza with her myself.
ESTER. (*Shocked*) Oooh, you couldn't do that!
ABEL. If he could, I could. (*The girls shriek with merriment.*)
    And what's so funny about that?
CONCHA. Don't you know what walking three times around the plaza with a girl means?
ABEL. What does it mean?
ESTER. That the two are engaged.
ABEL. Very well, we'll mark Lola off. But that still leaves Carmen and Rosa. I can sing it to them.

CONCHA. (*Laughing*) Not that song!

ABEL. What's the matter with that song? I think it's beautiful. (*He hums the tune.*) It sounds like the most weird and mournful air that the mind of man could invent.

ESTER. Because that song means you're engaged to the girl.

ABEL. Ah . . . you have too many rules and regulations in this valley.

ESTER. We'll teach you another one. Carlos Balderas used to sing this one to Concha all the time.

CONCHA. Until I sent him about his business.

ESTER. Until Lupita came, you mean. . . .

The Ring of General Macías

The people of Mexico lived under miserable conditions until they overthrew their dictatorial government and established a democratic society. This play is written from the point of view of a member of the upper
class. The reader's sympathies are with her as she struggles, against a
background of bitter revolution, to defend the honor of the man she
loves. Nevertheless, both she and the reader recognize, before the play
is over, how desperate were the lives of the poor and how justified was
the revolution.

CHARACTERS

>   MARCIA, the sister of General Macías
>   RAQUEL, the wife of General Macías
>   ANDRÉS DE LA O, a captain in the Revolutionary Army
>   CLETO, a private in the Revolutionary Army
>   BASILIO FLORES, a captain in the Federal Army

SETTING

>   Just outside Mexico City; a night in April, 1912

*The living room of General Macías's home is luxuriously furnished in
the gold and ornate style of Louis XVI. In the right wall are French
windows leading into the patio. Flanking these windows are low book-
cases. In the back wall is, Right, a closet door; and, Center, a table
holding a wine decanter and glasses. The left wall has a door Upstage,
and Downstage a writing desk with a straight chair in front of it. Near
the desk is an armchair. Down Right is a small sofa with a table holding a lamp at the Upstage end of it. There are pictures on the wall. The
room looks rather stuffy and unlived in.*

>   *When the curtains part, the stage is in darkness save for the*

moonlight that comes through the French windows. Then the house door opens and a young girl in negligee enters stealthily. She is carrying a lighted candle. She stands at the door a moment listening for possible pursuit, then moves quickly across to the bookcase Down Right. She puts the candle on top of the bookcase and begins searching behind the books. She finally finds what she wants: a small bottle.

While she is searching, the house door opens silently and a woman, also in negligee, enters. (These negligees are in the latest Parisian style.) She moves silently across the room to the table by the sofa, and as the girl turns with the bottle, the woman switches on the light. The girl gives a half-scream and draws back, frightened. The light reveals her to be quite young—no more than twenty—a timid, dovelike creature. The woman has a queenly air, and whether she is actually beautiful or not, people think she is. She is about thirty-two.

MARICA. (*Trying to hide the bottle behind her*). Raquel! What are you doing here?

RAQUEL. What did you have hidden behind the books, Marica?

MARICA. (*Attempting a forced laugh*). I? Nothing. Why do you think I have anything?

RAQUEL. (*Taking a step toward her*). Give it to me.

MARICA. (*Backing away from her*). No. No, I won't.

RAQUEL. (*Stretching out her hand*). I demand that you give it to me.

MARICA. You have no right to order me about. I'm a married woman. I . . . I . . . (*She begins to sob, and flings herself down on the sofa.*)

RAQUEL. (*Much gentler*). You shouldn't be up. The doctor told you to stay in bed. (*She bends over Marica and gently takes the bottle out of the girl's hand.*) It was poison. I thought so.

MARICA. (*Frightened*). You won't tell the priest, will you?

RAQUEL. Suicide is a sin, Marica. A sin against God.

MARICA. I know. I . . . (*She catches Raquel's hand.*) Oh, Raquel, why do we have to have wars? Why do men have to go to war and be killed?

RAQUEL. Men must fight for what they believe is right. It is an honorable thing to die for your country as a soldier.

MARICA. How can you say that with Domingo out there fighting, too? And fighting what? Men who aren't even men. Peasants. Ranch slaves. Men who shouldn't be allowed to fight.

RAQUEL. Peasants are men, Marica. Not animals.

MARICA. Men. It's always men. But how about the women? What becomes of us?

RAQUEL. We can pray.

MARICA. (*Bitterly*). Yes, we can pray. And then comes the terrible news, and it's no use praying any more. All the reason for our praying is dead. Why should I go on living with Tomás dead?

RAQUEL. Living is a duty.

MARICA. How can you be so cold, so hard? You are a cold and hard woman, Raquel. My brother worships you. He has never even looked at another woman since the first day he saw you. Does he know how cold and hard you are?

RAQUEL. Domingo is my—honored husband.

MARICA. You've been married for ten years. And I've been married for three months. If Domingo is killed, it won't be the same for you. You've had ten years. (*She is crying wildly.*) I haven't anything . . . anything at all.

RAQUEL. You've had three months—three months of laughter. And now you have tears. How lucky you are. You have tears. Perhaps five months of tears. Not more. You're only twenty. And in five months Tomás will become just a lovely memory.

MARICA. I'll remember Tomás all my life.

RAQUEL. Of course. But he'll be distant and far away. But you're young . . . and the young need laughter. The young can't live on tears. And one day in Paris, or Rome, or even Mexico City, you'll meet another man. You'll marry again. There will be children in your house. How lucky you are.

MARICA. I'll never marry again.

RAQUEL. You're only twenty. You'll think differently when you're twenty-eight, or nine, or thirty.

MARICA. What will you do if Domingo is killed?

RAQUEL. I shall be very proud that he died in all his courage . . . in all the greatness of a hero.

MARICA. But you'd not weep, would you? Not you! I don't think there are any tears in you.

RAQUEL. No, I'd not weep. I'd sit here in this empty house and wait.

MARICA. Wait for what?

RAQUEL. For the jingle of his spurs as he walks across the tiled hall. For the sound of his laughter in the patio. For the echo of his voice as he shouts to the groom to put away his horse. For the feel of his hand . . .

MARICA. (*Screams*). Stop it!

RAQUEL. I'm sorry.

MARICA. You do love him, don't you?

RAQUEL. I don't think he knows how much.

MARICA. I thought that after ten years people slid away from love. But you and Domingo—why, you're all he thinks about. When he's away from you he talks about you all the time. I heard him say once that when you were out of his sight he was like a man without eyes or ears or hands.

RAQUEL. I know. I, too, know that feeling.

MARICA. Then how could you let him go to war? Perhaps to be killed? How could you?

RAQUEL. (*Sharply*). Marica, you are of the family Macías. Your family is a family of great warriors. A Macías man was with Ferdinand when the Moors were driven out of Spain. A Macías man was with Cortés when the Aztecans surrendered. Your grandfather fought in the War of Independence. Your own father was executed not twenty miles from this house by the French. Shall his son be any less brave because he loves a woman?

MARICA. But Domingo loved you enough to forget that. If you had asked him, he wouldn't have gone to war. He would have stayed here with you.

RAQUEL. No, he would not have stayed. Your brother is a man of honor, not a whining, creeping coward.

MARICA. (*Beginning to cry again*). I begged Tomás not to go. I begged him.

RAQUEL. Would you have loved him if he had stayed?

MARICA. I don't know. I don't know.

RAQUEL. There is your answer. You'd have despised him. Loved and despised him. Now come, Marica, it's time for you to go to bed.

MARICA. You won't tell the priest—about the poison, I mean?

RAQUEL. No, I won't tell him.

MARICA. Thank you, Raquel. How good you are. How kind and good.

RAQUEL. A moment ago I was hard and cruel. What a baby you are. Now, off to bed with you.

MARICA. Aren't you coming upstairs, too?

RAQUEL. No . . . I haven't been sleeping very well lately. I think I'll read for a little while.

MARICA. Good night, Raquel. And thank you.

RAQUEL. Good night, little one.

(*Marica goes out through the house door Left, taking her candle with her. Raquel stares down at the bottle of poison in her hand, then puts it away in one of the small drawers of the desk. She next selects a book from the Downstage case, and sits on the sofa to read it, but feeling chilly, she rises and goes to the closet, Back Right, and takes out an afghan. Coming back to the sofa, she makes herself comfortable, with the afghan across her knees. Suddenly she hears a noise in the patio. She listens, then convinced it is nothing, returns to her reading. But she hears the noise again. She goes to the patio door and peers out.*)

RAQUEL. (*Calling softly*). Who's there? Who's out there? Oh!

(*She gasps and backs into the room. Two men—or rather a man and a young boy—dressed in the white pajama suits of the Mexican peasants, with their sombreros tipped low over their faces, come into the room. Raquel draws herself up regally. Her voice is cold and commanding.*) Who are you, and what do want here?

ANDRES. We are hunting for the wife of General Macías.

RAQUEL. I am Raquel Rivera de Macías.

ANDRES. Cleto, stand guard in the patio. If you hear any suspicious noise, warn me at once.

CLETO. Yes, my captain. (*The boy returns to the patio.*)

(*The man, hooking his thumbs in his belt, strolls around the room looking it over. When he reaches the table at the back he sees the wine. With a small bow to Raquel he pours himself a glass of wine and drains it. He wipes his mouth with the back of his hand.*)

RAQUEL. How very interesting.

ANDRES. (*Startled*) What?

RAQUEL. To be able to drink wine with that hat on.

ANDRES. The hat? Oh, forgive me, señora. (*He flicks the brim with his fingers so that it drops off his head and dangles down his back from the neck cord.*) In a military camp one forgets one's polite manners. Would you care to join me in another glass?

RAQUEL. (*Sitting on the sofa*). Why not? It's my wine.

ANDRES. And very excellent wine. (*He pours two glasses and gives her one while he is talking.*) I would say Amontillado of the vintage of '87.

RAQUEL. Did you learn that in a military camp?

ANDRES. I used to sell wines . . . among other things.

RAQUEL. (*Ostentatiously hiding a yawn*). I am devastated.

ANDRES. (*Pulls over the armchair and makes himself comfortable in it.*) You don't mind, do you?

RAQUEL. Would it make any difference if I did?

ANDRES. No. The Federals are searching the streets for us and we have to stay somewhere. But women of your class seem to expect that senseless sort of question.

RAQUEL. Of course I suppose I could scream.

ANDRES. Naturally.

RAQUEL. My sister-in-law is upstairs asleep. And there are several servants in the back of the house. Mostly men servants. Very big men.

ANDRES. Very interesting. (*He is drinking the wine in small sips with much enjoyment.*)

RAQUEL. What would you do if I screamed?

ANDRES. (*Considering the request as though it were another glass of wine.*) Nothing.

RAQUEL. I am afraid you are lying to me.

ANDRES. Women of your class seem to expect polite little lies.

RAQUEL. Stop calling me "women of your class."

ANDRES. Forgive me.

RAQUEL. You are one of the fighting peasants, aren't you?

ANDRES. I am a captain in the Revolutionary Army.

RAQUEL. This house is completely loyal to the Federal government.

ANDRES. I know. That's why I'm here.

RAQUEL. And now that you are here, just what do you expect me to do?

ANDRES. I expect you to offer sanctuary to myself and to Cleto.

RAQUEL. Cleto? (*She looks toward the patio and adds sarcastically*) Oh, your army.

CLETO. (*Appearing in the doorway*) I'm sorry, my captain. I just heard a noise. (*Raquel stands. Andrés moves quickly to her and puts his hands on her arms from the back. Cleto has turned and is peering into the patio. Then the boy relaxes.*) We're still safe, my captain. It was only a rabbit. (*He goes back into the patio. Raquel pulls away from Andrés and goes to the desk.*)

RAQUEL. What a magnificent army you have. So clever. I'm sure you must win many victories.

ANDRES. We do. And we will win the greatest victory, remember that.

RAQUEL. This farce has gone on long enough. Will you please take your army and climb over the patio wall with it?

ANDRES. I told you that we came here so that you could give us sanctuary.

RAQUEL. My dear captain—captain without a name . . .

ANDRES. Andrés de la O, your servant. (*He makes a bow.*)

RAQUEL. (*Startled*). Andrés de la O!

ANDRES. I am flattered. You have heard of me.

RAQUEL. Naturally. Everyone in the city has heard of you. You have a reputation for politeness—especially to women.

ANDRES. I see that the tales about me have lost nothing in the telling.

RAQUEL. I can't say. I'm not interested in gossip about your type of soldier.

ANDRES. Then let me give you something to heighten your interest. (*He suddenly takes her in his arms and kisses her. She stiffens for a moment, then remains perfectly still. He steps away from her.*)

RAQUEL. (*Rage forcing her to whisper*) Get out of here—at once!

ANDRES. (*Staring at her in admiration*) I can understand why Macías loves you. I couldn't before, but now I can understand it.

RAQUEL. Get out of my house.

ANDRES. (*Sits on the sofa and pulls a small leather pouch out of his shirt. He pours its contents into his hand*). So cruel, señora, and I with a present for you? Here is a holy medal. My mother gave me this medal. She died when I was ten. She was a street beggar. She died of starvation. But I wasn't there. I was in jail. I had been sentenced to five years in prison for stealing five oranges. The judge thought it a great joke. One year for each orange. He laughed. He had a very loud laugh. (*Pause.*) I killed him two months ago. I hanged him to the telephone pole in front of his house. And I laughed. (*Pause.*) I also have a very loud laugh. (*Raquel abruptly turns her back on him.*) I told that story to a girl the other night and she thought it very funny. But of course she was a peasant girl—a girl who could neither read nor write. She hadn't been born in a great house in Tabasco. She didn't have an English governess. She didn't go to school to the nuns in Paris. She didn't marry one of the richest young men in the Republic. But she thought my story very funny. Of course she could understand it. Her brother had been whipped to death because he had run away from the plantation that owned him. (*He pauses and looks at her. She does not move.*) Are you still angry with me? Even though I have brought you a present? (*He holds out his hand.*) A very nice present—from your husband.

RAQUEL. (*Turns and stares at him in amazement.*) A present! From Domingo?

ANDRES. I don't know him that well. I call him the General Macías.

RAQUEL (*Excitedly*). Is he well? How does he look? (*With horrified comprehension*) He's a prisoner . . . your prisoner!

ANDRES. Naturally. That's why I know so much about you. He talks about you constantly.

RAQUEL. You know nothing about him. You're lying to me.

(*Cleto comes to the window.*)

ANDRES. I assure you, señora . . .

CLETO. (*Interrupting*). My captain . . .

ANDRES. What is it, Cleto? Another rabbit?

CLETO. No, my captain. There are soldiers at the end of the street. They are searching all the houses. They will be here soon.

ANDRES. Don't worry. We are quite safe here. Stay in the patio until I call you.

CLETO. Yes, my captain. (*He returns to the patio.*)

RAQUEL. You are not safe here. When those soldiers come I shall turn you over to them.

ANDRES. I think not.

RAQUEL. You can't escape from them. And they are not kind to you peasant prisoners. They have good reason not to be.

ANDRES. Look at this ring. (*He holds his hand out, with the ring on his palm.*)

RAQUEL. Why, it's—a wedding ring.

ANDRES. Read the inscription inside of it. (*As she hesitates, he adds sharply.*) Read it!

RAQUEL. (*Slowly takes the ring. While she is reading her voice fades to a whisper*). "D.M.—R.R.—June 2, 1901." Where did you get this?

ANDRES. General Macías gave it to me.

RAQUEL. I don't believe you. I don't believe you. You're lying to me.

ANDRES. This house is famous for its loyalty to the Federal government. You will hide me until those soldiers get out of this district. When it is safe enough, Cleto and I will leave. But if you betray me to them, your husband will be shot tomorrow evening at sunset. Do you understand? (*He shakes her arm. Raquel looks dazedly at him. Cleto comes to the window.*)

CLETO. The soldiers are coming closer, my captain. They are at the next house.

ANDRES. (*To Raquel*). Where shall we hide? (*Raquel is still dazed. He gives her another little shake.*) Think, woman! If you love your husband at all—think!

RAQUEL. I don't know. Marica upstairs—the servants in the rest of the house—I don't know.

ANDRES. The General has bragged to us about you. He says you are braver than most men. He says you are very clever. This is a time to be both brave and clever.

CLETO. (*Pointing to the closet*). What door is that?

RAQUEL. It's a closet . . . a storage closet.

ANDRES. We'll hide in there.

RAQUEL. It's very small. It's not big enough for both of you.

ANDRES. Cleto, hide yourself in there.

CLETO. But, my captain . . .

ANDRES. That's an order! Hide yourself.

CLETO. Yes, sir. (*He steps inside the closet.*)

ANDRES. And now, señora, where are you going to hide me?

RAQUEL. How did you persuade my husband to give you his ring?

ANDRES. That's a very long story, señora, for which we have no time just now. (*He puts the ring and medal back in the pouch and thrusts it inside his shirt*.) Later I will be glad to give you all the details. But at present it is only necessary for you to remember that his life depends upon mine.

RAQUEL. Yes—yes, of course. (*She loses her dazed expression and seems to grow more queenly as she takes command of the situation.*) Give me your hat. (*Andrés shrugs and passes it over to her. She takes it to the closet and hands it to Cleto.*) There is a smoking jacket hanging up in there. Hand it to me. (*Cleto hands her a man's velvet smoking jacket. She brings it to Andrés.*) Put this on.

ANDRES. (*Puts it on and looks down at himself*). Such a pity my shoes are not comfortable slippers.

RAQUEL. Sit in that chair. (*She points to the armchair.*)

ANDRES. My dear lady . . .

RAQUEL. If I must save your life, allow me to do it in my own way. Sit down. (*Andrés sits. She picks up the afghan from the couch and throws it over his feet and legs, carefully tucking it in so that his body is covered to the waist.*) If anyone speaks to you, don't answer. Don't turn your head. As far as you are concerned, there is no one in this room—not even me. Just look straight ahead of you and . . .

ANDRES. (*As she pauses.*) And what?

RAQUEL. I started to say "and pray," but since you're a member of the Revolutionary Army I don't suppose you believe in God and prayer.

ANDRES. My mother left me a holy medal.

RAQUEL. Oh, yes, I remember. A very amusing story. (*There is the sound of men's voices in the patio.*) The Federal soldiers are here. If you can pray, ask God to keep Marica upstairs. She is very young and very stupid. She'll betray you before I can shut her mouth.

ANDRES. I'll . . .

RAQUEL. Silence! Stare straight ahead of you and pray. (*She goes to the French window and speaks loudly to the soldiers.*) Really! What is the meaning of this uproar?

FIORES. (*Off*). Do not alarm yourself, señora. (*He comes into the room. He wears the uniform of a Federal officer.*) I am Captain Basilio Flores, at your service, señora.

RAQUEL. What do you mean, invading my house and making so much noise at this hour of the night?

FLORES. We are hunting for two spies. One of them is the notorious Andrés de la O. You may have heard of him, señora.

RAQUEL. (*Looking at Andrés*). Considering what he did to my cousin— yes, I've heard of him.

FLORES. Your cousin, señora?

RAQUEL. (*Comes to Andrés and puts her hand on his shoulder. He stares woodenly in front of him.*) Felipe was his prisoner before the poor boy managed to escape.

FLORES. Is it possible? (*He crosses to Andrés.*) Captain Basilio Flores, at your service. (*He salutes.*)

RAQUEL. Felipe doesn't hear you. He doesn't even know you are in the room.

FLORES. Eh, it is a sad thing.

RAQUEL. Must your men make so much noise?

FLORES. The hunt must be thorough, señora. And now if some of my men can go through here to the rest of the house . . .

RAQUEL. Why?

FLORES. But I told you, señora. We are hunting for two spies . . .

RAQUEL. (*Speaking quickly from controlled nervousness*). And do you think I have them hidden someplace, and I the wife of General Macías?

FLORES. General Macías! But I didn't know . . .

RAQUEL. Now that you do know, I suggest you remove your men and their noise at once.

FLORES. But, señora, I regret—I still have to search this house.

RAQUEL. I can assure you, captain, that I have been sitting here all evening, and no spy has passed me and gone into the rest of the house.

FLORES. Several rooms open off the patio, señora. They needn't have come through here.

RAQUEL. So . . . you do think I conceal spies in this house. Then search it by all means. Look under the sofa . . . under the table. In the drawers of the desk. And don't miss that closet, captain. Inside that closet is hidden a very fierce and wicked spy.

FLORES. Please, señora . . .

RAQUEL. (*Goes to the closet door*). Or do you prefer me to open it for you?

FLORES. I am only doing my duty, señora. You are making it very difficult.

RAQUEL. (*Relaxing against the door*). I'm sorry. My sister-in-law is upstairs. She has just received word that her husband has been killed. They were married three months ago. She's only twenty. I didn't want . . .

MARICA. (*Calling off*). Raquel, what is all that noise downstairs?

RAQUEL. (*Goes to the house door and calls*). It is nothing. Go back to bed.

MARICA. But I can hear men's voices in the patio.

RAQUEL. It is only some Federal soldiers hunting for two peasant spies. (*She turns and speaks rapidly to Flores.*) If she comes down here, she must not see my cousin. Felipe escaped, but her husband was killed. The doctor thinks the sight of my poor cousin might affect her mind. You understand?

FLORES. Certainly, señora. What a sad thing.

MARICA. (*Still off*). Raquel, I'm afraid! (*She tries to push past Raquel into the room. Raquel and Flores stand between her and Andrés.*) Spies! In this house. Oh, Raquel!

RAQUEL. The doctor will be very angry if you don't return to bed at once.

MARICA. But those terrible men will kill us. What is the matter with you two? Why are you standing there like that? (*She tries to see past them, but they both move so that she can't see Andrés.*)

FLORES. It is better that you go back to your room, señora.

MARICA. But why? Upstairs I am alone. Those terrible men will kill me. I know they will.

FLORES. Don't be afraid, señora. There are no spies in this house.

MARICA. Are you sure?

RAQUEL. Captain Flores means that no spy would dare to take refuge in the house of General Macías. Isn't that right, captain?

FLORES. (*Laughing*) Of course. All the world knows of the brave General Macías.

RAQUEL. Now go back to bed, Marica. Please, for my sake.

MARICA. You are both acting very strangely. I think you have something hidden in this room you don't want me to see.

RAQUEL. (*Sharply*) You are quite right. Captain Flores has captured one of the spies. He is sitting in the chair behind me. He is dead. Now will you please go upstairs!

MARICA. (*Gives a stifled sob*). Oh! That such a terrible thing could happen in this house. (*She runs out of the room, still sobbing.*)

FLORES. (*Worried*) Was it wise to tell her such a story, señora?

RAQUEL. (*Tense with repressed relief*) Better that than the truth. Good night, captain, and thank you.

FLORES. Good night, señora. And don't worry. Those spies won't bother you. If they were anywhere in this district, my men would have found them.

RAQUEL. I'm sure of it.

(*The Captain salutes her, looks toward Andrés and salutes him, then goes into the patio. He can be heard calling his men. Neither Andrés nor Raquel moves until the voices outside die away. Then Raquel staggers and nearly falls, but Andrés catches her in time.*)

ANDRES. (*Calling softly*) They've gone, Cleto. (*Andrés carries Raquel to the sofa as Cleto comes out of the closet.*) Bring a glass of wine. Quickly.

CLETO. (*As he gets the wine*) What happened?

ANDRES. It's nothing. Just a faint. (*He holds the wine to her lips.*)

CLETO. She's a great lady, that one. When she wanted to open the closet door my knees were trembling, I can tell you.

ANDRES. My own bones were playing a pretty tune.

CLETO. Why do you think she married Macías?

ANDRES. Love is a peculiar thing, Cleto.

CLETO. I don't understand it.

RAQUEL. (*Moans and sits up*). Are they—are they gone?

ANDRES. Yes, they're gone. (*He kisses her hand*). I've never known a braver lady.

RAQUEL. (*Pulling her hand away*). Will you go now, please?

ANDRES. We'll have to wait until the district is free of them—but if you'd like to write a letter to your husband while we're waiting . . .

RAQUEL. (*Surprised at his kindness*). You'd take it to him? You'd really give it to him?

ANDRES. Of course.

RAQUEL. Thank you. (*She goes to the writing desk and sits down.*)

ANDRES. (*To Cleto, who has been staring steadily at Raquel all the while.*)
You stay here with the señora. I'm going to find out how much of the
district has been cleared.

CLETO. (*Still staring at Raquel*). Yes, my captain.

RAQUEL. (*Irritated*) Why do you keep staring at me?

CLETO. Why did you marry a man like that one, señora?

RAQUEL. You're very impertinent.

CLETO. (*Shyly*) I'm sorry, señora.

RAQUEL. (*After a brief pause*). What do you mean: "a man like that
one"?

CLETO. Well, you're very brave, señora.

RAQUEL. (*Lightly*). And don't you think the general is very brave?

CLETO. No, señora. Not very.

RAQUEL. (*Staring at him with bewilderment*). What are you trying to
tell me?

CLETO. Nothing, señora. It is none of my affair.

RAQUEL. Come here. (*He comes slowly up to her.*) Tell me what is in
your mind.

CLETO. I don't know, señora. I don't understand it. The captain says
love is a peculiar thing, but I don't understand it.

RAQUEL. Cleto, did the general willingly give that ring to your
captain?

CLETO. Yes, señora.

RAQUEL. Why?

CLETO. The general wanted to save his own life. He said he loved you
and he wanted to save his life.

RAQUEL. How would giving that ring to your captain save the general's
life?

CLETO. The general's supposed to be shot tomorrow afternoon. But he's
talked about you a lot, and when my captain knew we had to come
into the city, he thought perhaps we might take refuge here if the
Federals got on our trail. So he went to the general and said that if
he fixed it so we'd be safe here, my captain would save him from the
firing squad.

RAQUEL. Was your trip here to the city very important—to your cause,
I mean?

CLETO. Indeed yes, señora. The captain got a lot of fine information. It means we'll win the next big battle. My captain is a very clever man, señora.

RAQUEL. Did the general know about this information when he gave his ring to your captain?

CLETO. I don't see how he could help knowing it, señora. He heard us talking about it enough.

RAQUEL. Who knows about that bargain to save the general's life besides you and your captain?

CLETO. No one, señora. The captain isn't one to talk, and I didn't have time to.

RAQUEL. (*While the boy has been talking, the life seems to have drained completely out of her*). How old are you, Cleto?

CLETO. I don't know, señora. I think I'm twenty, but I don't know.

RAQUEL. (*Speaking more to herself than to him*). Tomás was twenty.

CLETO. Who is Tomás?

RAQUEL. He was married to my sister-in-law. Cleto, you think my husband is a coward, don't you?

CLETO. (*With embarrassment*). Yes, señora.

RAQUEL. You don't think any woman is worth it, do you? Worth the price of a great battle, I mean?

CLETO. No, señora. But as the captain says, love is a very peculiar thing.

RAQUEL. If your captain loved a woman as much as the general loves me, would he have given an enemy his ring?

CLETO. Ah, but the captain is a great man, señora.

RAQUEL. And so is my husband a great man. He is of the family Macías. All of that family have been great men. All of them—brave and honorable men. They have always held their honor to be greater than their lives. That is a tradition of their family.

CLETO. Perhaps none of them loved a woman like you, señora.

RAQUEL. How strange you are. I saved you from the Federals because I want to save my husband's life. You call me brave and yet you call him a coward. There is no difference in what we have done.

CLETO. But you are a woman, señora.

RAQUEL. Has a woman less honor than a man, then?

CLETO. No, señora. Please, I don't know how to say it. The general is a soldier. He has a duty to his own cause. You are a woman. You have a duty to your husband. It is right that you should try to save him. It is not right that he should try to save himself.

RAQUEL. (*Dully*). Yes, of course. It is right that I should save him. (*Becoming practical again*). Your captain has been gone some time, Cleto. You'd better find out if he is still safe.

CLETO. Yes, señora. (*As he reaches the French windows she stops him*).

RAQUEL. Wait, Cleto. Have you a mother—or a wife, perhaps?

CLETO. Oh, no, señora. I haven't anyone but the captain.

RAQUEL. But the captain is a soldier. What would you do if he should be killed?

CLETO. It is very simple, señora. I should be killed, too.

RAQUEL. You speak about death so calmly. Aren't you afraid of it, Cleto?

CLETO. No, señora. It's like the captain says, dying for what you believe in, that's the finest death of all.

RAQUEL. And you believe in the Revolutionary cause?

CLETO. Yes, señora. I am a poor peasant, that's true. But still I have a right to live like a man, with my own ground, and my own family, and my own future. (*He stops speaking abruptly*). I'm sorry, señora. You are a fine lady. You don't understand these things. I must go and find my captain. (*He goes out*)

RAQUEL. (*Rests her face against her hand*) He's so young. But Tomás was no older. And he's not afraid. He said so. Oh Domingo—Domingo! (*She straightens abruptly, takes the bottle of poison from the desk drawer and stares at it. Then she crosses to the decanter and laces the wine with the poison. She hurries back to the desk and is busy writing when Andrés and Cleto return.*)

ANDRES. You'll have to hurry that letter. The district is clear now.

RAQUEL. I'll be through in just a moment. You might as well finish the wine while you're waiting.

ANDRES. Thank you. A most excellent idea. (*He pours himself a glass of wine. As he lifts it to his lips she speaks.*)

RAQUEL. Why don't you give some to—Cleto?

ANDRES. This is too fine a wine to waste on that boy.

RAQUEL. He'll probably never have another chance to taste such wine.

ANDRES. Very well. Pour yourself a glass, Cleto.

CLETO. Thank you. (*He pours it*). Your health, my captain.

RAQUEL. (*Quickly*). Drink it outside, Cleto. I want to speak to your captain. (*The boy looks at Andrés, who jerks his head toward the patio. Cleto nods and goes out*). I want you to give my husband a message for me. I can't write it. You'll have to remember it. But first, give me a glass of wine, too.

ANDRES. (*Pouring the wine*). It might be easier for him if you wrote it.

RAQUEL. I think not. (*She takes the glass*). I want you to tell him that I never knew how much I loved him until tonight.

ANDRES. Is that all?

RAQUEL. Yes. Tell me, Captain, do you think it possible to love a person too much?

ANDRES. Yes, señora. I do.

RAQUEL. So do I. Let us drink a toast, Captain—to honor. To bright and shining honor.

ANDRES. (*Raises his glass*). To honor. (*He drains his glass. She lifts her almost to her lips and then puts it down. From the patio comes a faint cry*).

CLETO. (*Calling faintly in a cry that fades into silence*). Captain. Captain. (*Andrés sways, his hand trying to brush across his face as though trying to brush sense into his head. When he hears Cleto he tries to stagger toward the window but stumbles and can't quite make it. Hanging on to the table by the sofa he looks accusingly at her. She shrinks back against her chair*).

ANDRES. (*His voice weak from the poison*). Why?

RAQUEL. Because I love him. Can you understand that?

ANDRES. We'll win. The Revolution will win. You can't stop that.

RAQUEL. Yes, you'll win. I know that now.

ANDRES. That girl—she thought my story was funny—about the hanging. But you didn't . . .

RAQUEL. I'm glad you hanged him. I'm glad.

(*Andrés looks at her and tries to smile. He manages to pull the pouch from his shirt and extend it to her. But it drops from his hand*).

RAQUEL. (*Runs to French window and calls*). Cleto. Cleto! (*She buries her face in her hands for a moment, then comes back to Andrés. She kneels beside him and picks up the leather pouch. She opens it and, taking the ring, puts it on her finger. Then she sees the medal. She rises *and, pulling out the chain from her own throat, she slides the medal on to the chain. Then she walks to the sofa and sinks down on it.*)

MARICA. (*Calling off*). Raquel! Raquel! (*Raquel snaps off the lamp, leaving the room in darkness. Marica opens the house door. She is carrying a candle which she shades with her hand. The light is too dim to reveal the dead Andrés.*) What are you doing down here in the dark? Why don't you come to bed?

RAQUEL. (*Making an effort to speak*). I'll come in just a moment.

MARICA. But what are you doing, Raquel?

RAQUEL. Nothing. Just listening . . . listening to an empty house.

QUICK CURTAIN

Fragment from Earlier Draft of *The Ring of General Macías*

CHARACTERS:

CUCA, a maid.
EVA, wife to GENERAL MACIAS
JUVENCIO MARTÍNEZ, a Revolutionary spy
NICANOR, his companion
COLONEL CHAPA, of the Federal army
Two Federal Soldiers

PLACE:

A room in the house of GENERAL MACIAS

TIME:

An evening in the year 1915

SCENE:

It is a charming room in a house belonging to a family that for generations has been pleasant in their lives. At the back is a large square
window opening upon a patio. To the right of this window is hanging a portrait of the Blessed Virgin above a ledge on which burn two
vigilance lamps. In the right wall is a door leading to the rest of the
house. Near it is a table holding a cantalus filled with brandy, some
small glasses, and a prettily shaped vial. Close to this is a sofa. In the
left wall is a closet door. Below it stands a secretary with a chair, and
out from it is another chair with arms.

When the curtain opens we see EVA DE MACIAS standing at
the window looking out into the patio. She is dressed in negligee.
A beautiful woman of about twenty-five, suffering has haggered
[*sic*] her. Possessed of great poise and dignity she has two gods: one,

her husband, the other, her courage. Her servant and companion, CUCA, a solid motherly woman in her fifties, is sitting on the couch crocheting.

[SCENE 1]

CUCA. We may be having a revolution, I said to him, but that is no reason for the price of meat to be out of all reason. And then do you know what he said to me?

EVA. (*Without interest.*) What?

CUCA. He said the Revolutionists had stolen so many of our cows that soon we will be using meat to pay for things instead of money.

EVA. Did he?

CUCA. Eh, not a sentence of mine have you heard!

EVA. (*Forcing a smile, turning and trying to be pleasant.*) But I did hear you. You were speaking of the Revolutionists. (*With intense hatred.*) The Revolutionists! Ay, Cuca!

CUCA. (*Goes to her.*) Now, señora, you must not grieve so. The General is safe . . .

EVA. If I could only be sure. I have the strangest feeling here. (*She puts her hand against her heart.*) As though he were calling to me. I can hear his voice crying, "Eva, Eva! Help me!"

CUCA. Eh, what words you speak! After all, isn't he a general . . . a Federal general? And a very important man? The Revolutionists would be afraid to touch him.

EVA. (*Sitting on the couch.*) As plain as I hear your voice, I can hear his. Crying, he is . . . like a little baby.

CUCA. (*Coming down to her.*) Now you know that is a lie. Is not General Macías the bravest general in the north . . . in the south . . . in the whole of the Republic? He has only to make a face, and the Revolutionists would run like frightened rabbits . . .

EVA. (*Looking up at her with pride in her face.*) You are right . . . he is brave. The very blood in his veins boils with courage. If I can only be brave enough to meet his bravery.

CUCA. You can, child, you can.

EVA. No. Fear eats my heart. As each day passes with no message from him, I . . . (*She breaks off, biting her mouth to keep her lips from quivering.*)

CUCA. Señora, keep reason in your mind. How can he send us any messages with Revolutionists between his camp and this house?

EVA. But a whole month . . . thirty days . . . seven hundred and twenty hours . . . He might have found some way to let me know he was safe . . .

CUCA. Has he then nothing else to do but think of means to send you love notes?

EVA. (*With a sad smile.*) Now you make me sound a fool, Cuca.

CUCA. Are you not one?

EVA. Yes. A very great fool who loves a brave man very much. [. . . missing page 3]

CUCA. A brave man who will cut the heart out of my body if he comes home and finds you looking as you do. For three nights you've had no sleep. And all you do is weep and wail.

EVA. I think I've forgotten how to sleep.

CUCA. (*Jerks her head in a determined manner.*) Eh, and here is something to help you learn. (*She goes to the table.*) A glass of brandy . . . perhaps even two, and . . . eh . . . (*She sees the vial.*) and what is this pretty bottle that I've not seen before.

EVA. (*Quickly and harshly.*) Put that down, Cuca.

CUCA. (*As she slowly puts it down.*) What is it, senora?

EVA. (*Guiltily.*) It is a . . . a sleeping draught. I bought it at the chemist's this morning.

CUCA. (*Looking at her with slow comprehension.*) So . . . a sleeping draught. A sleep from which there is no waking!

EVA. Cuca . . .

CUCA. (*Interrupting.*) The Church forbids it. No masses could be sung for your soul. You would sleep in unhallowed ground . . .

EVA. But if there is a true God I would be with my husband! With my hand in his do you think I'd fear the seven kings of Hell?

CUCA. No. No, little one. (*With sudden fear.*) But you would not take it unless you knew.

EVA. My heart will tell me when he dies. He lives in my heart. Why should it not tell me.

[skip to arrival of Revolutionary soldiers]

JUVENCIO. I am Juvencio Martínez, señora, your servant. Once a
lawyer, today . . .

EVA. (*With loathing.*) A spy. A Revolutionary spy.

JUVENCIO. Then you have heard of me.

EVA. And so has all the world. (*Steps toward him.*) You are very
clever, señor Martínez, playing your little tricks with rings, but
this is a Federal house, and my husband makes no promises to
Revolutionists.

JUVENCIO. One little moment, señora. Perhaps you will understand
your husband's message better when I tell you that he is a prisoner
of my soldiers.

EVA. (*Horrified.*) A prisoner? That's a lie!

JUVENCIO. Perhaps you had better examine the ring again, señora . . .
to make certain.

EVA. Then you stole it from his dead body. He would never allow himself to be captured.

JUVENCIO. No? Do you hear that, Nicanor?

NICANOR. For a dead man he has a loud voice. Do ghosts roar with
anger, señora?

EVA. You are lying, both of you. Even if he were a prisoner he would
never send you to me for shelter . . . not Revolutionists . . . not
here!

JUVENCIO. He puts a value on his life, señora. And if I do not return to
camp by sundown tomorrow night . . . (*He flings out his hands.*)

EVA. You mean . . .

JUVENCIO. I believe it is the custom to shoot generals. Of course if
he were just a colonel we would hang him . . . but luckily he is a
general.

EVA. (*Sinking down on the sofa, her hands pressed to her face.*) Blessed
Mary . . . Holy Virgin . . .

JUVENCIO. And now, señora, will you give us food and lodging for the
night?

EVA. (*In a stifled voice.*) The kitchen is across the patio.

JUVENCIO. Thank you. (*Turns to NICANOR.*) Go and fix me
some . . . (*His voice dies into silence as men's voices can be heard
shouting outside.*)

MEN. (*Off left.*) They must have gone through here! Be careful of those horses! Surround the house!

EVA. (*Frightened.*) Who is that?

JUVENCIO. Federals, señora. Hunting for us. (*Catches her wrist.*) You must hide us!

EVA. Do you think me a traitor!

JUVENCIO. (*Quietly.*) Only a woman who loves her husband. And if I'm not back by sundown tomorrow evening . . . (*He makes a significant gesture across his throat.*)

EVA. (*Visibly pulls herself together.*) I'll hide you. . . .

CHAPTER THREE

Books and Novels and Hollywood

1942–1953

Niggli had taken on Paul Green's desk job at the University of North Carolina during the early 1940s (according to her correspondence with him), handling administrative and academic matters pertaining to the Carolina Playmakers. Green had gone to Hollywood for an indeterminate time. In her letters, Niggli discusses programmatic issues, facilitates business affairs by enclosing forms where he can simply "check off" or sign, and is always personable but efficient. She mentions the weather, or Navy trainees marching past her office window, then asks him to clarify who receives the insurance refund on a car that was sold. She occasionally jokes with Green, imploring him not "to elope with a Hollywood blond," or simply states that he is missed, signing off with either "love, Jo," or "affectionately," and at times simply "J."

Niggli refers to issues discussed in staff meetings, and steps taken by a committee (of which she is a full member) creating an interdisciplinary major between Sociology, Music, and Dramatic Arts, for a degree titled "Playground Recreation." She states that Sam (Selden) is drawing up a list of the required courses in time for spring quarter. A principal issue in her letters is the supervision of master's students in the play-writing program, their academic reviews and grades. Niggli appears to be assuming Green's role as principal thesis director. She consults with him on the approval of drafts of plays or assignments that he has also reviewed, adding her reflections. But it is left to her to assign follow-up work, to deal with exceptions requested by students, and to document their progress. Niggli is performing an academic role, as the following examples will show. She teaches classes, takes care of administrative needs, and, most significantly, reviews the progress of graduate students. Biographical sources state only that she was Green's secretary, but the era must be considered. Women were not hired by the university as full-time faculty, much less as administrators of a unit.

On March 2, 1943, Niggli says she has arranged hour-and-a-half conferences with each of the students during the coming week. In a previous letter, she stated that "everything is going ok down here,"[1] and that "I think D——C—— is finally straightened out," and then in a subsequent letter on March 8 she states that she has had a number of conferences with this student and is worried because "her characterization and dialogue are pretty poor. The trouble is that D—— thinks in a shallow manner, and when you try to dig for something deeper, you find the well-hole dry. A notice came in to the office today that her orals (on which you are supposed to serve) are set for the afternoon of March 18." She continues that the student is definitely putting in a lot of work, but that her work is simply substandard, and that "if a light, frothy little comedy, suitable for production in high schools is adequate, then she'll get by." Niggli discusses another student's work in the same letter, who is "writing the story of her own life, and she can't get a dramatic perspective on it. Couple this with the fact that she doesn't know a dramatic situation when it hits her in the face, and it reduces to another problem. But A—— has an intensity that D—— lacks, and I think if I push her enough she'll turn out a decent play. Anyway I'll push. It remains to be seen what comes out."

A week later she states that D—— has the first and third acts of her play typed and is working on the second. "I'm keeping my fingers crossed for that girl. I certainly hope she makes it." Two days later in a new letter she states that "D—— failed her writtens. Poor girl. She certainly gave it the old college try." Then Niggli cites a discussion with Sam about thesis plays and "just what is the standard we should set up in the department about them." He has suggested that the program require a minimum of three months' work on a play after the idea has been selected. She agrees, and asks Green's input. Since the cited student tried to do hers in less than three weeks, that "should have automatically eliminated her. It seems hard, but we do have to have standards that apply to all cases and not just the individuals." In a letter in April, Niggli gives an update on each of the students: some have completed, one will polish her play at home during the summer, the student named D—— failed, another chose to postpone commencing her thesis, and Niggli encloses the thesis outline for yet another student. Niggli herself has been "asked to stay here and teach this summer" and states she will remain in his office. She says she has registered the office phone in her name, and also appears to be facilitating a writer's club.

These examples clearly demonstrate Niggli's administrative efficiency, as well as her command of details and intelligence in dealing with academic administration and supervision of graduate-student projects. While some records indicate that Niggli served as Green's secretary, others simply show her as "instructor," after having worked as director of the radio division. It is apparent from these letters, however, that she was making decisions and collaborating professionally on academic matters that involved graduate students. In the current era, she would have been assigned an appropriate title.

Letters toward the end of spring state: "I'm glad you're pleased with the way I'm handling" one student (April 27), and that another, whose thesis was not submitted in time to send him a copy, "finished her thesis in fine shape." On May 14, Niggli relates in a handwritten note that "Proff pulled a fast one on me about A——. Without saying a word to me he called her in and told her she couldn't write a play. Well, she raised Cain, naturally. I told her to come and see me and I talked to her for over an hour," calming and helping her find direction again.

Green would remain in Los Angeles through the fall (his wife had joined him and they purchased a home), return for a few months, and leave again. Niggli asks him to pick up copies of three movie scripts when he is at that "shop" that sells them (her manuscripts show that she worked on screenplays during the 1940s, some time before her own time in Hollywood). On June 23, Niggli takes on a more authoritative tone. She describes a sudden decision by the university to move Green's offices to another building, so that the university printers can take over their offices. Since she teaches from 10:00 to 12:00 (she often taught summer school at UNC, but the graduate program appears to also be ongoing), she instructs "the girl in the office to throw them out on their ear if a thing in that office were touched before I got there." At noon she "marched" over and spoke to the head of the Buildings Department, asking "how come and why," and then proceeds to do the packing of Green's manuscripts and other items in the office. Niggli displays a self-confident and professional attitude about the needs of an academic office and matters concerning the playwriting program.

On July 2, Green sent a Western Union wire asking Niggli to confer with Proff about A——, as he just finished reading her thesis play and finds it below standard, both in quality and format. "If the rest of her work toward her degree is good," then he says he will okay her graduation only because of the war emergency. Two days later Niggli sent him a long letter stating that she spent time evaluating the play and "finally decided I could not, in honesty, pass her play." The situation is discussed in a staff meeting, and afterward she states Proff "called her in and told her the play failed." Niggli reports that the student came to see her and "kept insisting that you had told her it was a wonderful play, which—frankly—I doubted. Then your telegram came. Without saying a word to me she had sent all of her material off to you." The student was apparently trying to subvert the local advisers by sending her play out to Green. Niggli had previously tried to help the student; now she recognizes that she was used. She also comments that "If we allow any caliber of play at all to pass, the value of my M.A. naturally drops. Soon Carolina will have a pretty low M.A. value with other schools."

After two more paragraphs Niggli concludes that "the poor child" is not M.A. material. Green subsequently tells Niggli she has cleared up "a lot of things," and returns the play for "your and Proff's action there." He leaves the decision in Niggli and Proff's hands. Once again, Niggli's decision is equal to other faculty in the program.

Niggli's salary for these administrative chores was paid by Green. On July 8, 1943, Niggli writes to Green's accountant in Hollywood, Betty Stewart. Stating that she is an instructor at the university and that Green's checks to her are $25 per week, she provides the New York City address of the person who is Green's typist. Niggli further states that she does not have a social security number because employees of the University are not allowed to have one. She concludes with: "I pity you on trying to figure out his income tax."

On July 12, Niggli informs Green that "My father is still quite sick and shows little prospect of getting any better. Because of this I have accepted a job as radio editor with an advertising firm in San Antonio." She asks him to forward a letter of recommendation. Niggli departed two weeks later, leaving all academic matters in order. Her correspondence in the future would indicate her parents' King William Street address (also on several manuscripts and personal stationery from this decade, with her name as "Josephina"). That fall, her former mentor and writing coach Dr. Roehl, who was still teaching at Incarnate Word, died at age sixty-six. The tribute given him in *The Logos* says he was a scholar in philosophy, history, literature, and languages; a foremost Shakespearean critic; and a specialist on literature of the Southwest.

Return to San Antonio

Niggli's father had continued to work in Mexico; an article in Spanish of unknown date (but obviously during the war) in a Monterrey newspaper lauds him for his work ethic, even as "jefe" of his company, and for his commitment to help during the world war. Stating that he regularly listens to news updates in his own office, the reporter remarks that he not only heads his own company, he is treasurer and shareholder in another company (it does not cite the names of these businesses). He is described as never going out to movies or having other pastimes, instead using his lunch hour to write letters to U.S. citizens living throughout Mexico to encourage them to purchase war bonds, adding that he has raised thousands of dollars for the war effort (he and his elder brother William had done the same in Eagle Pass during World War I).

Niggli now settled in with her mother in San Antonio, helping care for her father and working on the final stages of *Mexican Village*. She took on various jobs, at first teaching speech and choir at the private girls' school St. Mary's Hall, where her group of seventy-three girls did a performance for Armistice Day. Niggli was also trying to get a writers' club going (in November). On January 6, 1944, she thanks Green for sending his new book, and mentions that her seniors at St. Mary's said they were not interested in Shakespeare, that they did not care for the language. "Modern education has indeed forgotten the things of the spirit," she retorts. The following month, Niggli says she is glad he liked *her* book (apparently she sent him an early version, for *Mexican Village* would be released in 1945). She tells him she was commissioned by *The Writer* to do two books on professional writing, which will give her enough money to travel to Mexico City that summer.

But it is her mother who became gravely ill in 1944. In a long, hand-written letter addressed to Betty Smith,[2] in care of Ana María Torres in Colonia del Valle in Mexico City (the date was assumed to be 1944 according to a librarian's notation; Smith's book was published in 1943), Niggli says her mother "almost died in February, which kept me running in circles," but that she is now doing well. Niggli apologizes for not writing sooner, but that she was busy finishing her own book, and had "come down here for a much needed rest." She is no longer "teaching brats," but instead "working in a very swanky bookshop in the afternoons only, which leaves mornings free." She describes not only selling books but also advising customers, and that she "simply love[s] it," adding an anecdote about a customer's request for Smith's book *A Tree Grows in Brooklyn* by description, without knowing its title. Niggli says she reread the book for the fifth time before leaving for San Antonio, and declares that she finds "The Tree, stylistically and emotionally, one of the great books of this generation. . . . All of the characters are ripe with life, each one clean-cut and well-rounded, none of them less than the other, and yet none overshadowing the other." Niggli continues with extensive analysis, and concludes the letter, "and I honestly believe that you now have an established place in American literature."

Niggli held three different jobs in San Antonio between 1943 and 1946 (while dealing with both her parents' and her grandmother's illnesses): radio work for an advertising agency, teaching at the private girls' school, and working for the landmark, independent Rosengren's Bookstore, which hosted literary discussions with well-known authors (including Niggli a few years later). She established a close relationship with the owners of the bookstore, Florence and Frank Rosengren, Sr., (who introduced her to John Igo, who later served as her chauffeur when she made visits to San Antonio). Niggli had a practice of scratching out ideas in hardbound journals (several are retained in her collection at Western Carolina University), and one such journal, with the date 1944, was donated to Igo, who provided it to the Niggli collection at Incarnate Word University. Like its counterparts, it is not a record of personal information, but instead a notebook where she elaborated story ideas. What is different about this one is that the first writings in the journal are titled "Dream I" and "Dream II." They read more like story ideas than dreams, and according to Igo, "she thought of it as experimental" work, but she called them dreams because the current trend was for psychology-oriented material. The two items were published in the San Antonio journal *PAX* in 1985, and are included here to demonstrate Niggli's writing during this stage of her life and the war era. The first is set in 1870 and includes excellent descriptions and a moment of tension imparting mystery. It seems to set a scenario for a television Western. This may be representative of her early TV ideas and exploration of a new genre, based on her professional writing classes in New York. The second, which is very brief, provides a reflection on personal life during the hardships of war.

During a period of three years in San Antonio, Niggli would remain busy, completing and publishing three books while making progress on writing her second novel. With her father's death, there is no longer any mention of a home in Mexico; instead, Niggli develops new friendships in San Antonio, including a Catholic priest. "At the Guadalupe shrine in San Antonio we had a wonderful priest who used to say to me, 'Your soul is in trouble because you write about these idols,'" she remarked during her 1980 interview. Niggli laughed and said she responded, "Father, just because I write it doesn't mean I believe it." He was possibly referring to the content of *Mexican Village*. But he apparently trusted her, because on another occasion he contacted her and said she might be interested in having an object he had found. Niggli states: "There had been a terrific hail storm and they had to change the cornerstone in the church, it had been loosened up by the storm. When they took out the cement around a particular cornerstone, they found a lot of things inside, including an image made out of black glass that had had pins in it. I said, 'Father, where are the pins?'" He declared to her he was not superstitious, but just in case, he thought it best to remove them. This anecdote shows what occurred often during the early years of the Spanish colony when, as churches were built by Indian labor, the natives found a way to incorporate their own beliefs within the new religious constructions.

Niggli did travel sporadically to Chapel Hill, principally for the release of her books. She made occasional trips to Mexico, perhaps settling her father's affairs. Her correspondence with Green breaks off for more than a year, but in early March 1945 a letter from Green expresses sadness over Proff's death. Green says he has been in Chapel Hill for a few months and now returns to California, and that he has switched to MGM, having spent the previous years writing for Columbia. Niggli responds that "since Papa's death in February, I have been running around in circles." She also says she is finishing the second book for *The Writer*. Then she and "Mamma plan to go to the south of Mexico for a while, and then I don't know what I'll do. I've had several requests for new books on Mexico, but I have a novel in mind, and I may do that." During the same month, Niggli wrote to Smith, first asking her permission to include "the enclosed page from our pamphlet on radio writing," in her second book for *The Writer*. Then she states: "There's not very much new with me. French is planning to bring out a special paper covered edition of SUNDAY COSTS [Samuel French was based in London, and published editions there and also in the United States], and two other plays are being reprinted in some new anthologies. If I don't write some new ones, the old ones will begin to creak at the seams with age." Niggli also makes reference to the fact that Charles Haubiel is writing an opera score for *Sunday Costs* for the Metropolitan one-act contest, which requires "an all-American" opera, she says, wondering why he doesn't read the rules. Still, she calls him a "good composer with a fair reputation." (This musical would be performed in 1950 in North Carolina.) Niggli's concluding paragraph offers advice on Betty's relationships, admonishing her to stay with someone she likes but doesn't love, because the previous person she "loved" but did not like would have spent all her money, taken credit for her work, and she would have ended up "a beaten woman."

Pointers on Playwriting

Although Niggli reports nothing "new" about herself, *Pointers on Playwriting* would soon be released in Boston, and her somewhat fictionalized stories of northern Mexico, *Mexican Village*, was at press in Chapel Hill. Despite her personal sadness, 1945 was a big publishing year for Niggli. That fall, a review in the *New York Times* called *Pointers* a breakthrough guide for the neophyte. "Here, in brief chapters that go straight to the heart of the matter, is pure gold for anyone interested in the mysteries of dramaturgy," says C. V. Terry, adding that Niggli regularly reminds readers of the "grim fact" that the best plots "derive from life," concluding that "If Miss Niggli's book doesn't inspire you to a determined effort to get it out—then Thespis is probably not your muse."

Written in a personal and somewhat chatty style, *Pointers* offers several examples from Niggli's own plays, with the added key elements to her success: "Almost everything I have said throughout this book applies to suspense and surprise, because on these two things hinges the success or failure of your play. Keep them in suspense and surprise them at the end, is the basic pattern for all plays" (33). In another section, she criticizes misunderstandings of dialect often used in drama, and admonishes against attempting a dialect with which one is unfamiliar. She discusses dialects of the South (for both whites and blacks), and provides corrections—unique in that era—for how English speakers mistakenly use and pronounce Spanish-origin words: "The West has borrowed many speech habits from the Mexicans, but almost invariably the Spanish word is misused. For example, the Westerner will say, 'Well, let's vamoose,' meaning 'let's go.' In Spanish the word is 'Vámonos.' Using the same word, the Westerner will say, 'Go on, vamoose,' meaning, 'You go,' whereas the Spanish word is 'Vaya'" (68).

In describing character consistency, Niggli cites from what appears to be her unpublished play *The Fair God*, based on France's installation of Maximilian and Carlota as emperors of Mexico: "If one of your characters must make a sudden change, prepare for it earlier. I once did a short play on Carlota of Mexico's sudden attack of insanity, but something was wrong. At last it dawned on me that Carlota, up to the climax moment, was as sane as anybody else. I then [added] in a short scene where she accused her lady-in-waiting of stealing a brooch."

CARLOTA. (*Looking about her with distrusting eyes. She feels the brooch. Suddenly she clasps both hands tightly upon it, and speaks commandingly.*) Countess!

RAQUEL. Madame?

CARLOTA. My brooch, I've lost my brooch.

RAQUEL (*Puzzled*). But you are wearing it, madame.

CARLOTA. I tell you I've lost it. (*Crosses to Raquel.*) You have it. You stole it from me.

RAQUEL. (*Trying to control her anger*)You are mistaken, madame. I assure you that . . .

CARLOTA. Nothing is safe. Nothing is ever safe. (*She releases the brooch and sits on the couch, her head bowed in sorrow.*)

RAQUEL. (*Coldly.*) You are wearing the brooch now, madame.

CARLOTA. The brooch? Do you like it? It's very pretty. I've had it a long time—I think. I can't remember. It's my head. It aches so. I can't remember anything with this headache. [end of excerpt in book]

"That's all, but it served its purpose of establishing Carlota as a nervous, sick woman on the borderline of collapse. After that the insanity scene was perfectly convincing" (49–50).

Of note here is the fact that Mexican dramatist Rodolfo Usigli became famous for his play *Corona de sombra* (1943, later made into a Hollywood film), which is based on Maximilian and Carlota's reign. One has to wonder when the idea occurred to him, as Niggli's play was written much earlier than his (in 1935 or 1936). She met him in New York or Mexico City, and worked closely with him during the late 1930s. Niggli could have shared her idea with him, or this could be a simple coincidence, as the Maximilian era in Mexico has always been a topic of great interest. Usigli's play is part of a series of three historic plays. But the contemplation of Usigli's probable dedication to Niggli in his published book *Corona de sombra* makes it seem quite likely he borrowed the idea.

Mexican Village

Niggli's first novel was featured in successive display ads in the *New York Times*, with a book-jacket statement written by Betty Smith, who called *Mexican Village* "a gusty surprise," and "colorful story telling at its best." The novel was even reviewed twice in this prominent newspaper. Noted critic Orville Prescott, writing in his "Books of the Times" section, called it a "remarkable book by a greatly gifted Mexican writer" in October, and a shorter review in December by Mildred Adams asserted that *Mexican Village* makes "people come alive," describing a "part of Nuevo León's background, with North American influence." While Prescott's review is done with romantic flourish, Adams adopts a more serious tone, lauding the storytelling and "true flavor of human life," and aptly calling the title "unfortunate. It sounds like a sociological study and may prejudice readers fed on too many sociological studies of our neighbors to the south." The title, not selected by Niggli, likely sprouted from the original request by the university press for Niggli to create a work of nonfiction.

In North Carolina, a short article in the *Greensboro Daily News* (October 1945) celebrates Niggli as a "newcomer in the village's literary ranks" and calls her one of the Carolina Playmakers' *star students*, indicating that she currently works for a radio station in San Antonio. A photo accompanying the article shows Niggli seated, autographing books, while Betty Smith and the artist of drawings in *Mexican Village*, Marion Fitz-Simmons, stand at her side. Smith introduced Niggli at the reception held in Chapel Hill. This article quotes from a somewhat repetitive and gushing review in the *New York Herald-Tribune*, which considers the book "without a peer in its field. The American reader will understand this particular Mexico of the northern hills better, after he has read *Mexican Village*, than ever before; in many ways, indeed, he will understand all of Mexico better. That a single book can accomplish this is an achievement worth marking."

At the time *Mexican Village* was published, it was evaluated only for its Mexican attributes (although Texan folklorist J. Frank Dobie cited the about-to-be-published novel in terms of representing the Southwest in his 1943 book). Newspaper reviews called it a most convincing portrayal of Mexican village life, with depictions of tensions between traditional and modern society, and between Spanish and Indian cultures. Viewed decades later, it posits an interesting sociological study for Texas, principally for the inevitable Mexican-Anglo mixture that has occurred since the nineteenth century. This cultural fusion includes racial/ethnic intermarriage, which has resulted in the character Bob Webster's identity crisis, similarly depicted in the 1950s movie *Giant* (interestingly, the movie adapted from Niggli's book, *Sombrero*, did not include Bob Webster's story).

The extensive book can be considered a novel or a series of ten inter-related stories about life in a small village called "Hidalgo." The principal place of employment for the townsfolk in *Mexican Village* is a factory, where the foreman is modeled somewhat on Niggli's father. As a mystery unravels about the protagonist Bob Webster's origin, it is discovered that while his father is white (and Texan), his mother is Mexican of mixed Spanish and indigenous heritage. Thus, he represents the mixed racial/ethnic background of many people in Texas.

Decades later, *Mexican Village* was cited as an important cornerstone of early Mexican American literature. In his early assessment of Chicano literature, Raymund Paredes calls the novel a work of "great originality," which "was clearly intended to convey to American readers the distinctiveness of Mexican experience and expression." Recent critical references to the book consider it principally for its "folkloric" representation as it relates to Chicano literature, and do not mention her other two novels. Consideration of Niggli's three novels as a whole, however, makes apparent that her goal was not simply to re-create Mexican "folk life," but also to depict the tensions of mixed values and heritages within Mexican society in an era of rapid modernization. This applies as well to their inclusion in U.S. society.

In an introduction for the book's republication in 1994, María Herrera-Sobek states that Niggli's consistent "exploration of the history, psychology and folk ways of Mexican people . . . make her a direct precursor of Mexican American literature." She also cites what she calls Niggli's "special linguistic style," a style of English that seems to be a literal translation from Spanish—for example, "the family Castillo," "the house Castillo," or "the father of Severo." Herrera-Sobek further notes that this linguistic practice would occur in subsequent works by Chicana writers, such as Estela Portillo-Trambley, Helena María Viramontes, and Sandra Cisneros, capturing a nuance of Mexican culture in their use of English language.

Tey Diana Rebolledo (1995) says Niggli's first novel challenges the codes of conduct for women and posits a strong, independent woman in the role of curandera, possessing healing or seeing powers—aspects that are evident in some female characters of Niggli's other novels. Rebolledo also contrasts Niggli's "complex" characters with those of another Mexican-born writer, María Cristina Mena (who lived in New

York and published stories in English in magazines between 1913 and 1916), whose female characters are at times "presented as stereotypes in traditional love-story plots."

The year following its publication, academic journals also reviewed the novel in terms of its possibilities for use in the classroom. The Catholic journal *The Americas* saluted Niggli's technique of thoroughly describing characters, but felt that "her capital fault is that she cannot stop writing," concluding that the 491-page book was "tedious." The reviewer, Claude Kean, seemed even more disturbed, however, by the fact that religion hardly plays a vital role in this village. "Their real religion, we gather, is paganism, with its thousand and one taboos and superstitions. The village *padre*, though allegedly a personage of importance, counts for little among his people but as an expert at playing dominos and at dyeing birds. The fact that his parishioners number black witches, and cutthroats, and profligates by the score, does not in the least ruffle his serenity, holy man though he be." Read decades later, the reviewer's observation is amusing; Niggli's description of life in Mexico is no different than that revealed on contemporary telenovelas. Contemporary thought would refer to the village's practices as cultural syncretism.

Kean even suggests that Niggli herself cannot be Catholic, since she uses the phrase "to take communion" (it does not occur to him she is translating literally). This was likely amusing to Niggli, who remained Catholic all of her life, even dedicating her final novel to the Chapel of Our Lady of Guadalupe in Cherokee, North Carolina. Upon her death, her memorial services were performed by Catholic priests, and her will provided for the Catholic Student Center at Western Carolina University.

The academic journal *Social Forces* recommends Niggli's novel from the very first sentence, whether the reader "is interested in community studies or in Latin American life." Reviewer John Gillin feels that she has remarkable skill for capturing the main facets of "Ibero-American rural community life." While lauding her artistic skill, he critiques the fact that the people of Hidalgo have been represented in a novel rather than in a more scientific venue. Although other critical reviewers would refer to the book more as a collection of stories than as a novel, Gillin—who does not wish it to be labeled fiction—surprisingly considers the book a solidly connected entity, "sustaining reader interest from beginning to end," albeit "unnecessarily melodramatic." He recommends the book for an Introduction to Culture class, or as a good synthesis for those who are familiar only with the "dull 'facts' of the scientific field worker."

A review by Agapito Rey in the *Journal of American Folklore* in the summer of 1947 indicates that he likely conversed with Niggli. Rey states that Niggli's "big four" characters—the doctor, the priest, the mayor, and the judge—were drawn from real life. Three of these died during the 1930s, he says, but the real-life doctor is the one who induced Niggli's father to return to San Nicolás de Hidalgo, after renewing contact with him in El Paso. Rey points out that the village described in this novel is "typical," because it does not include Indian communities, but instead a "people who are a mixture of native and foreign elements well assimilated." He also appreciates the descriptions of courting and marriage customs, profound religious practices that mix pagan and Christian tenets, typical songs and dances, horse races and other pastimes, women's skills, and bullfight history. Rey concludes his review stating that her narrative preserves a passing era: "In a few more years these quaint little towns will give way to modern life and standardization."

A recent reading by Rita Keresztesi, who studied Niggli and other authors in her dissertation, considers *Mexican Village* much more than a "simple precursor to Chicano literature." Referring to the book as a "borderlands romance," she states that Niggli "displays an embellished and self-consciously fake 'travel poster' image of a region that cannot hide the ambiguously composite—racially and historically layered—picture of Mexico in the 1920s."

Keresztesi finds that Niggli appropriates the genre of the romance in order to historicize the Mexican people in a "hybrid text" where "conventional endings in death or marriage have already taken place before the story begins." Thus, information on specific Indians, the local Spanish colonial aristocracy, and the various mixtures in this village, both of custom and race or ethnicity, are all interrelated. The end result is more subtle than that of a "romantic, even quaint" story, as categorized by earlier critics. For her, the novel "sheds light on how to rethink identity, culture, and nation in a modern imperialist context," layered within the "colonized, recolonized, industrialized, transnational, and culturally hybrid Mexican-American contact zone." This reading would probably have appealed to Niggli, who consistently brought history into her creative works. Niggli's keen eye for observing and depicting

Mexican culture and history, together with Indian cultural practices, definitely lays a foundation for future creative works in English that depict Mexican Americans in the United States.

Her first novel sold well. According to records kept by the University of North Carolina Press, five subsequent reprintings followed a first release of 5,000 copies. A total of 22,253 copies sold during the decade after its release. Years later, the University of New Mexico Press reissued the novel in paperback (1994), with a foreword by María Herrera-Sobek.

The year after its release, in August, the *Greensboro Daily News* says fans enjoyed Niggli's *Mexican Village* enough to warrant a fourth printing in ten months. It is also reported that she is about to depart for Hollywood to work on a script for a movie version of the book. Here she is called "plump, jovial, Mexican-born Josephina." This first screenplay apparently didn't fly, as the movie version of *Mexican Village* would not come to fruition until years later with Norman Foster.

The state of North Carolina was also impressed with Niggli's book and awarded her its prestigious Mayflower Cup in 1946, for the best book written during the previous year by a North Carolinian. Sponsored by the North Carolina Literary and Historical Association, this tribute for original works in fiction or nonfiction of outstanding excellence did not require that candidates be natives of the state, but that they have established residency. Judges for the competition were professors of history and English at North Carolina colleges and universities; their selections highlight luminary arts and letters during the twentieth century (the award was retired in 2002). The honor elicited a telegram from Paul Green: "We are all delighted at the Mayflower award. This is one of the best decisions the judges have ever made. I kiss your hand. Paul." In her thank-you response, Niggli says she is glad that they will all be able to get together during Christmas that year, meaning he and his wife, she and her mother.

The Durham *News and Observer*, upon announcing Niggli as recipient of the award, states that she is a native of Monterrey, Mexico, who "now lives at Chapel Hill." While staying at the Hotel Majestic in Mexico City (use of its letterhead on April 12, 1946), Niggli informs Green that she and her mother have just purchased "the last house on the right side before entering Gimghoul Castle Drive" (bordering the UNC campus). Niggli says she is doing research on a new book "and working like a dog." She and her mother moved to Chapel Hill in the summer; then she made the trip to Hollywood to see about converting the novel to film, and visited with the Greens. Her follow-up letter to Elizabeth Green, with a return address of 746 Gimghoul Road, describes a smooth "trip home"; Niggli states that she has hired a secretary to get her manuscript typed. Since it is August 1946, she is obviously working on her second novel. In a letter to the Greens in October, Niggli comments on the Carolina Playmakers' choice for first play of the season, and states that she is striving to meet a November 1 deadline for the new book. Earlier in the year, she had published her second professional writing book.

Pointers on Radio Writing

The mid-1940s were surely a high point of Niggli's life. Already renowned for her plays, she published her first novel and a professional writing guide in 1945, followed by a second guide, *Pointers on Radio Writing*, the next year. Then, her novel *Step Down, Elder Brother* was released in late 1947, and at least two short stories would see publication that year. With two professional-writing books, Niggli would regularly be sought out for articles on writing strategies by *The Writer*'s monthly magazine, and occasionally by others, such as *Senior Scholastic*. Her writing books sold well. Twenty years later, the publisher of the first book asked Niggli to do a revised and expanded edition, which was released as *New Pointers on Playwriting*. She now had a solid reputation as a playwright and writing guide or instructor.

Niggli carried a heavy workload in the years before these publications, however, and states that she "broke down" in exhaustion in the late winter of 1945. But it was also emotional stress. Her father and grandmother died that year, and her mother had been seriously ill the previous year. It was a period of her life when she explored several avenues in her creative expression. Short stories found in her WCU archives were probably composed during the 1940s, when she had ceased creating plays and embarked on narrative.

In less than seven years, Niggli had written fourteen plays and produced most of them (the only play she never saw performed, as she stated later in life, was *The Ring*); then she completed two novels and two technical books in four years. It was too much of a pace to maintain without rest. The years in San Antonio were also intense—caring for her parents and grandmother, working various jobs as well as writing—and she suffered what she called later a "breakdown," although it was likely only fatigue. She had been living in the home next door to her parents, at 217 King William Street, and had likely just traveled to New York for the release of *Mexican Village*, shortly after losing both her father and grandmother. She describes her return to San Antonio to Julia Cauthorn, who recorded a conversation with her on April 30, 1979: "I came back to 217 . . . I returned just before Christmas, with a nervous breakdown. I was typing, there in your back kitchen was where I wrote *Mexican Village*, they called me to lunch [from her parents' house next door at 221 King William]. 'Weren't you afraid, upset by the hailstorm?' I was unaware of the hail. Lots of soldiers came to our house. They went to Florence Rosengren's—she made marvelous split pea soup."

Cauthorn, a prominent member of the San Antonio arts community, was at the time the resident of the house at 217 King William Street, where Niggli stopped on a visit to San Antonio in 1979, and she reflected on that period of her life. In this brief interview—some thirty-five years after the occurrences—Niggli confuses some of the facts, stating that her grandmother died in 1942 and that it was "A-Bomb Day," both of which occurred in 1945.[3]

The trip to Mexico City in 1946 probably occurred once she got enough rest to then begin tackling research for the next novel. Niggli and her mother left San Antonio in 1946, before publication of *Step Down, Elder Brother*. Her mother would not sell their family home for some years, and Niggli would continue in transition—between jobs and projects—for several years. Later, she would even indicate herself as "self-employed" between 1944 and 1954, although her self-appointed tasks were quite demanding. The new home in Chapel Hill provided the opportunity for a new stage in Niggli's life.

Early in 1947 she was saluted by a prestigious national group, the American Association of University Women. A dinner was held in her honor, sponsored by the Greensboro branch of the organization, and the award cited the imminent release of her second novel. Niggli delivered a talk at the Alumnae House of what was then called the Woman's College, now known as the University of North Carolina at Greensboro. This is related in an article in the *Greensboro Daily News* (March), which cites the great acclaim her first novel received, and her award of the Mayflower Cup.

Short Stories and Hollywood

Before the release of *Step Down, Elder Brother*, Niggli was submitting short stories to New York magazines, two of which were published and featured prominently during 1947. "Salt in the Air," published in *Collier's* in October, is an endearing tribute to the professional bullfighter, as well as a portrayal of how a young man living on the streets can find his destiny. It would be reissued the following year in a *Reader's Digest*–type book in Great Britain called *Argosy*, and also reprinted in translation in several Swedish and Norwegian magazines. The biographical note in *Collier's* states that Niggli is a member of the English faculty at UNC-Chapel Hill. The following summer she directed a creative-writing summer session at UNC. (Six years later she would participate in a writers conference in Hatteras, and ten years later she would organize a similar retreat at Western Carolina University).

"Salt in the Air" is a clever short piece where the aging bullfighter, Juanillo, observes the youngster sitting next to him, who reminds him of his own youth. He knows the boy is going to jump into the ring before the event starts, and that a good bull will be ruined for the starring *matador*. But he also recognizes it is how he got his own chance. Juanillo becomes a hero by rescuing the youngster, and a man with new resolve to become a teacher of such young people. Niggli's published short stories have similar themes as her novels—themes of Spanish and Indian heritage, and the Mexican Revolution.

"A Visitor for Domínguez" was published in an annual magazine featuring principal events of the year, '47, in August. This short story contains a dark sense of the inevitability of death and loss during war. In a rustic western setting, a "rebel" is being held in a jailhouse by government soldiers. He is to be hung the next morning, not even killed by firing squad as Domínguez states he should be in respect for military honor. But the "federals" do not demonstrate such respect during the Mexican Revolution. Niggli puts emphasis on the fact that the federal soldiers consider themselves too important to guard the prisoner, and therefore leave him under the watch of a single sergeant while they all sleep. When a woman arrives on foot with a note by "the big man, Huerta" that indicates she has permission to visit her husband, the sergeant allows her in and awakens the prisoner. He checks the contents of her basket and is amused when he discovers only a container of beans, disparaging the peasants who cannot bring something of better quality than what is already provided in jail. But the sergeant does not consider that there is a knife hidden in the beans and her "official" note is falsified.

The woman's description, with her head and face nearly covered by a shawl, evokes the Virgin of Guadalupe, and in fact she becomes her husband's salvation. The female character is extremely submissive, loving, and respectful to Domínguez. But he is verbally and physically abusive, although at the end grateful enough to take her with him as he escapes. The descriptions are somewhat cinematographic, and the vocabulary and setting similar to Niggli's "Dream" sketches. She may have written the story while she was living in San Antonio. The woman relates how federal soldiers looking for Domínguez destroyed his home and killed his favorite dog, and that they would have killed her had she not hidden. Niggli's principal discourse appears to be the extreme cruelty of the previous Mexican regime (although it also focuses on a rebel who is an abusive spouse), but the style of this story and others during this period show her to be leaning toward writing for cinema.

No year is indicated within either of these stories. An unpublished story, "The Runaway," which appears to be from the same era, gives a date of 1849—i.e., the Mexican War, in which Robert E. Lee did, in fact, participate. The setting for this story is an inn where a Union captain named Robert E. Lee buys a meal for a starving eleven-year-old boy. He and other soldiers are in the process of building a bridge across the Río Grande in Texas. The boy is wily and clever in evading the captain's query for information about his origin. The captain notes an almost musical quality to the boy's voice, who only reveals that he ran away from a stage after a fierce argument with his father over how King Arthur should be played. He is determined to make acting his career, and offers to entertain them to pay for his meal. The captain thinks about his own background and how he "ran away" from Virginia to "the wonderful land of Texas." He muses that perhaps someday he may have to make a choice between "the safe road and the dangerous path," for his own reasons. As the story ends, the captain stands up as "a leader of men" and walks out of the inn "into decision and the history of the world." It is an unusual story for its sensitivity and awareness of U.S. politics (somewhat related to the theme of "Saint's Day"), and more Texan than Mexican in this regard. Due to its notorious character, it is not surprising it was not published, but perhaps this and other short stories she explored found their way into movie scenes or episodes.

In 1947 Niggli was living the typical life of many writers: part-time instructor and freelance writer. Except, of course, she was very much in the limelight. She had achieved fame and would continue to be recognized as a talented writer for several years. By the following year, she would visit Hollywood for the first time and work for a year or so as a "stable" writer (a group of writers hired to write specific scenes on command and to rework scripts, and who received paychecks, not credits), an opportunity Green may have set up. Niggli worked for Twentieth-Century Fox and Metro-Goldwyn-Meyer. She wrote scenes for movies (her best-known and most often cited are the love scenes in *Seven Brides for Seven Brothers*) as well as episodes for various television series, including *The Mark of Zorro*, *Laramie*, *Paladin*, *Twilight Zone*, and *Have Gun, Will Travel*.

Since stable writers were not permanent employees, it is difficult to identify the specific years Niggli worked. It is evident, however, that she was there on two different occasions: one early on, and later when she developed her own screenplay. During her first period in Hollywood, however, she made a definite decision not to remain, following a famous person's advice. An article in the *Asheville Citizen-Times* (North Carolina) published March 19, 1978 quotes Niggli stating that she had become friends with Lionel Barrymore (who was confined to a wheelchair) at the studios: "'I would roll him to the commissary,' where they would chat. One day she told him that the studio wanted her to sign a contract, and he, knowing she wanted to teach, advised against it. He said, 'My advice to you is to go to England and learn stage and come back and teach.' So I said, 'Thank you, Mr. Lionel, I will see you tomorrow for the last time.'" She left, not realizing at that time that she would return in a few years to work on her own film.

Another probable influence on Niggli being hired in Hollywood was the impact of her second novel, published late in 1947, with very favorable reviews in major newspapers in early 1948.

Step Down, Elder Brother

Today, Niggli's second novel is hardly noticed, despite being one of her greatest contributions in terms of historical content and description. At the time of its publication, *Step Down, Elder Brother* received magnificent promotional attention. Advertisements by the publisher, a commercial press, ran in the *New York Times* every two weeks for a two-month period. The book was released in November of 1947 and selected immediately by the Book-of-the-Month Club for December, in a category for books situated outside the United States.

The novel takes place in the city of Monterrey and centers on the life of a prominent family during a winter period of the early 1940s. The extreme contrast between two levels of class is depicted, referred to as "the world above" and "the world below" (the latter evoking Mariano Azuela's title *Los de abajo*, translated to English as *The Underdogs*). The narrator and protagonist, Domingo Vázquez de Anda, is the eldest child in a family with holdings in both real estate and banking. He is thirty-five years old, about Niggli's age. As the novel opens he recalls his U.S. or American fiancée, Doris, whom he has left behind. He now faces an arranged marriage, as required by his elite class, with someone he does not love. His thoughts and observations demonstrate that Domingo feels intense love instead for his city; soon, however, he will experience similar passion for a woman forbidden to him by his class and status. *Step Down, Elder Brother* relates history and paints a highly descriptive portrait of the city. Landmark buildings and principal streets are defined, together with descriptions of life in plazas, restaurants, and bars that only a native of the region would know. The streets of this city, its cafés and businesses, the countryside as well as Monterrey's backdrop—the Sierra Madre range and its beautiful symbol, Saddle Mountain—provide a portrait of a serene era.

Domingo hires a mestizo chauffeur who represents the future "middle class." Mateo reads books on salesmanship in his time off, quickly becomes a salesman in the family's real estate firm, and gets involved with one of the family's daughters. They will sneak off and get married, shocking the family. This novel examines the shock being experienced by a long-entrenched elitist system, now being rocked by social changes as well as rapid modernization. Domingo's observations and reactions elucidate this clash. He tries to abide by traditional rules (while his sister defies them), but his noble nature supersedes his acquiescence to these rules.

Niggli aptly captured rapid economic change and growth in Monterrey (at one point Domingo remarks wryly that six hundred factories in this northern city do not seem to be enough) during the decades following the Revolution. Niggli's research in Mexico City in 1946 probably helped her define national politics that had a bearing on Monterrey in this era, but her father's own experience building companies likely also informed her work. In any case, the novel is highly representative of Mexican culture. The city's economic modernization is contrasted with old customs, such as the customary evening stroll around the public plaza as the only meeting place for young love interests, and "proper" conduct by females. Ancient lore of indigenous origin is shown to still hold importance.

The *New York Times* posted a review in January (by Charles Poore), stating that although "stiff and slow-going in spots," the novel "explores modern Mexican life in an exceptionally revealing way." Poore uses a significant quote from the novel to demonstrate Niggli's achievement in situating the post-Revolution era: "'Our world,' he tells his mother at one point, 'is finished. The old ideas no longer fit.'" He states that those "who have ever known Monterey [*sic*], whether as a tourist or not, will be delighted with Miss Niggli's sketches of the town; anyone who has never been there at all will feel fairly familiar with the place before closing her book." The reviewer cites her incredible accomplishment, but also criticizes her for writing too much: "If anything Miss Niggli has been too generous in showing modern Mexican life, tried to cram in too many characters illustrating various sides of it, the dreamers, the schemers, the idealists, the people on the way up and the people on the way down, and the plotting is sometimes heavy. In spite of that, *Step Down, Elder Brother* gives some memorable insights into Mexican life." He calls Niggli "a true novelist."

A second review in the *New York Times* the following month was posted by Mildred Adams, who also reviewed the first novel, which she now refers to as revealing "a close knowledge of rural Mexico." She states that Niggli "shows the same keen eye and acute understanding which distinguished her earlier book." The Revolution, Adams says, "becomes a thing seen through the pages of a photograph collection and the memories of old men." She also feels that the novel "moves too slowly, is too long drawn out," but nevertheless, "for all that, the skill with people, the sense of place and dialogue, the ability to make the reader smell and taste and feel which mark a born writer, are here."

Toward the end of February 1948, a review in the *Los Angeles Times* called the novel "a considerable triumph in story-telling," stating in its opening line: "Most books about Mexican life exploit the sensational and picturesque; few dig deeper into the struggle of a people in a process of great change. Josephina Niggli is one of these few."

Despite the negative comments on length (374 pages)—an odd criticism in light of many other lengthy books published in that era—*Step Down, Elder Brother* was definitely recognized as noteworthy. The *Los Angeles Times* reviewer, Edith L. Kelly, pinpoints Niggli's excellent construction of characters in the mestizo servants Mateo and Serafina, who "change the biological and the economic future of the [prominent] family." She also commends the contrasts drawn between Domingo and his former girlfriend Doris (Domingo defines himself as Mexican as tequila, and Doris as American as popcorn); and her portrayal of his clandestine lover, Márgara, the dangerous "Ixtabai" woman of Indian legend. She is the daughter of the revolutionary traitor Huerta's henchman. In fact, Kelly states that "one of Miss Niggli's strongest points is her analysis of human behavior." Weak points are "of minor importance," she adds, consisting of the introduction of short episodes for excitement or suspense that are unconvincing or unnecessary. Overall, Kelly considers the novel an excellent "rendezvous of both plebeian and aristocrat representatives," whose story is played out with the appropriate mixture of serious message and humorous or picturesque human element. Most significantly, Kelly sees the child of Domingo's brother and the servant Serafina posing as "the symbol of a new future" in the society—the mestizo, or person of mixed heritage.

The North Carolina newspaper *News and Observer* (William C. Parker) predicted new fame for "the Chapel Hill woman," saluting Niggli for "strong characterization" and a "stirring new novel," reporting that she did not "have to rewrite a single word." *Step Down, Elder Brother* is called "the story of the turning tide of the new generation, the revolt of the children of tradition."

Likely because of the Book-of-the-Month Club's categorization, William McFee writing for the *New York Sun* felt it necessary to point out that Niggli's novel was not a translation, and that she writes in English.

His was the most complex and meticulous of the reviews. He states that she approaches her characters from "the inside":

> Psychologically, she is at home with them as Henry James and Joseph Conrad never were at home with their English characters. Their art was that of the connoisseur in emotions examining, with immense curiosity, the working of an alien intelligence. Miss Niggli is depicting, with great skill, the inner life of a group of Mexicans as though they were her own flesh and blood. In that sense her novel is in the same class of those of Galsworthy in England and Sinclair Lewis in America. It is a very remarkable achievement."

McFee's analysis of her place in letters and psychology continues with his assertion that Niggli's description of the family unit made her novel "great":

> Latin-American family life is a far more integrated affair than with us. . . . The measure of our northern culture may well be the reception we accord this fine novel. Whether a public punch-drunk with second-rate historical fiction will perceive its qualities is not certain. This reviewer remains hopeful. Josephina Niggli sweeps into the discard a whole library of books by Americans purporting to tell us of Mexican life. We can see them for what they were, pretentious pseudo-romances which left the real Mexican culture untouched because their authors had never known it so as to understand it.

Observing that the novel provided an intricate yet absolutely uncontrived plot, specific conversations, scenes in the bar with political discussions, and scenes of family interactions that were all "brilliant," McFee concluded with a fantasy of Niggli's novel being appreciated by the avant-garde literary generation of the twentieth century. He further categorizes her work as equal to these major writers:

> Indeed, this reviewer likes to imagine Henry James and Conrad, Arnold Bennett and Ivan Turgeniev, Virginia Woolf

and Norman Douglas, all their differences settled, sitting in the Elysian Fields, reading this novel by a young woman of our time and agreeing unanimously that this is a first-rate piece of work. It will convince them that, in spite of their own enforced retirement from the arena, the art of fiction remains in good standing and not every writer has one eye on Hollywood.

Of course, Hollywood was a big deal in that era (and continues to be); all writers wanted their novels to make it to the big screen, but in effect, Niggli was probably not that concerned about whether her novels did. She certainly did not write with that intention, as McFee captures here. But his review is surely a work of art in itself, in salute to Niggli.

Step Down, Elder Brother was also reviewed by the Catholic academic journal *The Americas*, positively and with a much kinder tone than the one published two years earlier for *Mexican Village*.

Niggli's novels may also have been well received because the 1940s was a period when interest in Mexican or Latin American culture was strong (in the film *Sombrero* the rebellious character wickedly dances a *mambo*). In addition to the prevalence of Latin jazz and other Caribbean big band music, the trio *Los Panchos* had begun performing their "Mexican Love Songs" in New York City in 1944, and in 1947 were launched to national and international fame because of their unique instrumentation and harmony. This group established the sounds of Mexican nostalgia; they performed in New York, toured military bases, and expanded to international venues by the 1950s. Hollywood was releasing musicals and films with Latin characters, and Niggli's novels suited that audience. Her books interpreted the people and life of northern Mexico for an English-language public.

An Astute Reflection of Economic and Cultural History

The star of *Step Down, Elder Brother* is, in effect, Monterrey—in its historical transition immediately following the Mexican Revolution—an important city poised for change. The uncle and family patriarch in the novel states, "Monterrey is not beautiful. But to a man who loves power, she is magnificent" (207). New growth stimulated by construction of the Inter-American Highway, which began in 1930, led to Monterrey's arrival as Mexico's third largest city. Niggli may have purposefully selected the immediate post-Revolution in order to explore mestizo consciousness, but it was also her personal experience, the era when she came of age.

The city had experienced "growth since 1921 when the fighting days of the Great Revolution finished; [then] Monterrey shook herself, exchanged her rags for a fine new dress, and strung a chain of factories about her neck" (6). A character says, "The old must go to make way for the new." Modernization and a thriving economy were good for Monterrey, but they also threatened to destroy its inherent beauty, as Domingo observes. Like her character, Niggli perceived that the city would lose its uniqueness as it grew. She wanted to capture its heritage and customs at that very moment. By doing so, she created a lasting portrait not accomplished by any other novelist during this era, even in Spanish. Domingo sees with Niggli's eyes, as he describes the very heart of the city: "Hidalgo Street was the old Camino Real. Along it rode messengers from the Viceroy [in the colonial era] with orders for His Christian Majesty's most loyal Governor of the Province of Nuevo León. . . . In those days it took six months to travel from the Capital to Monterrey—six months of not knowing if your family would be alive to greet you when you returned. No, not six months, a year—more than a year." Fast-forwarding in his mind from the colonial to the nineteenth century, Domingo then states: "And what of the French soldiers who had marched down this street to capture the city for Maximilian?" (51).

He then reflects on another thoroughfare: Avenida Madero "was the real heart of Monterrey, although actually its three miles of parkway formed the city's northern boundary."

In the old days before the Great Revolution, when Morelos Street was called Commercial Street, it was too narrow to take care of the quickly growing business section brought into being by the railroad and the new factories, and many of the merchants had moved out here. Downtown property holders, horrified at losing so much good rent, widened the street, renamed it for the [Independence] patriot Morelos, and tried to entice the merchants back with modern buildings. But their efforts came too late. Tourists spent their money on Morelos Street; Monterrey spent hers on Avenida Madero.

Branching off from this street was the great Market of the North that imported southern folk art for Mexicans instead of tourists and also housed a branch of the liquor store that sold the same bottles downtown at four times the price.

Three miles of barbershops, hardware stores, leather workers, tinsmiths, fruit staffs, clothing stores, furniture stores, bookshops, music stores. . . . This street was Domingo's passion. . . . To him it symbolized Monterrey, clanging with music from a thousand radios and victrolas. It was as hard and garish as a painted woman, as full of laughter, as full of warmth. Lacking the subtlety, the charm, the sweet placidity of the south [of Mexico], it was frankly interested in one thing: money. (43–44)

Domingo expresses heartfelt love for the symbols of history and tradition, those things genuinely Mexican. Plaza Zaragoza, with bronze sculptures commemorating the four seasons (an Indian custom representing harmony in nature), is portrayed adoringly. The novel describes the university Domingo's younger brother attends, an institution that had previously been called the Colegio Civil. While it does not mention this, the Universidad de Nuevo León was founded in 1933. Prestigious Mexican writers and composers, such as Vicente Riva Palacio and Agustín Lara, are invoked, as characters listen to songs and sing their lyrics, or recite poetry by a revolutionary poet.

The surrounding region is described with geographic precision. Vivid descriptions include the highway north to the Texas border, with its steep downgrade shortly before Nuevo Laredo, and the pronounced mountain range and the route through it toward the city of Saltillo. Of special significance in the novel is the small village of Santa Catarina to the west, a model of many provincial areas of Mexico in the early twentieth century. The novel states that this small town was one of many temporary hiding places for Mexico's most-loved president, Benito Juárez, during his "presidency on wheels," as it was called, while Emperor Maximilian usurped the Mexico presidency. Niggli accurately depicts this charming country village (which also provided the setting for Niggli's play *Tooth or Shave*), to which Domingo travels by horse-drawn carriage to visit his *nana*:

Santa Catarina was the first town after leaving Monterrey for Saltillo. Here the mark of tourists could be seen only in a few highway saloons. This was the turning spot to reach the Huasteca cañon, that great gash in the side of the Sierra Madre range. It was on the guided tours of Monterrey, and many a boy with his burro had earned as high as a peso a photograph, posing with his animal against the backdrop of mountains.

But the town of Santa Catarina was as remote from tourists as though it had been completely off of the Saltillo highway map. No tourists ever walked through the narrow dirt packed streets, nor paused to admire the gaily painted houses.

A few guides would point to one house on the plaza, the bust of a man perched on its front wall. They would patter a small tale about this being the hiding spot during the French invasion of the Honorable Benito Juárez. As most of the tourists had never heard of Juárez, it made little impression. It never occurred to them to go and look at the house with the strange bas-reliefs of Spanish cavalier heads above the doors and windows, nor to realize that if this same Benito Juárez had not been so carefully sheltered here, the entire history of the North American continent might have been changed. For with Juárez' victory over the French-sponsored Maximilian, the United States did not have to go to war with France. (138–39)

Niggli thus provides a lesson on significant Mexican history, connecting to the celebration of *Cinco de mayo* through her character's reflections on what he loves about his native region.

Santa Catarina is no longer the enchanting village it was for decades; now it is only a neighborhood swallowed up into the expansive metropolis of Monterrey, which has grown out to enclose and reach beyond the former countryside.[4] Thus Niggli historically preserves an early twentieth-century countryside reality that now, for many people, only exists as a memory.

Family life is principal to this novel, and to Mexican culture. Niggli portrays the respect for elders and for family bonds. The family dinner hour is sacred, and Niggli converts the meals into an event to depict northern custom and tradition:

"The food of our childhood," Don Lucio sighed. "No matter how plain it is, no other food has ever quite the same familiar taste." Brunhilda obviously agreed with him, because as course followed course, she ate with exaggerated appetite. After the fruit cup came broiled trout, then *sopa de arroz:* rice fried with tomatoes and onions and topped by thin strips of banana. This was followed by filet mignon wrapped in bacon with a mushroom sauce, and served on rum soaked toast. Next was the *frijol*, the fat brown bean of Mexico, first stewed, then fried and mashed, with melted cheese poured over the top. Flaky French bread was on the table, but Brunhilda's hand reached again and again toward the *tortilla* plate. (108)

Analysis of other family members and their aristocratic background, as well as Domingo's propensity for intellectual reading, is related in the chapter from the novel included in the selections. This chapter gives evidence of Niggli's excellent assessment of a society comprised of two distinct class levels, the reading somewhat reminiscent of an Alfredo Bryce Echenique novel.

Indigenous Culture in *Step Down, Elder Brother*

Domingo falls madly in love with a woman who is at first only a shadowy figure behind a curtain. The intensity he feels is not an uncommon aspect of Mexican culture, if poetic indigenous lore is to be believed: "A woman would come into a man's life and without warning it would change into a strange and different pattern. . . . Márgara, indeed, she was the Xtabay and there would nevermore be rest for him anywhere. Of course, in the stories enchantment was a sharp sword that cut the victim off from contact with all former life; but in the real world, the victim had to continue in his ordinary fashion, doing the things he had to do: eating, sleeping and working in an office, and what person looking at him could say, 'He is crazed with love for the Xtabay'?" (138).

Although such a description may sound melodramatic to the English-speaking world, it is common popular belief in the Mexican world to consider that a man consumed with desire for a woman had seen the Ixtabai and fallen under a spell of enchantment (a recent telenovela titled *Apuesta por un amor* employs such a figure). She is a mysterious woman of Mayan legend, highly desirable and powerful enough to pull men in, draw them to her. Although in contemporary literature female images that can do harm are "la Llorona" or "la Malinche," in Yucatán and the Mexican gulf coast the more prevalent bewitching symbol is that of the Ixtabai. She is somewhat like the Llorona figure, a wailing ghost that comes out at night near bodies of water, searching for her lost children. Parents warn children not to go near water, or travel at night, because la Llorona could snatch them. The Ixtabai, on the other hand, is an attractive figure only interested in snatching men. She is also found near bodies of water and trees. A man can spot a beautiful woman, hear in the wind a whispering voice saying, "Stay," and feel in the branches of a tree her amorous arms hugging him. But the next day he could be found squeezed to death next to the tree.

References to indigenous lore or these types of images are common descriptors in Mexico and Mexican American literature. Even Domingo's sister Sofía is momentarily contemplated as the Ixtabai: As the gates are being closed to his family home as Domingo drives away, he catches a glimpse of a female in a near-transparent, long white gown, near the fountain in the center of the patio. He considers it an image produced by his state of mind and lack of sleep, not realizing at the time that his sister Sofía is sneaking out to be with Mateo.

Other cultural symbols figure in this story of contemporary Mexican society. Niggli aptly employs them to explore the basis upon which Mexican women are defined in Mexican culture. The Virgin Guadalupe is symbolized in Domingo's mother as advocate for her children and mediator between Domingo and his stern, disciplinarian father. While his forbidden love is the notorious Ixtabai creature, the female figure Domingo is actually most comfortable with is his nana, an Indian household servant and nanny, now retired and living in Santa Catarina. In Mexican elite families, an Indian nursemaid frequently "mothers" and raises the children. Often demonstrated this way in contemporary telenovelas, Domingo's nana is the one who instills values in him, lessons in life based on Indian lore. One evening when he is in a troubled state, he recalls one of her stories while meditating which steps to take next.

As Domingo sits on a ledge in front of a city building, he looks up at the moon, where "he could see the rabbit in it, squatting on its little haunches, its long ears tilted forward better to hear the voice of the Fair God" [referring to an Indian god]. As Domingo recalls the legend (included in its entirety in the selections here), Niggli recreates a story in oral history, and her account is far better than those related in children's books or fables published in recent years. Niggli's access to oral tradition always enhanced her research. The character in this legend is called "Hualpa," which is also the name of a male character in her play *Azteca*, but the latter is a very different personage. During the immediate post-Revolution, Indian warrior figures of great valor, who faced death triumphantly, were often exemplified in such modern counterparts as Emiliano Zapata or Pancho Villa. Thus, it is quite logical that a young man during the 1930s or 1940s would find strength in a legend about an Indian hero.

Mayan legends are often present in Domingo's consciousness, especially because he likes to read in his free time. Niggli accurately portrays, through Domingo, the cultural transformation being experienced in Mexican society. Diego Rivera and others began painting murals during the 1920s with depictions of indigenous history. By the 1930s, some of the first large temples and other excavations were opened to the public. Artists visited Teotihuacán and other sites to better understand their rich heritage. Anthropologists and various literary writers published books explicating their assessments and studies of early cultures. A prominent name cited by Niggli in *Step Down, Elder Brother* is that of Antonio Mediz Bolio (1884–1957), who studied the legends, history, and language of the Maya.[5] A diplomat and the author of several books of poetry, he achieved major attention with his book on the origins and philosophies of the Maya, *La tierra del faisán y del venado* (The Land of the Pheasant and the Deer), published in 1922. Born in Mérida, Yucatán, he was not ethnically Maya, but was fluent in the Mayan language and dedicated as a scholar to depicting the beauty, intelligence, and heritage of this region. Domingo rereads portions of this particular book when he needs to relax and de-stress. Later, he "is anxious to read the new book of Maya legends" by Mediz Bolio. This could have been *Introducción al estudio de la lengua maya*, hot off the press in 1943, although Mediz Bolio also published the first translation to Spanish of the Mayan *Chilam Balam de Chumayel* (1930), and *Síntesis mística de la historia maya, según el Chilam Balam de Chumayel* (1935).[6]

Niggli is the first Mexican American writer to describe and depict indigenous lore and traditions (legends and lessons of morality and learning) in English-language fiction. She herself was an avid reader. Her library during the 1950s contained as many resource books in Spanish as in English (see chapter 4). She also made careful translations of original texts in Spanish in order to inform herself, and at times adapted the information into her writings. An item in her manuscript collection at Western Carolina University demonstrates poetic analysis of a basic philosophy in Mayan culture. The poem could be either a translation from Mediz Bolio's writings, or her own creation based on her research; it contains descriptions that are common in works translated from the Mayan language. To one side at the top of her transcript is "The Book of Chilam Balam of Chumayel," followed by her name. The Chilam Balam, or books of the wise ones, is a series of texts that have only begun to be translated and decoded. Chumayel is an ancient Mayan group. Niggli was possibly reflecting on her research and created the poem, about four pages long, which carries the title "Chant to the Four World Quarters." A beautiful tribute to the creation of the earth, the poem designates and describes the four directions and cardinal points by their traditional indigenous colors: red for the East, black for the West, white for the North, and gold for the South. The colors are related to specific examples of flora and fauna, and to the people's journeys and settlements. The Guatemalan novelist Miguel Ángel Asturias also depicted these colors, in representation of the four directions, in his play *Cuculcán, serpiente-envuelta-en-plumas*, published in the book *Leyendas de Guatemala* in 1930. Niggli's poem is included in these selections because it demonstrates her close attention to Mayan and indigenous explanations of culture and origin. If it is her own composition, it demonstrates a higher quality of poetry writing attained by Niggli. Even if it is translated from Spanish, it is a very excellent translation. Either way, Niggli elucidates the high level of art and philosophy in autochthonous culture.

Other Influences on her Second Novel

Step Down, Elder Brother is a masterpiece, a creation that not only preserves a specific historic moment but also comprises a fascinating story, as noted in the book reviews following its release. It is further a cultural treasure, eloquently relating Indian legends, symbols such as the Ixtabai figure, and other uniquely Mexican cultural practices and beliefs. This novel evenly balances folk beliefs and traditions against rapid modernization and intellectual change in twentieth-century society. Niggli displays a keen reporter's eye as she scans and describes each aspect of life at a moment that can only be the late 1930s or early 1940s.[7] Obviously, various specifics could only have been experienced personally, but several books published in the 1930s and early 1940s may have contributed to her research. A notable book's historic images may also have inspired her story.

Rich descriptions of characters, and references to Mexico City in *Step Down, Elder Brother* directly correlate with images in the historic Casasola photographic archives, now one of Mexico's most valuable journalistic records. In fact, "the Casasola collection" is mentioned at various times in the novel, when characters peruse the faces of memorable figures involved in the political struggles of the Revolution. A book titled *The Casasola Collection* was published in Mexico in 1942, a time when Niggli was writing her first novel and may have also developed ideas for the second. This release was the first of a series of books published by Casasola's son Gustavo, who began a profitable production of visual histories from his father's archives. The issuing of this new Casasola book may have sparked an idea for Niggli. During the early 1940s, the Casasola book was frequently discussed in Mexican social life, and this sense is portrayed in *Step Down, Elder Brother*. The characters in Niggli's novel are enthralled by the photographs in various issues of "the collection," which were kept by the protagonist's uncle and passed around in a sort of men's-club environment (the cantina). In the novel, they appear to be magazine issues that are no long in print. This fits with the history of early Casasola compilations of photographs.

Born in 1874 in Mexico City, Agustín Víctor Casasola worked as a newspaper reporter and then entered the new field of photography at the turn of the century, which replaced newspaper sketch artists (of which José Guadalupe Posada, who died in 1913, was the most famous). While artistic photography was launched in the 1920s and 1930s through such well-known names as Edward Weston, Tina Modotti, and Manuel Álvarez Bravo, Casasola's photographs are always journalistic, records of meetings and important moments in Mexico's early twentieth century.

A photojournalist and entrepreneur, in 1912 he founded the Casasola Newsphoto Agency in order to compete with photographers who streamed into Mexico to cover the Revolution (which was a magnet for international journalists). His agency was very effective, and now his name encapsulates the only historic preservation of photographs of this era.

Casasola photographs reveal the Mexican people in late nineteenth- and early twentieth-century attire, often with resolute and hopeful expressions. It also depicts Mexico City street scenes, with street cars and automobiles of the era, as well as scenes in factories, cafés, government buildings, and jails. His work historically captures revolutionary figures, whether leaders or average people, both the victors and victims (in jail or after having been murdered, such as the famous Zapata photo). His collection also includes the only photographs of the women soldaderas.[8]

In 1921 Casasola initiated publication of an *Álbum histórico gráfico*, which was to be published in installments. The first issue covered the end of the *Porfiriato*, moments of triumphal arrival in Mexico City by insurgents, as well as jail incarcerations and firing-squad scenes, and ended with photographs of the inauguration of the new president, Francisco I. Madero, and his successor. The magazine was a commercial failure, however, delaying publication of further installments until after Casasola's death in 1938.[9] Niggli appears to have invented the publication of further installments (which Domingo's uncle possesses), unless a small number were released in limited distribution. If the latter is true, she further preserved a privileged moment in political history.

Niggli assuredly heightens interest by adding an element of mystery to the real-life Casasola photographs in her narrative, where male characters sneak into a back room to look up the faces of people who may be disguised and posing as members of their society. In fact, it leads to the unraveling of a secret about Márgara's father. Domingo feels that he has seen his face somewhere before; in time he realizes it was in his uncle's magazine, that the man was in fact Huerta's evil henchman, who tortured people. This is a clever mixture of history and literature, and probably not understood by anyone in the United States.10

An extensive text that included many Casasola photographs may also have influenced Niggli as she contemplated her second novel. This

was *The Wind That Swept Mexico: The History of the Revolution*, published by Anita Brenner in 1943. It would have been noticed by anyone
interested in Mexico, and was released in New York while Niggli was
teaching and holding down Paul Green's job at Chapel Hill. Brenner's
book is one of the first in English that explains historical reasons for the
Mexican Revolution, as well as conflicts between the victors and leaders
who sought to establish the new government.

Much like Casasola's photographs, Niggli's portrait-in-words of
Monterrey and its surrounding area forever preserves a passing era. Her
second novel was a great accomplishment, demonstrating that she had
as much affinity for a metropolitan ambience as for the peasant life she
related in her first novel and some of her plays. Niggli had completed
Mexican Village while living in San Antonio, and dedicated it to her
family members who died earlier the same year it was released—her
father, at age sixty-nine, and her grandmother, at age ninety-four. *Step
Down, Elder Brother* was dedicated to "mi comadre, Elsita Larralde,"
a close girlfriend since childhood whom Niggli probably visited regularly while she created the novel. While it is typical Mexican custom for
women to call a close friend *comadre* (and a male friend *compadre*), the
Larralde parents were probably Niggli's godparents, whom she has said
she visited regularly during the 1930s and 1940s. Therefore, Elsita would
have been like a sister to her.

Niggli's close relationship with the Monterrey area would start to dissolve once she and her mother settled into residence on the East Coast.
For a few years, however, her life remained rather in limbo—between
Hollywood and the East Coast, as well as a year in England. First, as she
transitioned out of Hollywood, she was invited to participate in a prestigious academic conference, a final professional stint in Monterrey.

A Conference in Monterrey and an Unpublished Novel

In 1949, an article in the North Carolina *News and Observer* announced
that Niggli would be one of the guest speakers specially invited to the
first Congress of Historians of Mexico and the United States. This significant binational conference was convened in the city of her birth,
Monterrey, in early September 1949, and hosted by such academic
and governmental institutions as the Mexican National Institute of

Anthropology and History, the Academy of Historical Sciences of Monterrey, and the prestigious Colegio de México. Principal U.S. sponsors included the Hispanic Foundation of the Library of Congress, the American Historical Association, and a group of Texas business leaders. The receptions and dining at the convention were covered by various Monterrey businesses. Grants from the Carnegie Endowment for International Peace and La Academia de Ciencias Históricas de Monterrey made possible the publication of a book of *Proceedings* of selected presentations (of which Niggli's was one of only eighteen papers selected), which was published in 1950. Reviews evaluating the event as well as the *Proceedings* appeared soon after in several journals, including the *Library of Congress Information Bulletin*, *Revista de Historia de México*, and *Cuadernos Americanos*.

It was an important intellectual event, featuring such notables as Alfonso Reyes (also born in Monterrey, in 1889) and Leopoldo Zea. Niggli and other presenters were feted with lavish banquets and a *merienda*, or formal tea, put on by the important ladies of Monterrey. Exhibits of Indian crafts and high Mexican art, including a huge reproduction of the Bonampak drawings, complemented the intellectual discussions. High-level government officials attending included the U.S. ambassador to Mexico, the U.S. consul in Monterrey, and the president of the Universidad de Nuevo León. During a day trip to Saltillo, the delegates were honored at a reception by the governor of Coahuila.

Niggli's participation in an international academic conference of this magnitude demonstrates her reception and inclusion in Mexican intellectual society. It is noticeable that others who write about Mexico in English were not invited. Anita Brenner's books, for example, have a certain political slant that may have limited her academic acceptance, whereas Niggli had made her mark as a literary professional. And she was surely invited for having recently published a novel on Monterrey.

Forming part of a panel on literary history, her talk (in English) was titled "The Importance of History and the Novel for Better Relationships between Countries." Niggli first discusses the idea of the "historical novel" and the fact that in the United States it only conjures up thoughts of something like *Gone with the Wind*, whereas "revolutionary novels of our time, and by revolutionary I mean change in a literary sense," such as James Joyce's *Ulysses* and Mariano Azuela's *Los de abajo*, are great "historical documents." She notes that the English translation of *Los de abajo* and other outstanding Mexican novels of the 1930s have not sold well, despite "magnificent" translations, and she feels it is because of the harmful stereotypical portrayals and "misinformation" propagated by U.S. writers who render a southern hemisphere "inhabited by sleepy Indians, bandits, velvet clothed young gentlemen with guitars, and shawled maidens who somehow manage to pass through the vicissitudes of eating and sleeping without ever removing a rose from their lips."

Writers such as Richard Harding Davis and O. Henry have done much damage with stories "in which one stalwart American stops a revolution with the aid of one machine gun and the knowledge that Señorita Carmen María de la Fuente del Castillo y Salvador y Fulano de Tal [a drawn-out play on the use of various names in Spanish culture] is waiting to bestow upon him the rose between her lips. . . . With these stories as conditioners, how can realistic novels such as *Los de abajo, El Resplandor* [and] *Nayar* hope to find an audience in the U.S., in Canada, or even England? There is no point of contact, because the Latin American scene has come to be recognized as either the background for bandits, revolutions or a long siesta."

While these comments are directed at the U.S. reading public, Niggli also admonishes Mexican writers to create historical fiction with a "selection of detail, in the choice of descriptive material which has universal meaning rather than merely local application."

I think my proudest moment was when the reviewers of *Step down, Elder Brother* pointed out that although the story was set in Monterrey, it could have been laid in Minneapolis, Montreal, or Manchester. I had told my readers that Mexico was not a strange, exotic land, a romantic Banana Republic, but a country whose beliefs, ideals and desires were identical with human problems everywhere. A woman in Durham, North Carolina, said to me after one of my lectures: "After I went to Mexico last summer I read one of your books, and you know, I realized that the people I saw down there were human."

Believe me, this is not a laughing matter. It is extremely serious. . . .

In my new novel I draw copiously from the ideas of Leopoldo

Zea and Jiménez Rueda. Without don Alfonso Reyes' fine essays
on bullfighting, I would have done a much inferior job on the bullfighting story in *Mexican Village*. Señor Saldaña, Licenciado Roel
and don Carlos Pérez-Maldonado, in their studies of Monterrey
history gave me much of the background material for *Step down,
Elder Brother*. But I hope I am not too much of a parasite. I hope
that my work paves the way, opens the door so that you, who are
historians, can walk through and say, "In this novel, you have met
the people as individuals. Listen to their history as a nation."

With this concluding comment, Niggli demonstrates her own intellect
and awareness of the need for better representation of Mexican culture in
the United States. Hers was a minority voice, however, for in the ensuing
decades, representations of Mexican culture in the greater media, and even
in academic departments in the United States, did little to dispel the idea of
a caricatured Mexico. In fact, true "Spanish" culture is considered to only
derive from Spain. Niggli credits great thinkers such as Reyes and Zea, and
yet little has been published on their work in the United States. Her effective declarations show that Niggli is an avid reader and researcher, that she
is academically sophisticated, and that she always attempts to accurately
depict the Mexican *human being* and Mexican history.

Surprisingly, she cites a "new novel" in progress. This correlates with
a newspaper account at this time about an imminent novel. Days before
Niggli's departure for Monterrey (August 30, 1949), the *New York Times*,
in its column "Books, Authors," states: "A new novel by Josephina Niggli,
'Farewell, Mama Carlotta,' will be brought out in January by Rinehart.
Set in Mexico at the turn of the century, the story deals with two brothers and the legend of Mama Carlotta, symbol of Imperial Mexico kept
alive by the upper 5 per cent of the Mexican people so that the 95 per cent
might be held in subjection."

An intriguing statement since this novel was never published, and
yet an arrangement had occurred between author and publisher or the
latter would not have released this information. One is left to speculate
whether Niggli simply did not complete it, or whether the publisher canceled it. A phone conversation with the publishing heir Rick Rinehart,
located in Colorado, elicited no information but the suggestion to check
with Holt, because "that side of the family" had kept the New York rights.

The Holt Company in New York, now part of a conglomerate, could provide no older records.

The theme of this unpublished novel appears to be fixed in the interesting turn-of-the-century era, after Maximilian's reign and Juárez's restoration, and during the Porfiriato—in fact, the era just prior to the outbreak of the Mexican Revolution. It is a period of time for which she made numerous notes, evidenced by her WCU records. It also reflects her ongoing theme on class relations, those above and below, in society.

In 1955, as Niggli prepared to depart for England, a San Antonio newspaper reported that she was writing "another historical novel of Mexico," stating it was set in the eighteenth century. It is difficult to determine whether this refers to the same novel reported earlier, or if she had embarked on an entirely different novel. The drafts for more than 100 pages of a novel carrying the title *Beat the Drum Slowly* (found in her WCU records) may represent the work of this era.

First Novel in Translation

Coincidentally, Niggli could have been attending the historians conference in Monterrey at about the time her first novel was released in Spanish translation. A condensed version of the English original, *Un pueblo mexicano*, was published by Norton in late 1949, the translation done by a Wellesley professor born in Spain, Justina Ruíz-de-Conde.

This appearance of Niggli stories in Spanish was highly acclaimed by two major academic journals. In April 1950, the *Modern Language Journal* calls it a "noteworthy" translation, with "amazingly well written stories based on carefully observed individuals." William A. Beardsley likes the fact that each section or story provides a "particularly dramatic moment in the life of one or two individuals." He also declares it an excellent book for classroom teaching, and that "just as story material, this text is unusually effective," with "notes not so numerous as some editors prefer, but adequate." This interest in Niggli's novel for classroom purposes signals an absence of books on Mexican culture in mainstream publications during this era (likely because Latino/Hispanic writers in Texas or other places could not access such venues). It cannot be stated that the movie of *Mexican Village* drew attention to this translation, as the film had not yet been made.

Two months earlier, a review in the journal *Hispania* opens with, "If you are looking for something thoroughly readable for intermediate Spanish classes, consider seriously this abridged translation of Josephina Niggli's popular *Mexican Village*." Reviewer R. H. Armitage commends the original charming illustrations, and states, "The student will witness weddings, funerals, serenades, brawls, bullfights, and fiestas," all elements of Mexican culture. He does take issue, however, with the editing, declaring that several unnecessary and overstated footnotes have been added, and providing examples of a few minor errors or confusions. Even so, he calls the translation "excellent" and of great value for teachers "interested in the cultural approach and in need of stimulating material."

This editing reflects a propensity to *explain* Mexican culture, even to Spanish-speakers, something only needed if the approach is from Spain. These tendencies greatly disappointed Niggli. Always polite and respectful, she did not make her feelings known publicly; in fact, she stated that when the translator came to meet her in Chapel Hill, she was polite but could not "thank her." In the 1980 interview, Niggli recalls the experience clearly and painfully. She refers to the translator as "Head of a Spanish department at a quality northern school [and] a very nice person," when Niggli met her at that time. She further states: "It was done unfortunately, and I say unfortunately because she translated it as a Spaniard. For instance, she would translate 'a young girl' as 'la joven,' and [her voice rising], when in Mexico do you ever say *la joven*? It lost its Mexican flavor. What I had was real, it was right" (Shirley).

In further discussion, Niggli stated that "I didn't have to look up anything," meaning, make things up. For example, "We had a very good witch doctor when I grew up, and I used to go see her. We all did." This becomes the *curandera* character in *Mexican Village*. After the novel's publication, Niggli was contacted by an academic at the University of Pittsburgh who "had made quite a study on witch doctors in Mexico and that of all the books he had read, mine was true," she said. An additional aspect of *Mexican Village* that greatly impresses folklorists is Niggli's facility for adapting English language to suit Spanish lingo in small-town communities. Even the daily practices and beliefs portrayed in *Mexican Village* are always reported as "true" in terms of folklore.

This is how Niggli wanted her works to be received—not to be altered, as was done with the translation, nor considered inventions,

but to be studied and understood as true reflections of Mexican culture. Since its publication, she noted bluntly, the "critical evaluations of
[*Mexican Village* are] not on the basis of the story, only critical evaluations on the folklore." This assessment, late in her life, leads quickly to
an acknowledgement that Niggli's novels, with the exception of the folklore, have not been adequately studied by scholars.

Travel in Europe

Upon her return to Chapel Hill, Niggli readied herself for her first
trip abroad. She was following Lionel Barrymore's counsel, and had
obtained a fellowship from the Theatre Guild in Ireland, as well as a
Rockefeller Fellowship (her third) for study in Europe. In late summer
of 1950, her departure for Ireland was documented by journalist Wink
Locklair, posting articles in both the *Chapel Hill Weekly* on August 25
and the *Durham Morning Herald* on September 10, 1950. He states that
Niggli will sail on the steamship USS *America*, and has received a three-
month travel fellowship. Her plan is to study at the Abbey and Dublin
Gate theaters at the invitation of the director of the Abbey Theatre, who
had been in Chapel Hill in 1947. Due to postwar scarcities, this director
has asked Niggli to please bring with her "two pounds of rice." Niggli
remarks that she will visit UNC faculty members currently in Paris and
London, who have each asked her to bring soap and rice. During this
trip she will also study directing at the Théâtre de l'Ouest in France, as
well as playwriting in London.

Locklair states that she lives on Gimghoul Road in Chapel Hill, and
in one article provides a hint of the difficulty Niggli may have experienced trying to publish during the years after the war ended: "She
describes the last year as a lean one for many writers and attributes
this, in part, to unsettled world conditions and to the fact that many
magazines are changing staffs and in some cases altering their story
requirements." This journalist also describes her writing habits, stating
that Niggli had been typing since she was twelve years old, and that as
of six months ago, she had begun using an electric typewriter, but she
used Gregg shorthand for note-taking in libraries. He notes that she is
"working on a new book but she doesn't care to reveal any of the details
just now."

An Opera

Shortly after her departure, the one-act opera version of Niggli's play *Sunday Costs Five Pesos* would be performed by Charles Haubiel—with a libretto written by Niggli—and serve as the premiere of the Charlotte Opera Association (the city of Charlotte is to the south of Chapel Hill). This premiere was announced in a *New York Times* article in September about upcoming events, but no follow-up review was done after its premiere. The local newspaper, however, published a long article the day after the performance, including a photo. Calling it a "Mexican opera," Helen Fetter Cook finds "typical Latin flavor" in the choral numbers, and states that the musical play "brought a rainbow of color and gaiety to the stage before an unusually attractive and artistic set." "Señor and Señora" Justo Sierra (well-known Mexican writer), who were in the audience, were introduced as personal representatives of the Mexican ambassador in Washington, who was unable to attend. Niggli may or may not have liked the caption below the photo, which asks, "Have you ever witnessed a hair-pulling, ear-pinching battle between a couple of Mexican spitfires?"

The opera was presented in November, according to the weekly newspaper *Asheville Citizen-Times* (in a column titled "Literary Lantern"): "Charlotte saw the premiere this week of a new opera based on the one-act Mexican play, *Sunday Costs Five Pesos*, written by Carolina Author Josephina Niggli." However, she is not discussed in the body of the newspaper article.

And a Movie

After her year abroad, Niggli returned to North Carolina, but was soon summoned to California by a movie studio that would now produce a Technicolor movie of her first novel. An article in the *Raleigh News and Observer* in January 1952 states that the screen rights "came with swiftness and financial impact for the rosy-cheeked, brown-eyed writer, who dwells here quietly with her mother. . . .'I had been making a speech in Corpus Christi, Texas, at the Southwestern Writers Conference last June [1951].' [When she returned to Chapel Hill, her mother said:] 'Don't settle yourself, you're leaving for California tomorrow. Your agent just long-distanced to say that MGM has bought your book and wants you to do the screenplay." The reporter, Carol Leh, says Niggli took the same unpacked three suitcases from her Texas trip with her to California. "Los Angeles wasn't new to Miss Niggli—she had visited with Mr. and Mrs. Paul Green when he was on assignment for Metro. But being there as a unit in a motion picture production was a new experience. 'I never worked so hard in my life; every day from 10 to five except weekends,' she declared."

Niggli's script for the film is stored in the Niggli collection at Western Carolina University. Dated October 31, 1951, this represents her completed screenplay, but it underwent new revisions before filming began in 1952. It is interesting to compare hers with the final script (available through Loew's Incorporated). Most significant is that the movie studio's legal team changed various names of people and towns, so there would be no confusion with real people. Hidalgo, the principal city in her book and in her own script, morphs into a nonexistent town, "Columba." The rival town, San Juan, becomes "Milpa Verde." Although the hero, Pepe—disguised in the scene included here as "Rubén Alejandro"—keeps Niggli's original name, the heroine's lovely name of Sarita is changed to "Eufemia," a very odd choice (perhaps suggesting euphemism). The hero's rival, Napoleon, also keeps his name, but the controversial Linares goat cheese is now from "Toluca."

Upon her return, Niggli described the writing process. To the *Greensboro Daily News*, she said, "The secret to really effective writing is rewriting until you have something that really satisfies you." A short piece on February 12, 1952, by Bill Peacock quotes Niggli extensively, describing her work as arduous: "'I rewrote the opening of the script 22 times and I know of one writer who rewrote his opening 65 times.

"'The opening is the most important part of a movie script, or any form—book, play, or short story,' Miss Niggli said. 'In Hollywood, the people know that if they fail to capture the audience in the first five minutes, the audience is lost. So the opening is even more important than the climax and close.'" He notes that "several special conditions must be met in writing for the movies. Miss Niggli emphasizes that the writer 'must think visually—not audially [*sic*]. . . . You must also keep in mind the extreme limitations of the camera. In a play, characters may enter from all sides of the stage, but in a movie, the range is quite restricted and the action must be concentrated to be effective.'" Peacock ends the article with Niggli's assertion that scenes often have to be written to fit a particular actor, especially in the case of a musical.

Leh says Niggli discovered that "'they knew a lot more about the book at Metro than I did. I wrote it ten years ago and hadn't read it since. Once I've finished a job, I'm through with it. But the producer and director quoted whole passages by heart. And when they threw some lines at me in an unsuspecting moment I said, 'That's pretty. Where's it from?' 'Mexican Village,' they answered."

Filming occurred that summer in California, then the crew was moved to Mexico; Niggli joined them at each location. In a photo accompanying a new article by Leh in the *Durham Morning Herald* in February 1953 (a month before the film's release), Niggli is shown laughing happily while conferring on site with Ricardo Montalbán and director Norman Foster (who had a permanent home near Mexico City). Niggli declares that "her goal in writing the screenplay like the book was to reveal the real Mexicans of various social strata, as she came to know them during the years she lived in Monterrey." Niggli wanted "'neither to idealize the poor downtrodden Indian nor to make a political issue of him.' She admits she wrote the book originally because of resentment over previous works that had done just those things."

Leh also discusses the reason for a different title: "At first the studio retained the book title for the cinema version, then decided 'Sombrero' would have more box office appeal than 'Mexican Village.'" In California, Niggli's name, the reporter says, "underwent a slight revision. She phoneticized it from 'Josephina,' printed on the jacket of her novels, to 'Josefina,' used in Hollywood." Of course, it had been spelled with an "f" as early as the 1930s by Niggli herself.

A similar article was published by the same reporter in the *Raleigh News and Observer*, filed from the Hollywood movie set. This article includes gossip about the stars' romances and marriages occurring around the time of filming in Mexico. Leh also relates more background on Niggli, that her paternal ancestors are "Mexican and Catholic," and Episcopalian on her mother's side from Alexandria, Virginia, with a great-great-grandfather who "ran guns for the Confederacy."

An article in the same newspaper by Jack Claiborne on March 29, 1953, declares that Niggli was "spoiled" by the treatment she received in Hollywood. Not only was she attended to in terms of her needs, she was greatly respected: "'One day during a script conference I noticed Jack [Cummings, the producer] and Norman Foster, the film director, sort of beaming at me. I would comment on the weather and they would rave right along with me. Pretty soon I began to think that 'well, look at me. I've got a couple of yes men right here in the highest brackets. But it turned out later that they were just admiring my MA degree. That little bit of sheepskin is heavenly in Hollywood.

"'People in Hollywood are like that,' she said. 'Just the slightest bit of education commands respect from them. That's because so few of them—I don't mean the stars, but the people who really do the making of the pictures—are not formally educated, although they have the best brains in the business.'"

In Claiborne's article, Niggli describes an economic downturn in Hollywood, with production costs being stripped in order to survive. "'When I was in Hollywood before, there were more than 350 writers working outside the MGM studio gates—they keep the writers outside the gates so they may be fired more easily, I guess—and now there are only 165 in all the studios.'" She said no one could explain the downturn, only that people were not going to the movies. A similar article by Claiborne published in the *Winston-Salem Journal-Sentinel* quotes Niggli on the high expenses that accompany a high income:

Then it costs a great deal to live in Hollywood. In order to be in on the social life—and business out there stems from social life—you have to live accordingly. So a great deal of that fabulous salary also goes toward paying such an ordinary thing as rent. Clothes, too, cost a great deal. . . . When I went out I was proud of my little wardrobe. But when I got out there I found that it was far inadequate. I had always figured that if you were a writer then you didn't have to dress too much, that writers weren't seen and, well, it didn't make too much difference about what they wore. But after production they would come to me and say, "Miss Niggli, the Mexican Consul General requests lunch with you today," or "the Mexican such-and-such would like you for lunch." Pretty soon I found myself dressing up everyday and running out of nice clothes. But one thing is sure. Now that I'm back I don't have to worry about clothes.

On location in Mexico the previous fall, John Rothwell, writing for the *New York Times* (dateline Cuernavaca, September 18, 1952), states: "That there has been no hint of the antagonism displayed at the treatment of Mexico and its nationals in some previous Hollywood productions can be attributed, however, to the recent arrival on the scene of Josefina Niggli, the author, and a producer-director team recognized as being sympathetically understanding of the Mexicans. Miss Niggli came from her home in Chapel Hill to view the filming based on her book."

Rothwell says Niggli was "surprised when Producer Jack Cummings became interested in her novel last year and induced MGM to purchase it." In addition, she was "amazed when he wanted no changes in it for pictures. Unlike the first publishers to whom she submitted her writings, he didn't even request that a North American hero be added. During six months in Hollywood as collaborator with Director Norman Foster on the screenplay, she found herself in the unique position of being an author who wanted to make some alterations while the studio folk were insisting upon sticking to her original story." Surprisingly, the *New York Times* review by Bosley Crowther in April 1953 calls the film "ostentatious and full of torpid hot air," making Niggli herself responsible for the fact no changes were made. "It is utterly lacking in excitement and dramatic character. Miss Niggli and her associate, Norman Foster, who also directed, are to blame." Apparently he did not read his colleague's article a few months earlier. Crowther also criticizes the film's creative angle of bouncing back and forth between three different stories.

A *Los Angeles Times* review was more gracious: "While hardly the best made picture," the film "provides an impression of Mexico that is unique." The "cutting" (editing) is considered abrupt, but the photography and vistas of Mexico are "intriguing." Niggli was in San Antonio when the movie was released, according to her 1980 interview, and claims she could not see it at that time. "I went to the theater the next day, and couldn't get into the theater because all the Chicanos were there.[11] It was that way every day." Ricardo Montalbán was a big draw, she added—someone she knew would be perfect for the role when she had seen him the previous year in a Spanish-language film (adapted from the novel *Santa*), where he also played a bullfighter.

The Actors in Mexico

Lead actors included MGM stars Montalbán and Pier Angeli, as well as Yvonne de Carlo, Cyd Charisse, and newcomers Vittorio Gassman (with acting experience in Italy, and the new bridegroom of Shelley Winters), and Rick Jason (who was put in at the last minute when Fernando Lamas opted out). The studio sought "an actor to play an authentic Mexican," Jason wrote in his memoir, for this musical of "three love stories intertwined among three amigos in a small Mexican town, from a novel by Josefina Nigli [sic]." Norman Foster was pleased after only one take, and Jason was offered the role of "Rubén." Jason recalls: "The film's musical and dance numbers were shot prior to leaving for Mexico. José Greco, the great Flamenco dancer, who played my brother-in-law (and the role of a gypsy *matador*), did a dance that I was privileged to be on the sound stage to watch. The routine he devised for the film was outstanding."

The cast then moved to filming on location in Mexico City and Cuernavaca. Jason's memoir continues:

> We worked for ten days in Mexico City in the Plaza de Toros. When I first walked into the bull ring, I made it my business to go over to the camera and introduce myself to the operator. I don't know why—instinct maybe. . . . He was a little surprised and introduced me to the assistant cameraman (who pulled the focus) and the second assistant who kept the slate, helped load the three reels of film, and measured the distance from the lens to the actor with a tape. . . . The electricians and grips were all Mexican, as well as a Mexican Assistant Director (A.D.) who translated for the American A.D. The key grip and his assistant (Best Boy) and the gaffer (head electrician) and his assistant were from MGM, as was the dolly grip (also in charge of the crane). Those were the people I hung out with behind the camera when I wasn't in a scene. It was the smartest thing I ever did in the picture business.

His memoir goes on to state that these key employees then favored him, putting him in better lighting and making his scenes much more impressive than those of the star, Montalbán (who was director Norman

Foster's brother-in-law). He also won friends by determining to work on his Spanish: "I'd studied three years of Spanish in prep school and decided this was my opportunity to learn to speak the language. I had my lunches with the Mexican crew. A station wagon would pull up and we'd stand around eating spicy (HOT!) soft tacos out of a huge cardboard carton, with jalapeño peppers and sodas or beer. I could barely feel my lips for an hour or so after lunch each day, but I stuck to Spanish (none of them could speak English) and about ten days later, started to think in the language. From then on, it was just a matter of learning a growing vocabulary and idiomatic sayings."

In fact, Rick Jason's Spanish improved so much while he was in Mexico that he had trouble getting cast afterward. According to his memoir, his agent had difficulty convincing a producer that he was simply a Jewish boy from New York. The producer did not want to "hire a Mexican."

A Final California Production

Although Niggli was in San Antonio when the film opened, she returned to California that year, apparently to work on another screenplay from *Mexican Village*. A brief note September 18, 1952 in the *New York Times* states that "three more of Josephina Niggli's short stories [will] be filmed as follow-up to 'Sombrero,'" not yet in release. "Now Jack Cummings, who produced 'Sombrero' from a screen play by Norman Foster, has commissioned Mr. Foster to begin work on another batch of three stories from the book. The new venture most likely will be called 'Mexican Village.' Pier Angeli and Ricardo Montalbán, who appeared in 'Sombrero,' are in line for the new picture."

Such a second film was never produced. But while Niggli was in California, she traveled up north and took a class at Stanford University in advanced playwriting (indicated on her resume the following year). Avid interest during the 1950s for musicals, and her knowledge of Mexican culture opened up opportunities for productions. It has been stated by various sources that her play *The Ring of General Macías* was performed as an opera by the San Francisco Symphony, but no record of this appears in San Francisco newspaper archives or in the city's Performing Arts Library. But she did write a new musical, with Paul Green, for a special festival in Santa Barbara.

This production, *Serenata*, was created in the spring, as noted in an article in the Santa Barbara newspaper under *Noticias de la Fiesta*, dated March 1, 1953: Niggli "found much of the old ways of Santa Barbara" when she toured the hacienda San Julián in Santa Barbara County, for many years the land grant of Spanish Captain José De la Guerra. She walked "in and out of dozens of old rooms, admiring deep recessed windows and fine old furniture and studying the differences between the oldest left hand wing built by Indian labor, when this was the dwelling of soldier-servants of King Ferdinand [*sic*], and the additions made by the De la Guerras and the Dibbles [the current owners of this "summer home"]. From the wall of the family's diningroom the portrait of Captain De la Guerra looked down upon us. Wonder if Señorita Niggli realized what an important job the captain did for Santa Barbara in his role as padrino of our pueblo so long ago. . . . He was a strong man, defeated in his most cherished ambitions because he was born in Spain, but he built an empire of power and land, such as no other Santa Barbaran has ever achieved."

The musical was based on Spanish-era history and featured as the highlight of the *Old Fiesta Days* event in Santa Barbara (near Los Angeles), held annually in August. Billed as a collaboration between Niggli and Paul Green, Niggli appears to have done the research and writing; her name alone is credited for the lyrics.

The program states that *Serenata* is "the most ambitious theatrical production ever undertaken" for the festival. The cast included some 30 actors, a chorus of about 70 people, 25 equestrian riders, and a ballet corps of another 60 dancers, featuring flamenco dancer José Manero (a principal dancer and choreographer in the San Francisco Ballet), who was then director of the Santa Barbara Ballet School. A full orchestra directed the music, and three performances were presented on an outdoor stage. Divided into six scenes, separated evenly between December 1821 and April 1822, the story line depicts the precise moment of change in government from Spanish to Mexican authority, upon victory of the colonial struggle for independence from Spain. A report from Mexico City imposes new levies on the Indians, and they react by preparing an uprising, while two characters prepare for their wedding. A pageant is presented within the play (again, Niggli's propensity to create a play within a play) on "the martyrdom of Santa Barbara," the village's patron saint.

The *Los Angeles Times* highlighted the ongoing event in a series of articles. The first, accompanying a photograph taken during dance rehearsals (Manero in grand display), depicts a Manifest Destiny sense of colonization: "In songs, dances and words *Serenata* describes the early-day life, philosophy and faith, the dreams and struggles of the Spanish soldiers, missionaries, aristocrats and artisans who brought civilization to the Golden State. It also tells of the joys and tragedies and workday life of the Indians who were converted by the padres."

Later, the newspaper filed a series of reports from Santa Barbara, the first citing Niggli as collaborator with Green (who had a lucrative record of creating historical pageants, including *The Lost Colony*) and referencing her as author of the original stories in the film *Sombrero*. On August 16, the reporter says a crowd of between 15,000 and 20,000 is expected for opening night festivities of the "world premier." However, on August 21, it is reported that there were 100,000 people in attendance for the first performance. On August 18, a description is made of the more than 150-member cast, accompanied by a photo of acting rehearsals. From records reviewed on the history of this annual event, *Serenata* appears to be one of few such elaborate presentations. Niggli would create another musical play based on Spanish history for a festival in San Antonio, ten years later.

Ironically, Niggli did not remain and view the final performance. In July 1953 she sent postcards to Paul Green from her travels in New York and Pennsylvania, stating it's "so nice not to have to hurry through every spot," and that "We're seeing so much and the scenery is truly beautiful!" The "we" could have been a companion or her mother.

Although she left the West Coast behind, Niggli would continue to contribute plot ideas or serial episodes to Hollywood, of which many drafts and outlines remain in bound journals or working notebooks in her WCU archives. Most are plots and ideas for "Westerns," but some are directed to specific television series of the 1950s.

Niggli may have planned to return, for many of her personal research books stayed behind (unless they were donated and sent there after her death). She could have left the books with Paul Green. In 1959, her former professor Samuel Selden became head of the drama department at the University of California, Los Angeles (UCLA), and the books could also have been in his custody and years later made their way to a storage basement at UCLA. Only in 2006 were they removed from storage by the UCLA Chicano Studies Research Center library, which has now cataloged them as an archival collection. Labeled the "Josefina Niggli Book Collection," the archive consists of sixty-eight books on a variety of topics—from religious practices, philosophy, and shrines; to Mexican history, politics, botany, and geography; to cults, witchcraft, tarot, and other fortune-telling practices. Old calendars and maps reveal background research for most of her published writings. Books on acting and staging scenes, including a publication in Italian of Luigi Pirandello's *Six Characters in Search of an Author*, informed her playwriting. None of the books have notes in the margins, and no personal notebooks were left with these (Niggli's habit was to make initial notes in workbooks, then transfer these to typed lists and pages of character and plot development). Most are in Spanish—fifty-seven, in fact—with only eleven in English, demonstrating Niggli's Spanish fluency and her procedure of going to original sources for research.

Their dates of publication represent an extensive range, from the nineteenth century to beyond the time Niggli was in California. Books on Catholic customs, saints, the Basilica in Los Angeles and other shrines, date from 1882 to the early twentieth century. Books on Mexico's natural beauty, recent political history, Spain's heroes and history, as well as books that would have informed her creation of characters—on human roles in love and homemaking, spy and detective writing, logic and ethics—all range between 1919 and the early 1950s. The remarkable fact is that a few date past the time Niggli was in California, including a book on the California missions (1961), and books on the early colonial era and Guadalajara and Baja California (i.e., Nuño de Guzmán's travels), which obviously helped inform her novel on the Miracle of Guadalupe. How did five books get there *after* Niggli's departure?

My theory is that some or all of the books were sent to UCLA after her death. A letter to John Igo (see chapter 4) from a person handling her estate indicates that Niggli's books in Spanish will probably be sent to San Antonio, a more appropriate place than North Carolina. Later, those disposing of her belongings may have decided on Los Angeles. Of those in question, some are in English, but have to do with Mexico or Latin America. If they were shipped to UCLA by WCU archivists, they made a mistake in separating Niggli's journals and extensive typed notes in preparation for novels from her research library. Her unpublished manuscripts, archived in numerous boxes and by manuscript numbers rather than themes or titles, could possibly be better understood if her books at UCLA were connected to her notes. The small WCU library did not, and does not, have a historian or archivist of Mexican expertise who could make better sense of Niggli's collected manuscripts—an effort that begs to be undertaken.

"Dream I"
dated September 14, 1944
(from journal in special collection at Incarnate Word)

This dream was strongly characterized by feeling that I had "read" the story before and that there was a good twist ending to it. Unfortunately I was artificially awkward before the dream could reach completion.

I have a sense that a good deal had gone on before my memory begins. All I can remember is the last scene.

It was a costume piece of the Old West—somewhere around 1870. The setting was a place much like Eagle Pass (as I remember it from a little girl). My house—or rather where I was, was a clapboard office on a street housed on only one side. The other side is dim—seemingly open fields. At the corner was a cross street, which ran East and West. Traffic went west toward the town. I remember the rays of the setting sun: a golden red, on faces. My street therefore ran North and South.

I am "aware" that a man—my lover—had been unjustly accused of something and was in jail. For some reason the town was much incensed, not only against him, but also against a friend: a man in his fifties, who owned a dry-goods store.

I was pacing up and down the sidewalk, which was at street-level at the crossing and rose along a bank so that four houses north it was some distance off the ground. This bank was very vivid, being built of yellow clay. It had been raining and the bank was slippery. During my pacing I never became muddy, but I was very aware of the mud.

There is a vague memory that I was in a large house on the SE corner of the crossing when the news of the town uprising occurred. I remember thinking, "Why, that house was like the Pingenot's." I ran across the street and started pacing. I felt terribly worried and helpless (due to my being female). I was aware of my lover's damages, but as I neither visualized him or his name, I have no recollection of either.

I seemed to be wearing a white lawn or mull dress with a white shawl. I remember the skirts swirling about my ankles and pulling the shawl tight about my shoulders.

My friend arrived. He was tall and thin, and I have an impression that he wore a flannel shirt and cowboy boots. His face and other descriptions desert me. He said something about the lynching and that "they" were going to burn his store.

We had walked to the corner. "There goes my wife," he said. A buckboard passed us with a woman sitting in the front seat. I remember her quite clearly. She was slender, in a gray taffeta dress, quite tailored, with a pleated yoke and leg'o'mutton sleeves. Her small brimmed sailor [sic] was fastened to her pompadour with two large crossed hat-pins. Her face was delicate with a small, pointed chin. The setting sun was a golden splash on her gray dress. I remember that I did not like her, and both my friend and I thought she had deserted our side.

My friend ran off down the street. Suddenly I could stand it no longer, and even though I knew I was courting danger, I hurried to town also.

His store was on a corner. All of these buildings had changed from clapboard to adobe, and I was reminded of the dry-goods store in Hidalgo. About seven women and two men were burning a bale of silk shawls. The store itself was not being burned, only the merchandise. The memory of the shawled women is very clear. The shawls were those cheap silk *rebozos* and were wrapped over shoulders and head like old Mexican women wear them. They were that poisonous green and dark red (a silk shawl I particularly dislike both asleep and awake). It was shawls of this type they were burning. Obviously the women had taken them as loot.

The next bit of dialogue was enclosed in a circle of my knowledge that small store-owners in the West at that time knew nothing of fire insurance.

Me: I hope you are insured against loss (meaning philosophically).

Him: Well-insured (meaning money).

We were both aware of the double implication and thought ourselves very witty in spite of our troubles.

I cannot remember the next sequence. An important bit of information reached us, but it is gone.

Then we were in a church—a definitely Protestant church, and everyone, including my friend, definitely thought I was Protestant. That is, they thought the person whose body I now inhabited was Protestant.

We had come there to pray that my lover would be spared from the mob. My friend's wife was also there. She had changed her dress for a white one with a high choker collar, and her hair was in a tall marceled [*sic*] pompadour. She wore no hat. Neither did many of the other women.

Someplace I had lost my shoulder shawl. When we knelt in the wooden pews to pray, I took a black lace flounce (dress trimming of some sort) from the woman in front of me. My friend whispered, "What are you going to do with it?" and seemed much surprised when I put it on my head. More people knelt in the pew and we were pressed so close together it was difficult to raise my arms, but I pulled until my right arm was free. (I was aware that I was going contrary to the established character of the person I represented, but I stubbornly insisted on praying like a Catholic.) "In the name of the Father, the Son, and the Holy Ghost." Everyone, specifically my friend, was much startled by this. At this moment I was awakened.

"Dream II"
dated September 14, 1944

Nothing but a fragment.

A lounge room in a store something like Solo Serve. Behind the counter seats for trying on shoes at Andrew-Henigens in Chapel Hill. Immediately in front of me was a glass showcase filled with women's lingerie. I explained that I wanted two jersey slips. She took out of the showcase one pink slip and one black one—the latter a waist petticoat. I liked it the best but it was too small around the waist. The pink slip was then transformed into the twin of the petticoat and I could buy neither.

As I started to leave the counter, I saw that the case was now filled with shoes—all of them black, but some in satin, some in leather, etc. I asked the clerk if they were non-rationed. She was furious. I can't remember her words but I am aware of their content. She implied that Sears Roebucks would never sell anything but rationed goods, and even as she spoke I realized how stupid she sounded when I knew so many good non-rationed shoes were on sale. Dream ended.

Note: Yesterday the gasoline ration quarter expired, and I had to make a special trip home from the store to get the tickets and have my car tank filled. This may have brought on the rationing sequence.

"Salt in the Air"

Juanillo, hat pulled low on his forehead, shoulders hunched forward to disguise his body, let the crowd surge around him.

"Don't let them recognize me," he prayed silently to his patron saint. "Not today. Not this particular day." From the bull ring came the sound of music. The words slid easily into his mind:

He takes up the sword
And walks to glory.

Once that had been his song. When he went into a restaurant, or passed a *mariachi* band on the street, it was played as a signal of the great Juanillo's presence. Even in Spain they had played it. But now Juanillo was only legend and his song was just another bull-ring tune.

But there might be some people here in this crowd who would recognize him. They would nudge their neighbors, who in turn would nudge others, and soon everyone would be looking at him. No, not at him—at his feet, his coward's feet, which had carried him away from his last two bulls and ruined him forever as a great sword.

Feet did that many times when the body had been too often torn by the curved horns. It was the nightmare of every fighter: the betrayal of the feet. There was no place in the arena for cowards. After that he had retired. Well, why not? He had money, he had known fame, and he was forty years old. Fatigue was in him, he told the newspapermen. It was time for him to retire. But even as he told it he could see the smile in their eyes, and the casual little glances they had flicked toward his feet.

Any man, he told himself defensively, has the right to retire. But it was no good. No matter what he told himself it was no good. The truth was always there. He had not retired; the ring had rejected him, exiled him for cowardice.

Juanillo took another step forward in the line toward the ticket box. To the right was another box with a much shorter line. That was for tickets in the royal elegance of shade. His own line was for the democratic sun. And too, the sun side was for those who really loved good fighting; for those who knew the worth of a bull as it came, black as death, from the tumbrel; for those who knew at a casual glance whether the *torero* was only a stuffed doll in pretty silks, or a good sword. Yes, the sun side was for those to whom bullfighting was a wine in the blood, those who could taste the salt in the air.

Juanillo lifted his chin to look at the blue-bright sky, then hastily hid his face. It was wicked luck that Sandoval was selling tickets for the sun side. Twenty-eight years ago this afternoon Sandoval had paid homage, had said royally, "for Juanillo today there is salt in the air." And then, at the last fight, the same Sandoval had looked at his feet and said tauntingly, "Salt."

Fortunately, Sandoval hated the sun box. He much preferred to sell tickets for the shade. The tinkle of the silver in his till was his delight; on the sun side the coins were copper. He did not even look up as Juanillo pushed his money across the opening.

As quickly as possible, without seeming in haste, Juanillo made his way to the sun entrance. His body moved easily through the crowd, swerving just enough to escape a push. Years of swerving—the body had prepared him for this. His mouth twisted ironically. What an end to ambition: years of dieting, of exercise, of facing the black bull in the arena—that at the end he must pass easily through a crowd.

The gatekeeper was new, so there was no danger of pitying recognition from him. Juanillo extended his ticket and walked quickly through the wide door. The smell of sun on closely packed bodies struck him with full force. For a moment he was young again.

There had truly been salt in the air then, and sun, and the gleam of blue silk on his body. Already famous as a *novillero*, a killer of small bulls, he was coming into the ring to meet the great black bull itself and to take up the title of *matador*, the killer, in place of *novillero*, the novice.

But that was twenty-eight years ago, and today was only sun and a facility for passing through crowds. But, thought Juanillo defensively, as he slid into a seat next to two young boys, a man has the right to relive his first triumphs. If he paid for his seat and behaved himself, what difference did it make to anyone that he was seeing, not the Sultan of Saltillo, who was fighting today, but a slim eager shadow named Juanillo in a *torero* costume twenty-eight years out of date?

The musicians were playing another piece now, and the boy on Juanillo's left said harshly, "I wish they'd play Juanillo's song again. It is my luck."

His own name attracted the man. He turned his head slightly and glanced along his eyelids. He noticed automatically that the boy had a good body and, more important, that his hands were small with strong wrists.

The other boy said sharply, "You are too superstitious, Ratón."

"Leave me alone!" snapped the Ratón, his hands wiping off palm sweat against his ragged yellow shirt.

The mind of the body stepped into the mind of the man. Realizing the Ratón's intentions, Juanillo half rose to call a policeman and put the boy in charge but he sank back again. How could he tell the policeman, "this boy plans to leap into the ring; he is an extemporaneous one."? The Ratón had only to deny it, and put off his performance for another Sunday. Nothing could stop these roosters once they had the ideas in their minds. They would go again and again to the ring until they got their chance, and once they took it, what good did it do them? If they escaped without a wound they were shut up in jail until some friends found enough money to bail them out.

Juanillo looked at the boy again, at the thick-nosed face, the slender body, the long fingers folding and refolding the coat in his lap. There was no doubt of it, he had the true fighter's wrists. He was wetting his lips, his eyes fixed on the president's box.

The great man was already entering. He was raising the white hand-kerchief. A trumpet's clear notes sliced the air. The fighters marched in to a burst of music, the Sultan of Saltillo in the center, his walk showing the proper arrogance. The men on either side of him were good fighters, but they lacked that final touch of pride that is prouder than death.

The parade reached the president's box. After the *toreros* gave the honorary salute, the first sword's pics rode to their places. In a moment the ring was cleared. All attention was fixed on the other door. Slowly it began to open. Juanillo could hear the Ratón's harsh breathing.

The crowd gave a long-drawn "Aah." The bull was in the ring. He ran around, blinded by the sun, and pawed at the sand. The horns were set too far back on the skull. When the ring servants gave him the preliminary passes, he hooked strongly to the right. A fair bull, thought Juanillo, very fair. He looked at the boy. The Ratón was shaking his head. "Not for me," he muttered. "Not this one."

Juanillo resented this boy's intrusion on his anniversary celebration. The devil take him, he thought crossly. The boy knows bulls. And when a good one comes out, this Ratón will jump into the arena, and the devil with the bull. He'll ruin the beast in three minutes. The Sultan will be very angry, very angry indeed. And why not? One good bull in an afternoon ruined by an extemporaneous one. To the devil with these boys and their ambition! I could tell him a thing about ambition!

The first fighter came out. The capework was fair. One good *verónica*, but nothing more. Juanillo snorted in exasperation. What had become of the good days—the days of Goana and Joselito, and Luis Freg? That was when a fight was really magnificent, and there was salt in the air. These men were all technique, with their constant talk of schools: the Sevilla school, the Córdoba school, the Ronda school. Who cared about schools? A great fighter knew the truth of the arena: It was the bull who was important, not the man. It was the bull who demanded and the man who gave. It was the bull who said, "This is my moment of truth, my moment of magnificent death." At the last, it was only the bull who should have pride. The fighter should have a humility greater than pride, an awareness of being more powerful than death, and, in the awareness, he should be humble. There was no such knowledge in these little men, with their technique and their schools.

Juanillo felt the Ratón relax against him. A new bull entered, head just small enough for the large body, the twitching ears saying, "I am a noble enemy." He charged straight, his thousand pounds of muscle dashing with full weight across the sand.

The Sultan was emerging from behind the *barrera* wall. This was naturally the Sultan's bull. This was a bull for sultans.

"This is my bull," whispered the Ratón. Juanillo put out his hand, but the boy had already leaped into the arena, using his coat for a cape.

There was a roar of rage from the crowd. They hated the extemporaneous ones almost as much as did the fighters. These boys were usually so bad, and they could ruin any bull in two minutes.

Juanillo found himself standing on his bench, his heart pounding against his rib case.

Memory peeled the covering from his mind. Juanillo was a boy of fourteen, muscles tensed, and waiting to leap into the ring. But a strong hand grasped his arm, pulled him back, did not relax under a storm of futile cursing. Later, in a restaurant, the man who had stopped him said quietly, while watching him wolf down needed food, "I could have let you leap into the ring. Why not? It was nothing to me."

"Why did you stop me, then?" Juanillo had asked.

The man played with some bread crumbs, his right arm stiff as it lay on the table. "When I was a kid I wanted the ring, too. Well, I jumped in, and when the police tried to drag me out I fought them. I got a broken arm for it. This arm." He touched it lightly with the fingers of his left hand. If that's what you want—no more fighting ever—"

"I am not a fool," Juanillo remembered he had said with vanity.

The man laughed, not in derision, but more as though the laughter were a shrug. "Fool or not, my chances were finished as yours might be. And you have wrists," he added slowly, "the strong supple wrists."

Watching the Ratón, a wave of sickness passed through Juanillo. Why did these city children never realize that the impresarios, whose nods made or broke a fighter, would have nothing to do with the extemporaneous ones? All they got for a brief moment of glory was a jail sentence and the ring closed to them forever. There was violence in the Ratón. When the police closed in he would surely fight—with the reward, perhaps, of a broken arm. And he had such good wrists. He had the arrogance, too. Here might be another Goana, another Sultan, another—yes—another Juanillo, and what had he done to save this talent? Nothing. He had sat placidly by, pretending it was none of his affair.

The sickness in him became an agony. He bit down on his lower lip until the blood came, but he was unaware of it. His attention was fixed entirely upon the drama playing itself out below him.

The Sultan tried to take the bull away, but the animal knew that the boy was his true enemy and refused the outer lure. The Ratón's feet went into position, his body bent slightly at the waist, the coat held with first wrists for a low *verónica*. The bull charged. Keeping his feet still, the boy curved his body to the right. As the bull passed, horns ripped the yellow shirt.

The crowd was kind now, yelling applause. Juanillo felt that he could breathe again. The Ratón's friend whimpered low in his throat.

Once more the Ratón addressed the bull, taking tiny enticing steps to one side. The animal's head lowered; he seemed to gather himself together. Juanillo's fine knowledge of bulls told him that this charge would kill the boy. The Ratón lacked the long years of training necessary to master this animal.

Blessed saints, the Sultan was moving in!

Juanillo forgot to breathe. If the Sultan went in now, he would be killed. Any man without a thorough knowledge of bulls who went in now would be killed. These stupid technical men! Why didn't the Sultan stay quiet? He was distracting the boy's attention. Yes, the Ratón had turned his face. Panic flashed across it. He obviously did not want the Sultan to be hurt.

The bull was pawing the sand now. If he charged—with the boy's mind distracted by the Sultan . . .

Unaware of what he was doing, Juanillo leaped into the ring, sprinted forward tearing off his coat as he ran. The Sultan was a good sword, in many ways a great sword, but he did not know—really know bulls. Left alone, he would get himself and the Ratón both killed. Here was a job for a true expert.

One stiff arm shot the Ratón off balance and out of harm's way. The ancient arrogance encased Juanillo as he faced the bull, watched muscles ripple under the curly hide. The serge coat lacked sufficient weight, but it would serve as a lure. Far in the distance he could hear a voice shout, "Juanillo!" but the shout was lost in the roar of the crowd. Then the voice of the crowd disappeared in a greater roaring. Some part of his mind told him that it was his own blood singing, but he had no time for music now. The bull was surging toward him, enlarging until the head filled his entire field of vision. Body muscles, flabby with disuse, tensed. His feet, his coward's feet, stayed still. Then the bull was on him. Automatically, Juanillo's hips curved to the right. The coat rose like a great wing, and for a brief moment the bull's side pressed his own side, and the heat of the animal passed into him and calmed him.

The twenty-eight years that lay between the great afternoon and this one flicked into nothingness. He could not comprehend why his shirt sleeves were pink. They should have been blue—blue silk. Then the chasm in time closed, and he was again a retired bullfighter.

The hovering swords had enticed the bull away. The Sultan was coming toward him with a smile, hand out-stretched. It must have been the Sultan who had screamed "Juanillo." No one else, seemingly, had recognized him.

Already the crowd was yelling for another bull. They were tired of this extemporaneous diversion and wanted to see what they had paid for: the great Sultan in a great fight. Instead of taking the Sultan's hand, Juanillo jerked his head toward the body-packed seats. "This is your afternoon," he said. "Forget you saw me." Then he darted across the ring, and allowed some laughing boys to haul him up to his own seat.

The Ratón's friend was still there, his eyes dark with terror. "The police got him," he said through stiffened lips. To this child of the streets the police were a far greater danger than the horns of the black bull.

Juanillo thrust some money into his hand. "Pay the Ratón's fine. And when you get him out of jail, take him to Juanillo to learn true fighting."

He had to scream to be heard above the orchestra, which had finished the applause music, and was now playing Juanillo's own song. It gave the man a warm feeling around the heart as he realized that the Sultan had ordered it to be played. The words followed him out of the arena and down the street:

He takes up the sword
And walks to glory.

Juanillo's feet touched the ground lightly in a true bullfighter's walk. What good was the celebration of an anniversary? What good were shadows of remembrances? They were dead things. Better to take what he knew and transfer it into the body of another—create from shadow a finer substance.

He tossed back his head and breathed deeply. There was indeed salt in the air.

"A Visitor for Domínguez"

The moonlight was a green cobweb on Mexican earth. A dog howled mournfully, and a coyote answered him from the low-lying hills, but the man inside the adobe hut heard neither the dog nor the coyote, and he was not aware of the moonlight.

He was stretched out on a cot, sound asleep, his breathing light and regular. The room was drab, and as barren of comfort as the desert landscape beyond the iron-barred window. The cot, a table, a bench were its only furniture. A prisoner captured in battle needs few comforts.

Slowly the moon drifted across the sky toward its home beyond the hills. In a little while it would disappear, leaving only the ruddy glow of the sentry fire to provide light. Men who should have been on guard were huddled in blankets. Their comrades were fighting beyond the hills, but these men were not at the moment concerned with battles. A few days ago they had fought, in a few days more they would fight again.

In the meantime they slept and ate and slept.

Soon their souls might be dancing in hell, never to rest again. Better to sleep while they could. Let the sergeant stay awake to see that their prisoner, the rebel Domínguez, did not escape. He was to be hanged in the morning, and men will try many foolish things to keep from being hanged. But he was the sergeant's responsibility. What else were sergeants for?

Domínguez rolled over on his cot. A little while ago his large hand, dangling over the cot's edge, had been in a pool of moonlight. Now it was in black shadow.

Death by hanging was a cruel thing to a man of 32, but Baltazar Domínguez was a peasant. He had fought Nature all his life, and Nature had conquered him with cruelty: with drought and flood and rock and barren soil. As a child he had learned to bind his own wounds, fight without comment, and accept the outcome with fatalistic calm. Fighting men was little different from fighting Nature, save that one had more chance to win.

So he fought, and was captured, and because he had been a great fighter, he was to die. His very ability to fight had trapped him into death. The Federals would not have bothered to hang a common soldier. The sentence had been passed. There was no hope of escape. What use to stay awake the last few hours thinking of a length of rope, a tree limb that would not break, a horse that walked slowly out from between tense knees, and feet that dangled too high above the earth?

So the rebel slept. Even the creaking of the hinges as the heavy wooden door swung open did not awaken him.

Sergeant Tomás Ala, his gun ready in his hand, came into the room. He lighted a stub of candle standing in its own grease on the table top, then prodded the sleeping man with the butt of his gun. "Domínguez! Wake up, you, Domínguez!"

"Eh?" the man muttered, half sitting up. "What do you want? Can't you let a man sleep in peace?"

"There's someone to see you. A woman."

Domínguez dropped his feet to the floor, and ground his fists against his eyes. "I don't want to see her."

"You have to see her." Ala backed toward the door, his gun ready to shoot in case Domínguez made too sudden a gesture.

"She has a letter from the big man." The rebel looked up at the stocky guard. "From the big man, eh? Who is she?"

Ala shrugged. "Says she's your wife." Turning to the door he called, "Come in."

A woman slipped past him like a flickering shadow. A shawl covered her head and swathed her face. Her long calico dress was wrinkled and stained with yellow desert earth. Over one arm was a basket covered with a towel. The sergeant spoke gruffly to her. "You'll have to talk fast. Half an hour is all you can stay. Orders."

"Here . . ." He pulled at the basket handle with his free hand. "What's in this?"

"Food, eh?" Ala jerked off the towel, thrust his hand into the basket, then snorted as he pulled it out and cleaned it by rubbing his palm up and down on his trouser leg. "Beans . . . nothing but beans . . . not even fine French bread for your man." He peered through the candle-lit gloom at Domínguez and laughed coarsely. "That's a wife for you. Can't bring you anything else to eat but what you get in prison anyway." As he backed through the door he said, "Remember, half an hour. Not one little minute more."

The door slammed, and the two people in the room heard the broad iron bar that locked it clang into place.

The woman made a half-frightened gesture toward Domínguez, then put the basket on the table and stepped back, her hands working nervously at the fringe of her long dark red shawl. The man, disregarding her, went to the table. The candlelight showed that his eyes and mouth were hard and cruel. Like the sergeant, he was a stocky man in dirty khaki, with sandals on his brown, bare feet. There was dignity in his slow movements, and a cold force of leadership that had thrust him into colonelship in the maelstrom of revolution. He did not look at the woman as he said, "Why did you come here?"

"I heard you were a prisoner."

He said harshly, "I told you to stay in the mountains. There's no place for you here."

She murmured something too low for him to hear, and he half-turned his head toward her. "What did you say?"

"I heard . . . they are going to kill you."

"Speak up. Speak up! Don't mumble. Come here to the light."

As she moved forward, he tossed the shawl back from her face, and stared thoughtfully at her face framed in two braids of heavy, glossy black hair. Her bones were delicate and fine, her skin the color of new honey. His gaze held interest but no emotion, and he disregarded the worshipful light in her dark brown eyes. "So you heard they were going to kill me, eh?" Then his tone harshened. "How did you get here?"

"Don Pablo lent me a donkey. At San Nicolás the soldiers stole him from me. Then I walked."

"And you brought this basket with you from the mountains?"

"I thought you would be hungry. The beans are cooked the way you like them, with garlic . . ." Her voice ended on a high note.

Domínguez caught her arm. She moaned and put her hand up over his but did not try to loosen his fingers. "Nothing else?" When she lowered her head, he shook her arm. "I said . . . nothing else?"

She whispered, "And steel." As he plunged his hand into the basket, and into the can that held the thick syrup of the beans, she added, gasping, "I wanted to bring it in a loaf of bread, but I had no money. It was the only way I knew. I'm so tired. So tired." She dropped her head toward one hunched-up shoulder and began to cry silently. He paid no attention to her. He wiped the knife off on the canvas covering of the cot, then sat on the bench near the table.

"Who knew you were bringing me this?"

"No one. I swear it. No one."

"In the morning when the sun rises I am going to be hanged. If I were going to be shot, that would be different. That's dying like a soldier. But, no. They are going to hang me just as though I were any rich citizen who wouldn't pay them money. Just as though I were a murderer or a thief. But I'm a soldier."

Not hearing his words, she squatted down on the hard-packed earthen floor near him, looking up into his face—just looking as though she could never see enough of him. He talked more to himself than to her. "I must escape. I have to escape. They can't hang me. Not this Baltazar Domínguez." He wiped a corner of his mouth with the back of his hand. "Did Don Pablo send me any word . . . any message?"

"Nothing. He said, 'God's hope.' That's all."

"'God's hope,' eh? Man's hope! My hope! I must get out of here." He walked to the window, peered out of it, then turned angrily to her. "This knife isn't enough! Why didn't you bring me a gun?"

"That was all I had. I didn't know if you'd be living when I came here. I thought . . . if you were dead . . . I could use that . . ."

"Women's thoughts! Soft thoughts! What good is a dead woman to the Revolution? I need a gun."

Her head drooped lower, and she pressed her palms against her mouth, half-sobbing. He went to her, looked down at her, his flat, broad face expressionless, then suddenly thrust out one arm. "Eh, you walked a long distance. You are tired. Here, you can kiss my hand."

She sprang to her feet, clutched at his hand, pressed it against her face, against her breast, covered it with both her own hands. He gazed at her dispassionately.

"You are a soft little thing, good for nothing but tears and laughter. Why did I marry you? Five pesos a month you cost me . . . that is Villa's law . . . every month out of my pay, five pesos to your fat pig of a mother. I was drunk when I married you. If I had been sober I would have thought of those five pesos, but I was drunk, eh . . . and a drunken man is a fool." He did not seem to notice as she dropped his hand and drew her shawl up to cover her pain-shot eyes. "Why didn't you bring me a gun?"

She said with quiet despair. "The Federals burned the town, burned our house. They killed your dog." Her back turned to him, she spoke rapidly in a low voice. "I tried to save him. but he ran back toward the house. I was hiding behind a little palm. The soldiers saw him. One of them laughed. He said, 'Here dies the soul of Baltazar Domínguez,' and shot him right between the eyes. He dropped like the red fruit of the cactus."

"What happened next?" asked the man in a dead voice.

"They threw his body inside the door. Then they set fire to the house. They said, 'Here burns the soul of Baltazar Domínguez.' They watched it burn. Then they went away."

"They didn't see you?"

She shook her head jerkily from side to side. "They didn't know about me. When they found out, they came back, but . . . I was gone. I was afraid of them. I went to Don Pablo. He gave me the knife . . . and the donkey."

Domínguez lifted his head slowly and stared at her with comprehension. "So that was why he sent me no message! He didn't know you were coming here."

The woman shook her head again. "No one knew. There were Federals all along the road." She turned toward him, lifted her face proudly. "I heard the soldiers say they were going to hang you. I had a right to be here. I'm your wife."

Slowly Domínguez rose to his feet, his hands clenching the edge of the table. He bent over it toward her. She looked bravely back at him. "The guard said you had a letter from the big man . . . from Huerta. How did you get it?"

She spoke without inflection, as though reciting a piece from memory. Her eyes were fixed on the table top. "When I reached Saltillo, I went to the great houses, talked to the servants. One of them said there was a fine lady with a letter giving her permission to see her brother. I stole it."

He reached across the table and grasped her shoulder. She kept her eyes fixed on the table, but the soft lips curled inward between her teeth. After a moment he slapped her across the mouth. She slumped backwards, out of his reach. He said hoarsely. "That's a lie."

"God's truth."

"Shall I beat it out of you? What man did you go to?"

"It was a woman. She had a brother . . ."

"What man?"

She whirled and flung up an arm to shield her face. Her voice was a low mutter, but he heard each word clear as a ringing bell. "This sergeant. He said if I wanted to see you . . . he said to tell you that story. It would be easier."

Domínguez did not move for a moment, then he slowly wiped his mouth and cheek on the sleeve of his upper arm, picked up the knife, and plunged it into the scarred gray wood of the table top, and stood there looking at its quivering handle. The woman watched this as a beaten dog watches its master. When he lifted his hand and beckoned to her, she moved forward, her feet dragging on the floor.

Slowly he reached out and grasped her by the throat with one hand. She clutched at his arm, her body bending back, giving at the knees. Then his hand opened and she slid to the floor, struggling to catch her breath, her fingers massaging her bruised throat. He jerked out the knife, weighed it in his palm. After a moment she dragged her body toward him, caught at his leg. As a man thrusts away a bothersome dog, he kicked himself free. She lay very still on the earthen floor.

Behind them they heard the clang of the iron bar as it fell against the door jamb. The door swung open and the sergeant said cheerfully as he came into the shadowy room, "Kiss your wife good-bye, Domínguez. You can kiss her again in . . ."

With a single fluid movement Domínguez threw the knife. The sergeant gave a sobbing gasp. He tried to pull the trigger of his gun but his finger would not obey him. He fell face forward to the floor. Domínguez did not move.

The woman pulled herself to her knees. She crossed herself, then peered up at her husband.

"The door is open," she whispered. Then louder, "The door is open." And louder still, "The door is open."

"Shut up," said Domínguez without inflection.

She edged toward him. "His hat on your head. His blanket high on your shoulders. Baltazar Domínguez or Federal? Who would know the difference?"

After a moment Domínguez walked steadily to the corpse, bent over it, took hat and blanket, and put them both on. Then he lifted the sergeant's gun, rubbed his hand over it. "If any Federal gets in front of this gun, he'll soon know whether I am Federal or Baltazar Domínguez." He gestured toward her with his chin. "Well, why are you waiting? Bring the beans with you."

The woman's voice was high with delight. "You want me?"

"I pay five pesos a month for you, don't I? That's the law. Whether you're here or in hell, I pay five pesos a month. Back to the mountain for the two of us."

As she picked up the basket he stared down at the dead sergeant, not seeing him, seeing instead a symbol of all Federals. "Steal my woman. Burn my house. Kill my dog. Kill my dog." He turned his head and spat. As the woman slipped up to him, the basket dangling from her arm, the shawl swathing her head and shoulders, he pushed her through the door, his hand at her back. "Hurry. We have a distance to walk in this darkness."

They passed the dim ruddy glow of the sentry fire. A sleeping man turned over, then turned back again. Baltazar Domínguez and the woman disappeared into the darkness of the Mexican desert. None of the sleepers awoke. In a few days they might be dead and dancing to the song of Grandfather Devil, never to sleep again through all eternity. Let the sergeant guard the prisoner. What else are sergeants for?

Step Down, Elder Brother
Chapter 7 (pp. 59–67)

The Vázquez de Anda house was very gay that afternoon. The sulpha had broken Cardito's fever, Brunhilda was home again, and don Agapito had left on the three o'clock plane to attend a bankers' convention in México City. For five days the family would be free of don Agapito's shadow. That alone, Domingo thought, was worth a celebration without all the added gladness.

Doña Otilia had been bustling about in the kitchen ever since she returned from church at five o'clock, where she had given thanks to the Blessed Virgin for saving her younger son.

Brunhilda spent the afternoon in her room resting from her journey, while Sofía rode back and forth from the house to the hospital, each time loaded with new instructions for Cardito's nurse. Domingo offered to perform this service, but Sofía told him rather cuttingly that women's instructions were too involved for the mind of man.

He did not like her riding alone so much with the new chauffeur; but he reasoned that Chapa's personal ambition to be a great real estate man would keep Sofía safer than any armed guard.

About six o'clock he wandered into the kitchen and teased doña Petra, the cook, who had come with doña Otilia from Veracruz when she moved to Monterrey as a bride.

He loved this kitchen. Its high ceiling and walls were washed in white, as was the chimney hood which came down over the long, tiled brasier. Little hooks had been screwed into the hood's plaster surface to hold cups and jugs from Guadalajara in such a fashion that the yellow pottery spelt out the word "Otilia," for all the world to see who was the mistress of the house. Other kitchens in Monterrey did not sport this magnificence. It was a custom that came from Michoacán. Doña Petra had a sister who lived in Michoacán, "And," said doña Petra, "if my sister can spell her name, then I can spell doña Otilia's."

The floor was unglazed red tile. Doña Petra was very strict with the kitchen maids, requiring that they get down on their knees and wash these tiles every day with stiff yellow brushes and soapy water. Early in the morning the girls could be heard at their scrubbing, the smell of strong soap invading both the great and small dining rooms.

A large black woodstove was a relic of old don Domingo's day, when it was not uncommon for fifty people to be entertained in the large dining room. There had been one banquet just after don Domingo returned from Germany of which doña Petra would often tell the Vázquez de Anda children. A hundred guests had been present, including handsome, dignified General Bernardo Reyes.[*]

"It was in nineteen hundred and eleven," she would sigh, "just after Porfirio Díaz fled to Paris. All Monterrey was certain General Reyes would be the next president. Ay, he was a beautiful man. And it was a beautiful meal: twenty-one courses. The wine flowed like water. Your grandfather looked very grand with his German mustaches. You had been born, niño Domingo, but the rest of you were all in the future. I can remember how your mother blushed when your grandfather gave a toast to Germany and said that her first daughter was to be named for a Brunhilda he had known there."

"I was named for a goddess in an opera," Brunhilda pouted, but doña Petra sniffed knowingly, with a wink to the more precocious Domingo.

"Goddess or woman, what difference, you were named Brunhilda just the same. And General Reyes applauded, and all the people. Germany was much loved in México in nineteen hundred and eleven. Well, that was a long time ago. It was the last great banquet held in this house."

"We have banquets now," Cardito always protested, then hid behind Domingo to escape a loving slap from doña Petra.

"Not as in those days. That was nineteen hundred and eleven. By nineteen hundred and fourteen General Reyes and your grandfather were dead. The Revolutionary general with the eyeglasses had captured

---

[*] Interestingly, Niggli uses the name of a principal Porfirian-era general, who was also Alfonso Reyes father. Since the latter, wellknown philosopher/writer was born in Monterrey, Gen. Reyes was obviously a known entity in Monterrey.

the city, and there were soldiers quartered in this house. Can you remember them, niño Domingo?"

"I remember a man who used to set tequila bottles up on the gallery railing and shot the tops off without spilling a drop of liquor."

"If that's all you remember, the saints be praised."

"I can remember horses in the patios . . ."

"Not the patios. The men stayed in the patios. The horses were kept in the formal parlor, and the top of your mother's French piano was used as a feeding bin. We of the family lived in the servants' quarters. Can you imagine your fine mother sleeping in the servants' quarters? Well, she did, and not a murmur of complaint did she ever make. Even your uncle Agapito must respect her for that. The woman he was married to at the time, God rest her soul in Paradise, made enough complaints to drive even your uncle Agapito crazy."

"I would like to have heard her," Domingo would say gleefully, promptly receiving a box on the ears from doña Petra for the sin of disrespect. But it was a gentle little slap in comparison with the spankings she administered if she found him flirting with the kitchen maids or stealing food from the icebox.

Remembering the old icebox, Domingo raised his brows in scorn at the fine new electrical machine which was the pride of doña Petra's heart. The old one had been a tremendous affair that opened from the top, so that the maids had to stand on a stool and go headforemost into its capacious insides in order to get out food or beer. The young Vázquez de Andas took malicious delight in catching the girls' heels and pushing them farther into the box than they had any intention of going. Muffled screams brought doña Petra with a flailing broom. She always said that when she reached Heaven and heard the angels scream she would automatically snatch up a broom, certain that the young Vázquez de Andas had followed her into the last retreat.

But the new box opened at the front, and Domingo privately decided, was not half so much fun.

A long table ran the length of the kitchen. On it were piled dishes filled with red and green chiles and small green tomatoes, boxes of garlic, strings of dried onions, and the baskets of *tortillas* which doña Petra herself patted out of finely ground cornmeal mash every morning. She heartily scorned the new custom of buying them from a *tortilla* woman.

Domingo took a paper thin *tortilla* out of the basket, rolled it up, and popped it into his mouth before doña Petra could snarl at him, "Hollow legs!" pushing him out of the way. Doña Otilia smiled at her older son while she measured rice on a small scale. All food in this house was portioned out daily in properly weighed amounts. Doña Otilia wore her pantry keys at her belt, and even the privileged doña Petra had to seek for her if an extra teaspoonful of flour was needed.

"Go away, Domingo," doña Petra snapped. "Can't you see that you are only in the way?"

"If you stay here," his mother said placidly, "there will not be enough food left for dinner. And don't forget, you are to go to Verónica Miranda's saint's day feast in an hour."

Domingo, who had forgotten all about it, grinned shamefacedly at her. He knew that his mother secretly harbored the thought that some day he would marry Verónica.

"Now go and see if Sofía has come back from the hospital."

He obediently went into the patio, to be halted by doña Petra near the fountain. "Eh, niño, one little moment."

As he turned to face her, she pulled her shawl tighter around her shoulders. At seventy she was as sturdy and agile as a woman of fifty. Her hair was black and glossy. Only the wrinkled skin betrayed her age. "What mischief are you up to now?"

"I, doña Petra? I don't know what you mean."

"And you so innocent! I've known you since the moment you were born. This is the second time you've had that look in your eyes. Who is she?"

"Doña Petra," he told her, amused, "you speak in riddles."

"Do I indeed? Perhaps you think I don't know about that pretty North American you were in love with ten years ago. And now you're in love again, praise the saints. When are you bringing her to call on your mother?"

Domingo stared moodily at the fountain. "Did I bring the North American girl to call on my mother?"

She shook her head at him but let him go without further protest.

Sofía had not yet returned, so he climbed the gallery stairs. As he passed his Uncle Lucio's door, it opened, and the little man's head popped out. Seeing that Domingo was alone, he opened the door wider and beckoned his nephew inside.

Don Lucio's room reflected all of his various interests. A miniature chemistry outfit was on its own table under the window. Another table was set up as an electrical workbench, while on yet another was laid out his carpenter's tools.

In place of pictures, his correspondence school diplomas were neatly framed on the walls, and his mandolin lay beside its case on the bed.

Don Lucio pushed some books off the only chair so that Domingo might sit down. "I want to ask you," he said importantly, "about this fellow, the Counselor Farías. What do you intend to do about him?"

"The Counselor Farías?" Domingo was puzzled. "Why should I do anything about him?"

"From what you told us, if he hadn't argued with the Rector, they might have called a doctor and gotten Cardito to the hospital sooner."

"I doubt it. You didn't meet the Rector."

"Hmmm." Don Lucio folded his hands behind his back and paced up and down the narrow space between his bed and the window. "Tell me about Farías, Domingo."

"There's nothing much to tell. He got a law degree through some miracle, set up a practice, failed at it, and finally persuaded the Governor to appoint him to the staff of the University. That's all I know, really."

"You certainly know more than that. Why does he hate Cardito?"

"I haven't the slightest idea unless . . . Let me try and remember."

Out of the haze of the past three years a memory came into focus. Cardito had been secretary of the students' syndicate. That was three— no, four years ago. The son of an old enemy was in Farías's class, and Farías failed him. Cardito, knowing the true circumstances, ordered all of the students to go on strike until the boy was passed. Domingo vaguely remembered attending one of the meetings and listening to Cardito's impassioned speeches larded with comments about government appointments. There was a strong demarcation in the school between men known as real professors and those called "the governor's friends." It had nothing to do with any governor personally but with the century old war between the University, which was not wealthy enough to support itself autonomously, and politics.

Domingo related as much as he knew of the case while don Lucio paced up and down. As he finished, the little man said, "He failed Cardito three times . . . deliberately kept him in the school of bachelors when he should have been in the law school. Why didn't the students go on strike for Cardito?"

"Cardito won't let them. He says it's a personal matter. He says he's going to force Farías to pass him."

Don Lucio came closer to Domingo. "Have you spoken to Farías?"

"No. It's Cardito's problem. I think he should fight it out himself."

"Does Agapito know about it?"

"Why should he? As long as the student strikes do not affect his bank, there's no need for him to be interested."

"Cardito is his nephew."

"A fact which I pray will not intrude too much upon his consciousness. I think he still sees Cardito as a ten-year-old child. May he forever continue to see him that way."

"Amen," don Lucio muttered. He struck his hands softly together. "But the matter is changed now, Domingo. Cardito can no longer take care of it himself. This fool Farías really almost killed him."

Domingo shook his head and rose. "I tell you it's Cardito's problem. The boy is twenty years old and must fight his own battles." Seeing his uncle frown, he added, "You think I'm being cruel, don't you?"

"Yes," don Lucio said slowly. "Or rather, let us phrase it that I think you are mistaken."

"I am not mistaken. I am simply tired of meddlers. It is a terrible thing to meddle in what is good. It is even worse to meddle in what is bad. When Cardito gets well, if he wants to go down and beat Farías to a pulp, I would be the first to shout 'Viva Cardito!' I will even pay his jail fine with pleasure. But I will not take care of his revenge for him. I am sorry, Uncle Lucio, but if you think about it for a while you will see I am right."

"I wonder," said don Lucio slowly, picking up his mandolin and fitting it carefully into its case. "Thank you for talking to me, Domingo. If any news comes of Cardito, I will be in don Primitivo's." His voice took on a casual tone and he carefully avoided looking at his nephew. "Did you know that don Primitivo was a good friend of the new commanding general of the military camp?"

"Of General Gil? What were they, old bullfighting comrades?"

"Do not be so cynical!" Don Lucio fitted his hat carefully on his round head and fastened his overcoat to the chin. "General Gil is a graduate of Chapultepec. He is of the Gil Treviño family from San Luis Potosí. Don Primitivo got his bullfight training on the ranch of General Gil's father."

Domingo pressed down on his lips to keep them from smiling, but he could not conceal the twinkle in his eyes. "Do not celebrate the general's arrival too much with don Primitivo. Remember that we are dining here at ten, and don't get too drunk."

"I never get drunk," Uncle Lucio told him with great dignity. He swished through the door like an angry turkey.

Domingo, much amused, went on to his own room. He lit the gas burner, then sat down in his comfortable armchair and stretched out his legs toward the flame. He decided that when Sofía came home for further instructions, he would return to the hospital with her after leaving Verónica's. Cardito, Sofía had reported several times that afternoon, was sleeping peacefully. The doctors seemed much relieved about his condition.

Domingo stretched his thin body and yawned. He had only to put out his hand to take any of several new books from the shelves. A shipment had arrived yesterday from Brentano's and this morning another from Mexico City. Since don Agapito deplored the money Domingo spent so foolishly on books, he consequently bought more than he could really afford.

His searching fingers hesitated over a new volume by Mediz Bolio which had arrived in the Mexico City shipment. Mediz Bolio was one of his favorite writers and this new book of Maya legends promised to be a great delight. But he knew that if he started it now, he would never reach Verónica's party, so he let his hand slide forward to a thin paper volume labeled *The Best Poems of the Best Mexican Poets*. His eyes wandered from page to page, finding verses read long ago and long ago forgotten. Two lines from Salvador Díaz Mirón, which in the old days had always amused him, now leaped out at him:

> If you are ice, why, then, am I not frozen?
> If I am fire, why are you not consumed?

And it occurred to him that the verses were no longer a matter of humor. He settled himself more comfortably in the chair and read the entire poem through:

> To sweeten for a little your indifference
> Turn on me your angel-borrowed eyes,
> And drown your death-pale fingers in my hair,
> In my dark and sorrow tumbled hair.
>
> But this is vanity, not consolation!
> We are separated by a world.
> If you are ice, why, then, am I not frozen
> If I am fire, why are you not consumed?
>
> Your graceful hand, slender and transparent,
> Rests too lightly on my slave-chained head.
> It is the glacial cup on flaming lava.
> It is the cup of snow on the volcano.

He had rejected poetry entirely after Doris left. The knife cut too deep. Then, with the turning of the years, with the dulling of pain, he had come back to it, but not to such sentimental verses as these. He preferred the mysticism of Ramón López Velarde, the modern sophistication of Xavier Villaurrutia. The older romantic lovers, who continually sang of broken hearted lovers and indifferent mistresses, had always amused him, possibly because he had never loved an indifferent woman.

Up to the time he met Doris he had divided all women into two types: the ones he might some day marry and the ones he would never think of marrying. Then Doris flamed to his flame, but he had been the one to turn away. The women he knew later were merely a searching after what he had rejected in Doris.

Verónica Miranda came the closest. She was a sweet, childlike creature whom he might have married had don Agapito not so completely approved of her. Domingo smiled wryly to himself. Like Sofía, he thought, I, too, have my small defiances.

Marriage to Verónica, he decided, however much it pleased the family, would be very dull. Her conversational powers were limited, and she irritated rather than soothed him.

What was the strange elixir in human chemistry which caused an explosion when one pair of individuals met, yet had no effect at the meeting of another? Márgara possessed this elixir for him; Verónica did not. But did the flow of time dull such excitement?

Márgara belonged to a world he had never known. Her background, her thought processes were completely strange to him, whereas Verónica was a part of his own environment. With Doris he had met this same problem and had intellectually solved it. Better to solve the problem of Márgara immediately before he became so emotionally involved that no application of cold logic would be possible.

He sat quietly in the big chair, his head bowed, his long arms drooping toward the floor. The poetry book, forgotten, dropped from his hand. Against the curtain of his closed lids he fastened Márgara's image. What did he know of her, really? That the Indian blood was strong in her veins? That poverty had bathed her in its boiling stream, searing away true pride until only false pride remained? That much and no more. And yet she had rippled his blood as no woman had done since the days of Doris.

His left arm stirred, remembering the feel of her body against it. The chill of terror had been in her, and that terror had come into his arm. Even her hair, soft under his cheek, had vibrated with nerves, and all because of the painted picture of a man.

He tried to visualize the miniature. The light had been bad, and Bárcenas had snatched it away before it had been possible to really see it. During the brief glimpse, however, he had been struck by something faintly familiar about it . . . not as a man remembered, but as a picture remembered. Somewhere, some place, he had seen a picture of that man, and with it went a story which made the picture memorable.

The photograph, the studio, the mystery of Márgara. Was he in love with her? No, not really. It was merely a sexual attraction, an experiment in chemistry . . . Márgara. Márgara . . .

As from a great distance he heard a scratching at the door. It sounded like a small kitten trying to get in, but there were no kittens in the house. Again came the scratching.

Domingo jerked free of his half doze and opened the door. A tear-stained Serafina looked pleadingly up at him.

Step Down, Elder Brother
Legend of the Rabbit in the Moon (pp. 217–19)

Domingo sat on a ledge thrust out by a corner of a building and watched the moon flirting with a nearby star. It was a full moon tonight and he could see the rabbit in it, squatting on its little haunches, its long ears tilted forward better to hear the voice of the Fair God. The old legend Tía Nicanora had told him as a child returned to him:

"There was this little boy, very selfish, very wicked. His name was Hualpa, and he killed small animals, not for food but for sport. Because he was so strong, so arrogant, the other boys who lived in his village thought him very grand, and all the things he did, they did. Then came the great feast of the Fair God. The village went on pilgrimage to the Temple in the City, but Hualpa would not go. He was so proud he said that he was equal to the Fair God, and would carry no fruits or vegetables to the Temple's altar. 'The War God is my god,' he cried, 'this god of the fields and streams, this god of small beasts and birds, this gentle peaceful god is not for me.'

The other boys were frightened by such blasphemy. His mother wept, and his father also. But Hualpa laughed, and ran away into the forests, and killed a rabbit because it gave him pleasure to see the tiny creature die.

As he went home that evening, swinging the dead rabbit by its ears, he saw an old woman crouched by the road that led into the deserted village, for, mind you, everyone in the village except Hualpa had gone to the festival. This old woman was weeping because she was hungry. She begged the rabbit of Hualpa that she might eat. He laughed at her and told her she was a weak thing, not worth staying alive. 'No one,' he said, 'should be alive but the strong and proud. Die then if you are too weak to find food for yourself.' He tossed the rabbit up on the roof of the house where she could not reach it, put his hands on his hips, flung back his head, and laughed at the old woman who was too weak to live.

The old woman said nothing. She merely looked at him. But he felt a grinding pain in his bones. He felt his ears stretch longer and longer. He felt his hands turn into paws. He felt himself shrink smaller and smaller, until every blade of grass widened to the size of a tree trunk, and every tree trunk widened to the size of a house, and every house widened beyond the reach of his eyesight. He tried to cry out, but there was only a squeak in his throat. He tried to run, but he found himself leaping in great bounds. At last he encountered a stream. He was afraid to peer into it, but he had to peer into it. Then he knew that what he had feared was really true. He had changed into a rabbit.

During the next year the arrogance, the pride of strength, was washed out of him. The boys he had taught so well were trying to trap him. The large animals were constantly on his trail to kill and eat him. Then, on the eve of the Fair God's festival, his own father attempted to catch him and take him as an offering to the Temple. He escaped, but he sat by the stream and added his tears to the water. He knew then that even the smallest beast has a right to the peace of freedom.

As the twilight darkened he thought perhaps, if he went humbly to the Temple, the Fair God might take pity upon him and change him back into a boy. He started off on the long journey to the city and the festival.

Many people were on the road, but they did not notice the tiny creature. The road was long, his legs were short, and after a while he grew very tired. He paused to rest, his heart pumping for fear someone would see him and trap him, now that he was too tired to evade them. But no one was near except an old beggar, crouching in a ditch.

From time to time the old man would call out, 'I am so hungry. Aid me or I will die.' But none of the marching pilgrims heard him. Or if they did, they paid him no attention.

Hualpa looked at the beggar for a long time. Once in the proud days he had refused an old woman food. Now he had no food to offer. He thought of the Fair God, so grand in the temple. In his tiredness he knew that the God had so many creatures to watch over that the problems of one rabbit were of no account. He crept closer to the old beggar. Pushing his nose against the beggar's hand, he remembered that the very young and the very old can hear the voices of the animals.

'Old man,' he whispered, 'eat me to cure your hunger.'

'Do you know what you are giving?' the old man asked. 'It is your life you are giving.'

Hualpa shivered in his rabbit's form. 'Tomorrow the boys will kill me for sport, or a pilgrim will kill me for food. They are clever, and I am no longer clever. They will know how to trap me. Better for you to eat me, than for them to have me for sport.'

'Where is the arrogance, where is the pride?' the old man asked. 'Is this a true humility?'

Hualpa, the rabbit, wanted to answer him, but he was afraid. The skin of the old man had begun to shine until it seemed the night was as bright as the sun-cradled day. He grew then, taller than the distant Temple, taller than the clouds. The stars were a necklace on his breast. Hualpa, crouching close to the earth, was gently lifted on one giant palm, drawn up to the face that was broader than the earth, whiter than the tender blossoms of the *yuca*. Trembling on that palm, Hualpa could see the eyes that were as blue as feathers from a peacock's tail, the hair that was yellow as cantalope meat. And Hualpa knew that this was the Fair God, and that he should be afraid, but he was not afraid. The love in the face that was broader than the earth, strengthened him, and he was not afraid.

Then the Fair God spoke and his voice was louder than the wind in a tempest, louder than the crash of thunder, and sweet as a birdsong. 'You have truly learned your lesson, my tiny servant, and so I am going to set you in the moon. Then all who see you sitting in the moon will remember your lesson; they will remember that when they harm my children they do even greater harm to themselves.'

That is why, on clear nights, when the moon is full, we can see Hualpa sitting there to remind us to love all things, not with arrogance, but with humility."

"Chant to the Four World Quarters"
Unpublished translation or creation of poem evoking Mayan philosophy, no date

Eyes. Turn first to the wild flying bees.
He is their lord, their king, their god.
The logwood tree is his hut. His
Is a flower, white cup on dark wood.
Of logwood, also, is the house of the green bird.

Eyes. Turn south, turn to the yellow bird.
He guards the mountains, the nine tall mountains.
Nine streams, nine rivers, nine flowing waters he guards.

Flint red, red flint, is the stone of the bee god.
Arbor red is his tree of the world.
Arching high, arching wide with its limbs and its branches. He
Flies with his news to the queen bee of the hive.
Red he is, red as the vine, the red vine of healing.
Red as the gourd, as tipped feathers of turkeys,
Of wild yellow turkeys, eating, eating the dark red corn.

Flint white, white flint is the stone of the north. Bees
Fly to their tree, tree arbor of white.
Breast white are their turkeys, eating white Limas.
White lima-beans are their corn.
Their corn is white.

Flint black, black flint is the stone of the west.
Arbor black, tree black, black are their turkeys. Black
Turkeys, the wild black pigeons. Black
Is their speckled corn.
They feed on the black spotted yams. Black
Are their limas. Black are all their black beans.

Flint gold, golden flint is the stone of the south.
Wild yellow birds nest in their tree. Gold
Trees of the world. Yellow turkeys nest high.
Yellow their flower cups, gold their pumpkins. They
Feed on their yellow corn.

Long ago came the people, bent down with their burdens,
Bent down, bent down.
They walked behind. In front walked the three who hunted.
Each carried his tall staff.
Hunters, the three, faces turned toward the distant land.
Each staff was torn, long ago, from the tree of the world.
The staff of the middle man measured and marked.
The staff of the middle man measured the leagues.
The staff of the right man cleared out the weeds,
Cleared the brush, cleared the leagues, cleared the land.
The staff of the left man swept clean the path for the people,
Swept the land clean.
Long were the leagues, leagues long, that they cleared,
Leagues long that they cleaned and they measured.
These three walked in front.
Behind them the people, bent down with their burdens,
Followed the path to the mouth of the well,
Followed the path to the island and sea.
Followed the path that was measured and cleared and clean . . .
Four voices they placed at the head of the mat. Four voices
That spoke for the people.
Four voices that spoke for the burdens and long leagues traveled.
Four voices that spoke.
Four voices.
A voice for the east and a voice for the north,
A voice for the west and a voice for the south.
Four voices that sang.
Four voices that sat at the mouth of the well.

Bees red. Bees that are wild, that are red, for the east.
Dark red is their honey flower.
Bees white. Bees that are wild, that are white, for the north.
White white is their honey cup.
Bees black. Bees that are wild, that are black, for the west,
Black, black above the black laurel.
Bees gold. Bees that are wild, that are gold, for the south.
Their flower is yellow.

Together they swarmed, together they flew to the island.
They found the sweet things of the land.
They found the yams and the pumpkins.
They found the tree of the world.

Their priest. Wind god, god of winds.
He commanded the humming warriors that guarded the arrow at
     the wall.
The arrow, the archer, he guarded.
He led the army above the tall grass.
He guarded the sun-eyed fire macaw. He
Gave the powdered red feathers, the feathers of macaw,
He gave to the people who carried their burdens,
He gave to the three who had cleared the land.
He laid out the mat, and appointed the voices.
He led the way to the well, to the mouth of the well, to the Archer.
He led the way to the sea and the island. Wind god,
God of winds. He was their priest.

Red, red for the east,
White, white for the north,
Black, black for the west.
Gold, gold for the south
Where the flowers are yellow.

**Fragment, Niggli's screenplay for *Sombrero*,
film based on *Mexican Village* (dated October 31, 1951).
Final filmed script is somewhat different.**

DON HOMERO
    Follows her gaze toward:
PEPE
    Nonchalantly drinking his wine.
DON HOMERO
CAMERA PANS him to don Daniel
DON HOMERO. Who's the stranger?
DON DANIEL. I don't know. I just noticed him.
CAMERA FOLLOWS don Homero over to Pepe.
DON HOMERO. Good evening, señor. This is your house. (*Bows formally*) Homero Calderón, mayor of San Juan.
PEPE. (*Shaking hands*) Rubén Alejandro, at your service. I am from Topo Grande.
DON HOMERO. We're always pleased to welcome strangers here, except, of course, those sons of mountain witches from Hidalgo.
(*Laughs loudly. Pepe's laugh is hollow.*)
    shot SARITA AND NAPOLEON DANCING
(*Her expression is apprehensive.*)
    shot DON HOMERO AND PEPE
Don Homero sizes him up. It is not suspicion—he considers him a good prospect for his daughter's hand.
DON HOMERO. You have many friends here in San Juan?
PEPE. (*Guardedly*) No. My last visit was rather brief.
DON HOMERO. That's a pity. Do you like cockfights?
PEPE. The very reason why I dared intrude on your hospitality. Even

Topo Grande has heard of Don Homero Calderón, breeder of the finest fighting cocks in the Republic.

DON HOMERO. Señor, I do not deserve such praise.

PEPE. You underestimate your fame, don Homero. I, too, raise the noble birds, but unfortunately I lack your talent for training them.

DON HOMERO. (*Overwhelmed*) Your glass is empty, señor Alejandro. You must drink a toast to Sarita, my beautiful daughter, whose birthday we are celebrating. (*Confidentially*) Incidentally, whoever wins her, wins my beautiful black Satan. (*Taking Pepe's glass*) Let me get you my personal wine.

PEPE. (*As music stops*) Thank you, but first permit me the honor of a dance with your charming daughter?

DON HOMERO. A pleasure. This night is for the young.

PEPE. With your permission. (*Bows and exits as don Daniel enters*)

DON HOMERO. (*Whispering*) Such good manners—and he also raises fighting cocks!

INTERIOR PARLOR—MEDIUM FULL

Napoleon escorts Sarita to her chair while other couples circle the room, waiting for the music to begin again. CAMERA MOVES IN with Pepe as he goes to Sarita, who, seeing him, self-consciously fans herself.

PEPE. (*With a flourish*) With your father's kind consent.

SARITA. (*Indignant*) What impudence! I don't ever remember meeting you.

PEPE. (*Lowering voice*) I'm sure your foot remembers my ankle.

SARITA. (*In a fierce whisper*) How dare you come here!

PEPE. The bee must return to the honey of your lips.

The orchestra plays "Recuerdo." Pepe lifts her to her feet and begins to waltz skillfully.

shot DON HOMERO AND DON DANIEL

DON HOMERO. (*Admiringly*) He also has a talent for the dance.

DON DANIEL. And for the ladies!

shot PEPE AND SARITA—DANCING

Sarita blossoms under his expert guidance.

PEPE. My arms love to hold you.

SARITA. (*Scandalized*) Don't say such things!

PEPE. You're even more graceful than the girls of . . .

SARITA. (*Interrupting*) Don't mention that word!

PEPE. (*Innocently*) What word?

SARITA. Hidalgo! (*Gasps as she realizes she has said it*) I have only to tell them your name, and they'll tear you to pieces. What is your name?

PEPE. Pepe Gonzalez

SARITA. Not the wild one who paints mustaches!

PEPE. The same. Also the son of the finest cheese maker in the north.
    Draws her close. She does not resist.

MEDIUM—DON HOMERO AND DON DANIEL

NAPOLEON. (*Entering*) Who is that rooster?

DON HOMERO. Rubén Alejandro from Topo Grande he said.

NAPOLEON. (*Suspiciously*) Alejandro? That's a peculiar last name.

DON HOMERO. Now, Napoleon, don't be jealous. He comes from a very fine family.

shot PEPE AND SARITA—DANCING

SARITA. (*Nervously*) Aren't you afraid someone might recognize you?

PEPE. To be so near you is worth any risk.
    The orchestra segues into the birthday song, "Las Mañanitas," and Pepe sings it.

FULL SHOT

Everyone joins in. At the end, Pepe kisses her hand to the disapproval of the chaperones. Her friends congratulate her.

ANGLE AT ORCHESTRA

Pepe whispers to the leader, slipping him a banknote.

CAMERA FOLLOWS as he pushes aside Napoleon who is talking to Sarita. A loud mambo blares forth, startling everyone. Pepe grabs Sarita and begins to dance. Embarrassed, she tries to disengage herself, but he pulls her back.

DON HOMERO AND DON DANIEL

Don Homero frowns at the display.

PEPE AND SARITA DANCING
Pepe's enthusiasm is contagious, and Sarita enters into the spirit of the jungle.

ROW OF CHAPERONES
Shocked and grim-faced.

FULL SHOT
Other couples get up nerve enough to dance the mambo, but Pepe and Sarita are the center of attention as he introduces some startling innovations. When the number reaches its strident climax, Pepe sweeps Sarita toward the balcony overlooking the street. Guests immediately start to gossip.

EXTERIOR BALCONY—NIGHT—MEDIUM
Sarita is dreadfully conscious of being alone on the balcony with Pepe.
SARITA. Ay! They are all watching us. You have danced me right into a scandal. You are truly a wild one.
PEPE. But I'm willing to be tamed.
The music begins a more sedate number.

EXTERIOR PATIO—NIGHT—MEDIUM AT TABLE
Don Homero fills his glass while don Daniel spreads white cheese on a tortilla.

DON DANIEL. Let those old hens cackle! But I remember when they danced the bunny hug! (*Takes a bite, says, with surprise*) This is a jewel of a cheese!
DON HOMERO. (*Expansively*) Only the best Linares cheese for my daughter's birthday.
DON DANIEL. This is no cheese from Linares.
DON HOMERO. You recognize the taste?
DON DANIEL. (*Tasting it*) I remember this savor.
EXTERIOR BALCONY—NIGHT—MEDIUM SHOT
SARITA. (*Pleadingly*) If you really like me, please go!
PEPE. Not until you promise to let me see you again.

SARITA. That's impossible! Have you forgotten there's a feud between us?

PEPE. Not between you and me. Which is your window?

SARITA. (*Pretending to be shocked*) To my room? I won't tell you!

PEPE. Why not?

SARITA. Why should an Hidalgo man need to know my room is in the back near the corral of the roosters?

EXTERIOR PATIO—DON HOMERO AND DON DANIEL

DON DANIEL. (*Excitedly*) Ah—now I remember!

DON HOMERO. (*Impatiently*) At last! Well?

DON DANIEL. Ask the cowboy on his horse in Sonora—ask the soldier on the bridge at Laredo—ask the sailor on his ship at Tampico: "Ola, friend—who makes the finest goat cheese?" And the answer will always be the same—"The family Gonzales of Hidalgo."

DON HOMERO. (*Double-take*) Hidalgo! (*Wildly*) How did it get here?

DON DANIEL. The stranger!

Don Homero makes a dash toward the parlour.

INTERIOR PARLOUR—FULL SHOT

Don Homero storms into the parlour.

DON HOMERO. Where is that devil from Hidalgo?

There is horror and consternation. Angry voices echo "Hidalgo!" All turn toward the window. Don Homero rushes forward, camera moving in with him to a CLOSE SHOT of Sarita, standing alone on the balcony, breathlessly fanning herself. She forces a pathetic little smile which fades as her father approaches. From the street comes a clatter of hoofbeats as Pepe yells derisively. Don Homero can only sputter in futile rage.

DISSOLVE TO:

EXTERIOR RIVER—DAY—WIDE ANGLE

A secluded spot where the bend of the river forms a deep pool shadowed by trees. A guitar leans against a tree trunk, near a lacquer tray filled with fruit. In the distance, jagged peaks push back the sky.

1. Baby Josefina in a cart being looked after by two family servants, on
   the grounds of her parents' country home in Hidalgo (early accounts
   refer to the house as having substantial grounds with planted gardens)
   circa 1912–13.

   (COURTESY BILL FISHER, FROM NIGGLI FAMILY SCRAPBOOK.)

2. Josefina with camera in San Pedro Park, San Antonio, age five, 1915
(other photos taken at the same time show Josefina photographing swans).
Interestingly, the San Pedro Playhouse, the home of San Antonio Little
Theater, was built on the grounds of San Pedro Park in 1929–1930.

(COURTESY BILL FISHER, FROM NIGGLI FAMILY SCRAPBOOK.)

3. Josefina and her grandmother Phoebe Morgan in front of the family home in Hidalgo, 1922.

(COURTESY BILL FISHER, FROM NIGGLI FAMILY SCRAPBOOK.)

4. Josefina in Hidalgo on Christmas Day, 1921. She had a pet donkey
named Sennacherib, which may be the donkey in this photo;
she once explained that the donkey was named for the only poem
that she could recite the whole way through (must refer to Lord
Byron's poem "The Destruction of Sennacherib.")

(COURTESY BILL FISHER, FROM NIGGLI FAMILY SCRAPBOOK.)

Moberly, *Devinney* Mo.

5. Portrait of Josefina's mother, Goldie Morgan, as a young girl, taken in her hometown of Moberly, Missouri. After training with a local violin instructor, she moved to New York to continue her training and became a professional violinist. It was her career as a violinist that brought her to San Antonio, Texas, where she met her future husband, F. F. Niggli.

(COURTESY BILL FISHER, FROM NIGGLI FAMILY SCRAPBOOK.)

6. Josefina dressed as a page to Oberon for a production of
Shakespeare's *A Midsummer Night's Dream* given in Eagle
Pass, circa 1918.

(COURTESY BILL FISHER, FROM NIGGLI FAMILY SCRAPBOOK.)

7. Portrait of Josefina's father, Frederick Ferdinand "Fritz" Niggli. He was a serious businessman, as his dress and countenance reflect.

(COURTESY BILL FISHER, FROM NIGGLI FAMILY SCRAPBOOK.)

8. Niggli (age fifteen) and Abraham Barrera wearing costumes demonstrating "El Jarabe Tapatío," the national dance of Mexico. San Antonio, Texas, published December 28, 1925. The *San Antonio Light* Collection. Permission granted by UTSA's Texas Institute of Cultures, no. L-0516-A.

(COURTESY OF THE HEARST CORPORATION.)

9. Josefina in festival dress worn as "María" in the play *Soldadera*,
published in her first book, *Mexican Folk Plays*.

(PERMISSION GRANTED BY WESTERN CAROLINA
UNIVERSITY FOUNDATION.)

10. Josefina in 1945 or 1946 (likely at the Rosengren's bookstore) in San Antonio, holding her first book, *Mexican Village*. The *San Antonio Light* Collection. Permission granted by UTSA's Texas Institute of Cultures, no. L-3176.

(COURTESY OF THE HEARST CORPORATION.)

11. Ricardo Montalbán, film director Norman Foster, and Josefina on the set
in Mexico for the filming of *Sombrero*, based on her book *Mexican Village*.
Montalbán played Pepe Gonzáles.

(COURTESY BILL FISHER, *SOMBRERO* ARCHIVE.)

Love from Tuffy, DeeDee,
baby white Zorro and me.
Josefina Niggli

12. Last formal photo of Josefina with pets Tuffy, DeeDee, and Zorro
from Christmas card 1980 (also appeared in the *Dictionary of
Literary Biography*).

(COURTESY JOHN IGO.)

CHAPTER FOUR

A Final Novel and Teaching

1953–1983

Despite the release of a major film, an opera in San Francisco, and a musical play in Santa Barbara, Niggli gave up on California and once again returned to Chapel Hill. Now in her forties, she desired a permanent teaching job above all other possibilities. But it was a period of U.S. history, known as the McCarthy era, that was not favorable to writers. In 1953, the House Un-American Activities Committee hearings were in full swing. Some writers left the country (like Joy Davidman, who married C .S. Lewis); many others had to find different avenues of work. Congress was issuing subpoenas and targeting writers in Hollywood, such as the famous husband-and-wife team of Dashiell Hammett and Lillian Hellman (the first served five months in jail for refusing to testify, while Hellman was forced to appear before the HUAC). While Niggli had not been associated with the pro-communist League of American Writers, her connection to Paul Green (who skirted the political witch hunt by leaving Hollywood, and even the United States), and a lack of work opportunities likely influenced Niggli's decision to abandon the glamour of California.

She was "home" (as she would continue to refer to North Carolina), writing articles and seeking a full-time teaching post by fall of 1953. An article published in the January 1953 issue of *The Writer* magazine demonstrates Niggli's continued talent for pedagogical writing. The biographical note with the article states that she is "now conducting courses in creative writing" at the University of North Carolina. In this concise piece, titled "Proportion in Writing," Niggli's comments provide a key to specific insights that made her an engaging instructor. She begins by discussing traditional rules and particular characteristics sought by editors evaluating creative writing. For "clarity," she says, the traditional beginning-middle-end concept could be conceived as "gestation, unfolding, and completion." A story cannot be "grasped, as can a painting, a statue, or a building, in a single glance." Niggli also explores her concept of the divisions of a story as past, present, and future, offering examples and reasons for varying lengths in each area, and concludes with the following:

> We might say, therefore, that while a story presents time past, time present and time future in the three sections of Germination (Cause), Unfolding (Transition) and Conclusion (Fulfillment of Cause), the contents of the story will determine which of the three is the most important, and how much space must be devoted to it for proper proportion.

Niggli's assessment provides direction and creative maneuverability for future writers who may not have understood why an editor rejects stories for lack of definable divisions.

A Tenure-Track Job

During the summer of 1954, Niggli was a featured speaker at the fourth annual North Carolina writer's conference, held at Hatteras (according to the *Greensboro Daily News*). She had also landed a full-time teaching post in dramatic art at the Woman's College of the University of North Carolina's multi-campus system, located in the city of Greensboro. This campus is now known as UNC-Greensboro.

Niggli's job application form (retained in that campus's archives, and permanently missing a page) indicates she has been hired to a tenure-track position as assistant professor in the Department of Dramatic Art. She cites her recreational interest as "photography," her religious affiliation as Catholic, and civil status as "unmarried." Typical for the era, her employment history is indicated in the usual submissive female fashion: Secretary to Dr. Roehl at Incarnate Word College, 1929–31; Instructor at the private girl's school St. Mary's Hall, 1943–44; Script-writer, MGM, Culver City, June–December 1951; and Self-employed as a Writer, 1944–54. Niggli either forgets, or does not consider it significant to list her two-year administrative role in the radio and play division of the university's Department of Dramatic Art, or her first period in Hollywood. While Niggli seems to neglect citing some of her important publications or jobs, she also appears never to have created a curriculum vitae or factual list of all of her published works. In fact, when resorting to memory, she often gets dates mixed up or leaves out significant items.

On this application, Niggli lists six short stories and numerous poems published in magazines between 1928 and 1935, principally *Mexican Life*, as her creative works. She does not cite her books. Other items may have been indicated on a page now misplaced (there are only three pages of her application in these archives), or Niggli may have wanted to indicate only the items best suited to a college teaching position.

In a letter to Paul Green dated October 20, 1954 (letterhead The Woman's College), Niggli formally thanks him for a talk he provided. "All of the girls were simply delighted—both with what you had to say and with you personally." She expresses hope that he will repeat the visit at the beginning of the following year. Niggli appears to be settling into academic life at this juncture. In a handwritten letter also penned at Greensboro, she again thanks Green, noting that everyone warned "that girls over here don't go to lectures," thus they were impressed that, while they expected "about 30, 120 showed up!" She expresses disappointment, however, that he and Elizabeth were not able to "get by to see my little apartment. I'd gotten it all fixed up for you." In the fall of 1954, Niggli was forty-four years old, but in her dialogue with Paul Green, he often seemed fatherly and she his student-protégée.

Niggli's experience in Hollywood made her a desirable attraction for special lectures in the local area as she settled into her new academic position. Niggli was asked to talk about the movies in an address to the "Lecture Club," a women's group that convened in private homes following a buffet luncheon (*Greensboro Daily News* on November 11, 1954). After "casually dropping such names as Loretta Young, Greer Garson, Betty Grable, Clark Gable, Gene Kelly and Red Skelton, [she said:] 'To those of the profession, Hollywood is a humdrum town,' hemmed in by the demands of their public and the demands of their work. She described the prodigious off-stage work that goes into any production," including the work of extras, mechanical horses, writers, guards, costumers, musicians, electricians, and producers, and the commissary where all staff ate and where the predilection was for chocolate ice cream sodas. Niggli used examples from "Seven Brides for Seven Brothers" to describe how Hollywood topped the world in musicals.

A New Collaboration

The state Historical Club invited Niggli to the sixth annual Book and Author Luncheon on January 8, 1955 (*Greensboro Daily News*). She was slated to talk about "something unusual and special," a "collaboration" with a well-known photographer of babies and young children, Josef Schneider of New York City. Although an unusual venture, Niggli's biographical references always indicate her hobby as photography (a photo of her as a five-year-old child in San Antonio shows her lugging around a camera). However, she never published or displayed her own photographs. And in this case, she was only sought for narrative to accompany Schneider's work. A month later, in the same paper (February 5), the reporter filed the following creatively written account:

> Josefina Niggli, who writes, met Josef Schneider, who photographs, in New York City, more than a year ago. A social encounter, it was. The two soon found that they had more in common than the use of an "f" where most folks put "ph." Miss Niggli has had photography for a hobby for a long, long time and Mr. Schneider was looking for someone with a neat way with words to help him with a book starring his pictures of children. Pretty soon they found themselves collaborators.

The book was to consist of photographs by Schneider and narrative by Niggli "interpreting the Schneider method." The journalist states that

Niggli had been "cramming every child psychology book she could lay her hands on" in preparation for her writing, although she was commissioned by Schneider for "her understanding of photography," since Schneider had already authored a book.[1] The new collaboration would be titled "A New Method of Photographing Babies." The project makes little sense for Niggli's career. In fact, said book was never published. A review of articles published in the *New York Times* about Josef Schneider never cites a second book, but instead only his awards received, workshops taught, various advertisements, and his 1949 book, which was reissued to even greater acclaim in 1953. During the early 1950s, Schneider did several art shows displaying his photos in New York City. He also garnered attention upon launching a correspondence course on child photography in 1955, with three "large, attractively-printed volumes" (see *New York Times* article by Jacob Deschin) that demonstrated his innovative lighting techniques. This may constitute the "book" Niggli collaborated on—as it would be somewhat similar to her writing-technique guides—but her name is not indicated in advertisements.

With no new novel and no additional movie screenplay, Niggli appears to have been floundering in finding her writing niche during the postwar era. She had always preferred realism to the romantics, and the strong interest during the 1930s for folk or regional adaptations suited her early playwriting. She favored Mexican topics and historical fiction for her novels, which led to her opportunities in screenwriting. She was also attracted to the creation of musical plays. But no new works were published during the 1950s. Her need for full-time employment and stability could account for this.

An unexpected invitation, however, and the opportunity to again travel to Europe, was about to change her present life.

An Invitation from England

During that first and only academic year she spent at the University of North Carolina Woman's College, Niggli acted as adviser to many students. In one case, she helped a student with information about prerequisites by writing a letter to the University of Bristol in England. The reply she received, however, was directed personally to her. Bristol officials said they had been looking for her for some time, and that they wanted to offer her a position. Niggli had forgotten about her international fame as a playwright. Now she would enjoy an opportunity like the one Paul Green and others had experienced during the past decade. It meant giving up her full-time job as professor, but Niggli accepted the offer.

> "It has been a very painful decision to make [she states on July 3, 1955 to the *News and Observer*], one which I didn't recognize fully until I took down some of my Mexican library and started to pack." Her workshop in the back yard of her home showed evidence of her packing, and during the interview a truck drove up and workers removed large boxes of books and manuscripts which she is giving to the University of North Carolina Library.

Niggli reflects on the experiences of her early training at UNC with the Carolina Playmakers, and gives tribute to two of her mentors:

> "Prof Koch was our teacher and his gift was inspirational. It was a subconscious quality he had. He drew out the talent in people. It was a very exciting period." About Chapel Hill, she added, "There is one thing that is characteristic of the writers here—they are so kind. They are so willing to help young writers that are coming along. Paul Green is one of them—he is so generous. And I don't know a writer here who isn't ready and willing to help young talent."

The article also states that Niggli had been "a resident of Chapel Hill for 20 years," apparently counting from the time she arrived in 1935.

The position she was offered at the University of Bristol was long-term. A 1955 article in the *San Antonio Express-News* titled "Teaching Job in Britain" (in the "Pot Pourri" column) is quoted in its entirety:

> San Antonio's Josephina Niggli, noted author and playwright, has just accepted a 3-year invitation by the Old Vic Theater School in Bristol, England to teach playwriting.
>
> Josephina and her mother, Mrs. G. Morgan Niggli, who have been making their home for the past few years at Chapel Hill, N.C., will leave Sept. 1 for England. They have sold their Chapel Hill home and spent last weekend here.

In addition to teaching playwriting in a college near Chapel Hill, Josephina has been writing another book—a historical novel of Mexico in the eighteenth century. It is about three-fourths finished and she is working hard to complete it before leaving here.

Lured by the greater limelight of teaching at the Old Vic and the excitement of living in London, Niggli left her new position. She sold the Chapel Hill home purchased after her father's death and embarked on a teaching position granted due to her prestige, but which also provided the opportunity to run her own student theater. On September 18, 1955, in a letter to the Greens, Niggli describes a smooth nonstop flight from New York to London, as well as the days of sightseeing and theatergoing upon their arrival. She talks about new plays, citing which ones she believes would go over well in New York, and closes by stating they will depart that week for Bristol. She asks Elizabeth to persuade Paul to "bring you over this year."

The Old Vic Theatre School in Bristol had been established by Laurence Olivier in 1946. After the war, the drama school sought new faculty of renown to further its mission to provide industry-led vocational training to prepare not only actors but also stage managers, carpenters, electricians, sound technicians, costumers, property designers, and directors. Its students worked not only in the theater, but also in radio, television, film, and recording studios. Several contemporary British movie actors have received their acting training at the Old Vic. Niggli was qualified to teach in several areas, and likely found it gratifying to be recognized for her diverse experience. But for unknown reasons, she did not remain in England for three years. Illness, or a desire to return to the United States could have been a factor, or her contract may not have been renewed. Further answers may lie in the archives of the Old Vic. No explanation has been found in U.S. newspaper articles.

By 1956, Niggli was again seeking work in North Carolina.

The Eternal Pursuit of a Teaching Job

According to accounts since the late 1950s, Niggli began her teaching career at Western Carolina College (now University) in Cullowhee, near the Tennessee border, in 1956, but it is probable the position was temporary or part-time at first. The notice released by that institution following her death states that she had taught at WCU for "nearly 18 years." Since she retired in 1975, Niggli began a full-time position there in 1958. During the late 1950s, the university recognized the need for a theater and a director of drama, and likely took advantage of the opportunity to hire someone of renown already locally available. This remote and small college (as compared to other campuses in the system) would have been unable to attract an equally recognized figure. Niggli was available and ready, and possessed recent experience at the prestigious Old Vic School. She would be an excellent candidate for the teaching directorship.

It did not occur immediately. Niggli therefore sought other permanent positions and found one in Texas. In letters left behind, it is apparent she was offered a position at the University of Texas, Austin in 1957. She even relocated to this job before she received the permanent offer from WCU. In a letter to Paul Green on May 6, 1957, from Cullowhee, Niggli states:

> Someone may have told you that Bob Schenkkan [a former Playmaker] telephoned me from Austin and made the proposition *so* attractive that I agreed to go down and spear some T.V. giants with him. I'm to head up the Script Department, and it sounds as though it will be quite interesting, although I do hate to get out of teaching. Mamma and I are driving down the end of the month to rent a house and get everything set for the July exodus.

Niggli's letter continues with comments on a mutual friend who has left Texas, then commendatory comments on a graduate from the University of Bristol, recommending him for a position as stage manager with Green. Niggli concludes by discussing her work at WCU during the previous academic year: "This year has been very successful, Paul, so successful that in many ways I hate to go away and leave the profits to be reaped by someone else. Dr. Bird, the president, bless him, said that if they didn't treat me right at Texas, I was to turn right around and come winging back like a little bird, and that's an awfully nice secure feeling." (Could she have made the pun on his name on purpose?)

A year after her return from England, Niggli was now preparing to move to Austin, Texas. She had accepted an offer, but she worried about her ability to do professional writing, according to a series of letters (in her WCU archives) between herself and the director of a writing correspondence school, the Maren Elwood College, Professional Training for Writers, in Hollywood, California. The first letter reveals a certain lack of self-confidence in terms of her "professional" ability, but also a perfectionist attitude, a desire to be fully prepared as a teacher. The first letter is dated April 28, 1957:

> I have a serious problem and would greatly appreciate your advice.
>
> In 1942 I took the CBS course in Radio Production, offered at that time by N.Y.U., which included two writing courses, one in the Radio Play and one in Documentary. During the war I worked for NBC International, doing radio propaganda scripts in Spanish (I happen to be bilingual) to Latin America. This is the full extent of my "formal" writing training, because the playwriting courses given at the University of North Carolina, where I took my M.A., could hardly be called professional.
>
> Nevertheless, I managed to write two books, *Mexican Village* and *Step Down, Elder Brother*. The former, published in 1945, is used by most universities in teaching Latin American studies; and the latter (1948) [*sic*] was a Book-of-the-Month Club choice. My one-act plays, which are in an anthology called *Mexican Folk Plays* are produced both in this country and England.
>
> All of this work, however, deals with Mexican material. My short stories were not successful because magazines, as you well know, insist on U.S. heroes.
>
> My agency, MCA, Ltd., and my publisher, Rinehart, have been most patient with me, especially since, for personal reasons, I have done almost no writing since 1949, devoting most of my time to teaching. At present I am head of the Drama Department at Western Carolina College.
>
> This month Texas University asked me to head up their script department in Educational Radio and T.V., the job beginning August first. While supervising the work of others, this

will also include a certain amount of original work by me. It's
a wonderful job with a wonderful salary, but I have never done
one line of T.V. writing in my life! [This seems odd because of
her experience in Hollywood.]

Now I have given this problem a great deal of thought. Since
I have accumulated 8 years of rust I thought it best to start at the
bottom. My solution, which may not be a good one—and for
that I would appreciate your advice—is as follows: Take Fiction
Fundamentals, Psychology of Learning and Directed Writing
together, beginning now. This would polish my rust.

After moving to Austin in late July, start the T.V. course, as I
will have a certain amount of additional free time due to the late
September opening of the University. When the three original
courses are finished, then add on Writing for Radio.

Niggli encloses payment for the three courses, again asking for Maren
Elwood's assessment. The director responded on May 6, 1957, with the
following first paragraph: "Thank you for your most interesting letter just
received. I did not see your first letter of inquiry because all requests for
information are handled by our registrar. On my part I am quite familiar
with your books, especially *Mexican Village*. This I enjoyed to the full."
Elwood then goes on to state that the courses Niggli has selected would
be "far too elementary for you," therefore she is re-registering Niggli in
two courses that will meet her specific needs: Advanced Fiction and TV
Writing (and enclosing first lectures for each). Elwood agrees that these
should then be followed by Directed Writing, and states that the time
for each course is approximately a year, "but without doubt you will not
require that long."

Most surprising in the initial letters is that Niggli does not mention
her work in Hollywood, even if only on her own film, nor does Elwood
bring it up. Niggli's insecurity about her experience is surprising, but
perhaps it is logical for a woman in this era. Niggli responds to Elwood
within days, stating that she has

a rather personal problem which I did not bother to mention in
my last letter to you. I see now, that I was wrong. I should have.

When I was a young kid, starting out as a writer, I had a

shining goal. I was going to present Mexico and the Mexicans as they had never before been presented. Well, I did. I made big time. I even made M.G.M. and Book of the Month. You see, I reached my goal and passed it.

Then I decided I would try the American fiction market, and I ran head on into a very interesting obstacle. I couldn't write about Americans. Their psychology completely baffled me.

Niggli further states that she does not read popular works, only technical books on playwriting, classical plays, technical photography magazines, and her "regular" reading of Shakespeare and the Bible. Her only exceptions are detective novels, which she devours. She then states,

You see, Miss Elwood, I don't have to write for a living. M.G.M. took care of my income, and I make a very good salary in my job, and I'll be making even more at the University of Texas. I write because I can't help writing. And since yesterday I've come to the conclusion that it's just plain foolish tieing [sic] myself down to something I'm simply not interested in: the average short story.

Now, keeping in mind the point that creating an American character is a real problem to me, do you think I'd be better off in Advanced Fiction—or could I exchange it for "The Detective and the Mystery Story"? You've delt [sic] with all sorts of writers. I've only delt [sic] with me. And you know your own courses.

Niggli appears to have used her correspondence with Elwood to self-analyze her midlife juncture. On May 13, Elwood replies (amazingly, two days after the date on Niggli's letter) that her advice is for Niggli to stay with the courses that she previously prescribed, that the Advanced Fiction course is helpful for any genre of writing, in terms of mechanics. She offers nurturing: "With your success in the past I am confident you can mount this hurdle and believe it can be accomplished best by the work entailed in this Advanced Fiction course," and concludes that "working with you is going to be fascinating."

This correspondence includes no further letters of Elwood's, but two additional letters to her from Niggli, who responds to other questions by Elwood. She discusses detective writing, stating that she doesn't "particularly care to write like" a person Elwood cites. "Unfortunately, like Tom Wolfe, she lacked that extra thing that playwrights need. I suppose you'd call it a sense of the stage. Ironic, isn't it? If we could only have traded talents." Now she begins to sound more like the confident Niggli. In terms of detectivesque narrative, Niggli says she likes the way "men think," and her favorite "detective story writer is Dashiell Hammett. However there is one woman whom I like very much indeed, but at the moment I simply can't remember her name. It's Dorothy something. She wrote "The So Blue Marble," "The Fallen Sparrow," and "The Body on the Beach."

Niggli's final letter to Elwood is dated July 13 (her forty-seventh birthday), indicating a new permanent address of 2506 Inwood Place in Austin, although she says she will not leave Cullowhee until July 23.

> A few weeks ago I went down to Texas to discuss the new job, and it was definitely settled that I was to teach Radio Writing, classes to begin in late September. As I wrote you before, I took a class in 1942 with Charlie Jackson, and worked at NBC International during the war. However, I've had absolutely nothing to do with Radio since then.
>
> My feeling about the courses I'm taking now is this: I shall probably teach Television Writing in Spring Semester, but the Advanced Fiction is purely a private affair, for my pleasure only. After giving the matter a good deal of thought, I've decided the best thing for me to do is shelve the Advanced Fiction for a little while, and start in as soon as possible on the Radio Course. Consequently, I'm enclosing a check for the amount listed in your catalogue, hoping that this plan will meet with your approval. If the Radio course is nearly as good as the T.V., it will be what my students call a "Real whopper!"
>
> Yesterday I mailed Assignment VI for T.V. The two remaining Lectures have no assignments, and I'm glad to have this small hiatus at this time since the end of my Summer School Course plus the long moving treck [sic] to Texas is going to keep me busy until after August 1.

Nothing further is stated (in correspondence left behind by Niggli) to indicate why she did not remain at UT-Austin. Despite the greater prestige of the University of Texas, and the likelihood Niggli would have received a higher salary, she instead chose to return to North Carolina, taking the president up on the offer to "fly" home. The professional insecurity she reveals in these letters could stem from her awareness of middle age, a concern for where she would spend the rest of her time, and the many years of job-hopping without a stable position. Obviously she did not require an income, since she declared, "I write because I can't help writing," but she felt the need to write for old-fashioned theater more than the desire to be involved in the new entertainment media.

Returning Home

A writer's conference was held in August at the WCU campus, and Niggli was indicated as a member "of the college English faculty" (May 1958, the *Asheville Citizen-Times*, dateline "Cullowhee"). She obviously planned this from Texas or returned early. Niggli had participated in similar workshops in recent years; she is quoted, "In planning this conference at WCU, we thought that writers could benefit from a two-weeks [*sic*] study in a delightful resort area." The session would include recreational activities and entertainment as well as writing practice.

Niggli would remain at this institution up to her retirement in 1975. It was a place considerably different from the region of her birth and upbringing—northern Mexico with its dry climate and desert environment—but somewhat similar to Texas in humidity, and familiar in terms of North Carolina terrain. The western region of North Carolina is a feast of green and blue layers upon layers of mountains, all thickly covered with trees. Extensive fields of wildflowers bloom during most of the year—some intensely yellow, others mixtures of pink, purple, and white—laying a carpet toward the mountain range. The magnificent Blue Ridge and other highways gently rise and fall as they wind through this part of the state, with frequent signs announcing cutoffs to waterfalls, lakes, and caves. In a letter to Elizabeth Green in 1959, Niggli states the following: "The other day I had to drive over to Asheville, and it suddenly struck me that Paul probably thinks we have the old-fashioned, two lane roads with a curve every quarter mile. My goodness, no! We're tourist country, so we've got a swanky new highway, at the narrowest three lanes, and everyone counts the 60 miles to Asheville as an hour and a quarter and you can't do better than that on flat land. I admit the road to Cherokee is full of twists, but the road forks at Waynesville, and for us you follow 23A right into Sylva. We've got plenty of room to put you up, and it's only 16 miles from here to Cherokee and then right straight across to Knoxville or however it is that Paul wants to go. We'd certainly love to have both of you." (Niggli's mother moved with her to Cullowhee, where she would continue in her daughter's company until her death in 1968.)

In the furthest western reaches of the state of North Carolina, Cullowhee's name is derived from a Native American word meaning "where the bird lands" (hence the president's statement to her?). An hour's drive from the historic and picturesque Asheville to its north, it is closer to the Cherokee Reservation on the southwestern border of the state, in the lowlands of the Great Smoky Mountains National Park. Known as the place of origin of those who embarked on the Trail of Tears, the Cherokee Reservation comprises 56,000 acres (originally 135,000 square miles covering parts of what are now eight states). The small town of Cherokee and its surrounding recreation area sit in the heart of the reservation. After the Blue Ridge Parkway was built in the 1940s, the Cherokees began encouraging tourism. A mountainside theater was built in Cherokee by a Carolina Playmakers alumnus, and was inaugurated in 1950 with the now well-known outdoor drama "Unto These Hills." There is no record at WCU of any of Niggli's plays being performed there, but her 1964 novel is dedicated to the parishioners of Our Lady of Guadalupe Catholic Church in Cherokee, so she was likely familiar with the church. Cherokee today houses an extensive museum, located across the street from the theater, that includes a replica of a seven-sided council house and typical homes as they were 250 years ago.

The town of Cullowhee consists of a minuscule strip with one restaurant, three small cafés (two closed during the summer), and homes scattered through the hills on one side, with modular homes and storage units on the opposite side near the bank of the Cullowhee River. The nearly 8,000-student WCU campus (experiencing its largest freshman class in 2004) is somewhat larger than it was at Niggli's arrival, but it still gives the impression of a small college. Its grounds hug a hill of private properties where Niggli had her small home. The house she owned and lived in is not marked, and nothing remains in her name but the Drama School Theater at WCU, to which she assigned scholarships, supported by future publishing royalties, upon her death. Founded in 1889, WCU became a state college in 1903, and would surely lack much recognition without the fame Niggli brought to the small institution. During her tenure there, she was humble in terms of her needs or her clout. Only a letter in the late 1970s hints at some frustration over the administration's promise of student-assistant help that had not materialized.

Niggli may not have purposefully selected this remote location to spend the last twenty-six years of her life, but North Carolina had always chosen Niggli, from her acceptance to the renowned Playmakers company, to the state's prestigious award for her first novel, to the constant support and companionship of friends and colleagues in the university system. She loved teaching—a profession for which she exhibited the same passion as for writing and revealing Mexico to English-language readers—and eventually found her permanent job at WCU. She continued as always, however, to remain in contact with Texas.

With her job secured, Niggli continued to travel to "the Hill," involve herself in regional committees, and conserve her lifelong friendships. In 1958 she attended the forty-year reunion dinner of the Carolina Playmakers, hosted at the Chapel Hill Country Club. It included some one hundred Playmakers and provided a tribute to Thomas Wolfe. Four years later, in 1962, another dinner was held in Chapel Hill to celebrate the fortieth anniversary of the Carolina Dramatic Association. Niggli had been elected president of this association in May 1960, and was completing her second year in that post. Together with several others, she was selected for special recognition.

Niggli stayed busy. While teaching, Niggli held memberships in the American Theatre Association, the American Educational Theatre Association, the Dramatists Guild, the Authors Guild, the Photographic Society of America, the Carolina Dramatic Association (for which she served one term as president), and the Appalachian Writer's group, which now sponsors a scholarship in her name.

An Unpublished Novel

Her writing also took on renewed impetus. Niggli's archives at WCU's Hunter Library contain numerous notes and manuscripts, some of which are drafts from earlier published works, including her manuscript revising *Pointers*. Many others are unpublished works that appear to date from the 1950s and 1960s. Niggli made extensive notes on historic periods and scientific facts connecting to specific eras. In several cases, she reworked what she had already created as a play into a narrative account. Most drafts are accompanied by character charts and notes, plot formulas and plot equations, and information for specific scenes.

An unfinished novel bears the title of *Green Grow the Rushes* (it is currently posted on the Alexander Street Press *Latino Literature* database), but close review indicates a plot similar to both her novel *Step Down, Elder Brother* and the three-act play *Singing Valley*. A housemaid named Doña Perfecta "flutters" around fixing up the household for the return home to Monterrey of the family's daughter, Rita, who has been in New York City. The elder brother travels to Mexico City on business, and will exert the authority in the household, as Rita's father had fallen in battle in 1915. A much more interesting plot is found in a novel of more than a hundred pages, extensively revised (there are various versions), with accompanying notes in one folder that indicate it was rejected by a publisher. There is also an extensive outline of scenes, indicating that she may also have drafted this plot as a screenplay.

Titled *Beat the Drum Slowly*, the novel features and contrasts two strong male characters, Ramón the Fair and Ramón the Dark—"name twins," as Niggli calls them (conjuring the indigenous idea of the *nahual*). They are in love with the same woman, Pola. It is an interesting play on good and evil in terms of human nature: the lighter-skinned character, of the upper class, possesses evil intentions, while the second is of Indian heritage (adopted when a young orphan by "the Fair's" family) and of noble intentions. But they will later change roles in terms of doing good or bad deeds, or at least Pola will suspect the wrong person.

The setting is a small village called Botón de Ancla, a fictional location in northern Mexico. Niggli refers to this novel as "Pola" in a letter dated February 26, 1981—"an, as yet, unpublished book"—but it is titled "Beat the Drum Slowly" in her manuscripts. It appears to be the same novel referred to in earlier biographical entries as "Red Amapola." A portion of a letter by her, located in a box of old manuscripts, and dated December 1952 in Chapel Hill, states: "I've got several ideas butting around in my head. I want to move [the plot] out of Monterrey into Botón de Ancla. Had idea of beginning it with bus stopping there, man gets off, finds out there is a town beyond the highway . . . perhaps cashier in restaurant would be involved in one of the episodes." She frequently thinks in terms of scenes, rather than chapters. Her stranger to the area is going to be from Mexico City. Niggli's idea may have simmered and changed throughout the 1950s and 1960s.

The project includes outlines, character symbolism and descriptions, and charts—with headings for cultural, sociological, and economic factors. "The Dark" is defined thus: "Created by the Creoles, he cannot be bound by them. He is the middle-class man who evolves of his own strength, because he can find no place: too educated for his own class, too low blood for the Creoles." Doña Brígida (the aunt and protector of the young woman in the novel) is defined as "Society, the decadence of the Etiquette." "The Fair" is "the worst of the Creoles. He only wants his own way and will try to destroy anyone who wants to prevent his getting it." There is a character defined as "the Commentator," who surveys history and Mexico's need for change. The very first item on this list is "Santa Fé, the dark side of Communism. Rhodalcanot [sic] is the Utopian Communism. Other students: the young intellectuals who have an idealistic view of the future but no practicality." Another character is defined as "violence," others as people who cannot change (with the times), "the past," those who are rebellious with no philosophy, and those who sway in the wind. Pola is defined as "Mexico itself. She passes through the pattern of the Creole, but when she comes into the peasant world, she can't accept it, and so, she, too, goes the way of the Middle Class. She can only find happiness with the Middle Class man."

Comprising two sections, labeled "Part I" and "Part II," the first begins in Paris in 1875, with an epigraph from a source by Joaquín Santos titled "Mexican Life at the End of the Nineteenth Century" states: "Creoles, of pure Spanish blood born in Mexico, despising the wealthy Mestizos, the 'mixed men,' half Spanish and half Indian, and especially the pure blooded Indians, fled to Europe after Maximilian's execution in 1867. Mexican Paris was finally large enough to constitute a small world of its own, as rigidly bound by rules of etiquette as any imperial court."

Her mother having died, Pola has been educated in Paris from age eleven. She returns home as the intended bride of Ramón the Fair, but falls in love instead with Ramón the Dark, becomes pregnant, and—after the mysterious death of Ramón the Dark—is forced to marry the Fair. Or, it occurs the other way around, in a different draft. Niggli appears to be working on capturing this irony between the two kinds of Mexicans, with changes of perception and twists within her novel. Part II begins on page 118, in a region not unlike her home village near Monterrey, with an excellent description of the Fair's inner thinking, as well as the countryside and the small town, as he rides his horse. The novel relates the stories of various other characters.

Fragments from both parts are included in the selections here. This manuscript corresponds to Niggli's interest in creating a novel based in the century before the Revolution. It would have worked well to publish such a novel during the 1940s or early 1950s, but after that, times were different. In the United States, at least, after the Second World War and with a Civil Rights Movement brewing, there was no longer any interest in a previous century and social revolutions to overthrow colonial institutions.

Obviously, Niggli's forte was historical fiction, incorporating mystery and suspense, and consistently with the intention of teaching English-language readers about the rich Mexican traditions. She prepared extensive notes and research on what she dubbed a series of books on Mexico's history, separating notes by decades between 1780 and 1945 based on her research. For example, in 1800, "Napoleonic victories cause upheaval" is under a "Sociological" category, while "Newspapers appear" is under a "Cultural" column. She also scratched out an "idea for a book [about] a family hotel in a border town in 1866 on land that the river surrounds so that one day it is American, the next Mexican. [The] family has been there since 1827." Her idea analysis continued, describing several characters' origins, including Irish, German-Prussian, Spanish, and Mexican. The setting and the era correspond loosely to her father's relatives, one of which moved to Eagle Pass right after the Civil War and married a hotelier.

Niggli never composed autobiographical accounts, nor did she write about the famous personalities she knew during her life. The few items of private correspondence in the WCU Hunter Library collection consist only of the series of letters between Niggli and Elwood, and one or two letters to acquaintances. These may have been overlooked in the process of destroying her personal correspondence (as required in her mother's will, in case her mother survived her, which did not occur). An extensive series of letters, principally to Paul Green, are archived at UNC-Chapel Hill.

A Miracle for Mexico

At Western Carolina, Niggli had shaken off "the rust" and recovered her creative-writing skills as well as a drive to publish. She wrote plays (although her own took back seat to her students' work), a few by request, mostly skits or commemoratory pieces for WCU, but she also created a major historical play that was produced in San Antonio.

Only a few years into her job at WCU, a new novel came to fruition, a rich cultural representation that in an earlier outline and short draft had been called "The Grace of Guadalupe." It became Niggli's third and final novel, but A Miracle for Mexico has always been erroneously cataloged as a children's book.[2] This book represents the first creative work in English on Mexico's patron saint and significant cultural symbol, the Virgen de Guadalupe. Even scholarship in English on the dark Virgin originating in this hemisphere has principally occurred since the 1990s, although several studies were published in Mexico during the 1930s and 1940s, when Niggli traveled frequently to Mexico. The idea may have occurred to her in late 1955, while she was in England. In this year, a Mexican archbishop announced that he was commissioning a scientific study to determine whether the Virgin's eyes—on the early sixteenth-century tilma (cloak) painting—truly reflect human figures (the Indian Juan Diego and others), as a scholar interpreted in the early twentieth century. Or perhaps it occurred to her in 1948, when an engraving of the Virgin's image by Flemish artist Samuel Stradanus—dated 1615—was donated to the Metropolitan Museum of Art in New York City (this was about the time of the fanfare around her second novel). On the other hand, the idea of writing about this hemisphere's Virgin could have rested with Niggli for some time, for Guadalupe has much to do with mestizo consciousness.

In Niggli's earlier work, she portrayed the importance of Guadalupe in her characters' lives—as the character's namesake in *Singing Valley*, or the shadowy idea of her in the wife character in her story "A Visitor for Domínguez."

While the Dark or Indian Virgin's miraculous appearance occurs only ten years after the Spanish conquest of Tenochtitlan (now Mexico City) in 1531, the occurrence remained shrouded in silence for well over a hundred years. The first known written account, *Imagen de la Virgen María, Madre de Diós de Guadalupe, Milagrosamente aparecida en la ciudad de México*, was published in 1648 by a Catholic priest, Miguel Sánchez. Almost simultaneously (six months later, in 1649) a separate account, *Huey tlamahuiçoltica*, was published by another criollo priest, Luis Laso de la Vega, at the time the vicar of the Ermita of Guadalupe. While Sánchez's account was written in Spanish, the second chronicle is in the Náhuatl language and consists of six parts, some of which probably document oral history. The first section, *Nican mopohua* ("Here it is told"), being the account of her apparitions, became the commonly known *official* story of Guadalupe's apparition in more recent years. At first, Sánchez's chronicle was highly influential, and the Church tried to discredit the Náhuatl account. The latter, however, was supported by the ruling-class *criollos* later on, when their fervor for independence increased. This account became their link to an autochthonous (native) cultural patriotism.

The fourth section of Laso de la Vega's *Huey tlamahuiçoltica* is a collection of miracle stories, titled *Nican motecpana*, and these have been related in various published sermons. The fifth section is a biography of Juan Diego, the Indian who became the Holy Virgin's emissary. Sánchez's account launched the long process whereby Guadalupe was fused with Mexican identity, but Laso de la Vega's account strove to connect the Nahua Indians of Mexico to the new Catholic practice. She appeared on the hill called Tepeyac on the outskirts of Mexico City, where an ancient goddess who spoke Náhuatl had been venerated. Modern scholars see her as a mixture of the traits of several female deities, including Coatlicue (the supreme goddess), Coatlalopeuh (for phonetic similarity), and Tonantzín (for her role as mediator and mother). The Indian Juan Diego knew only basic Spanish, therefore he required an interpreter in order to deliver her message to the bishop. The fact that she appeared to him, asking for a temple to be built to honor her, demonstrated the importance of "Indian" continuation and philosophy in the Mexican central valley.

Her miraculous apparition was finally proven and demonstrated by her image stamped on Juan Diego's tilma, provided upon his third visit to the bishop in Mexico City, but it was not an era in which the news was easily promulgated. It was more than a hundred years later when the two accounts were published, and not until the mid-eighteenth century that Guadalupe's image as a "native" patron saint had extended to all of New Spain (Mexico) and Guatemala. Laso de la Vega's account, which some modern scholars think could have been written by several scribes (as was common with indigenous pre-Hispanic books), has been considered the official source since Independence by contemporary Mexican scholarship. The *Nican mopohua* portion is said to have been the work of an Indian chronicler named Antonio Valeriano (1520–1605), which account had been lost and was retrieved and restored by Laso de la Vega. All scholars quickly make note of the fact that the text in Náhuatl is not in any way a translation of Sánchez's chronicle in Spanish; its style is strikingly different, and it varies somewhat in details (Poole 112). Thus, two different scribes were pulling the information together in the same time period, likely because dialogue was occurring about "the miracle."

Although it could be viewed as a ploy of Catholic maneuvering, the Dark Virgin's existence is of high cultural and political importance that has only increased over time. Her appearance to Indians now ruled by Spaniards signified the continuation of native philosophy and religious beliefs despite the insertion of European traditions. To others, her arrival blessed the mixed race that had resulted after the conquest. Niggli's portrayal of the Mexican representation of the Mother of God ties to her own Catholic faith, but also to her work as a cultural historian; she wanted to depict the origin of Mexico's emblem for its mestizo society.

History behind the Image

The espousing of Guadalupe as Mother of all Mexicans coincides with the late colonial era and an increased impetus to wrest itself free from Spain as the monarchy tightened its grip. She first came to represent resistance to efforts by the Spanish to maintain a distinction between *pure* European-derived citizens and people of mixed races, with full-blooded Indians at the bottom of the ranking. As late as 1776, a law on the sanction of marriages allowed parents and civil officials to prevent the legal union of a colonial citizen with mulatos, Blacks, *coyotes* (of Indian, Black, and Spanish mixture), or Indian persons, thus ensuring the maintenance of purity in Spanish blood (Carrera 118).

The Creoles, or *criollos*, were of untainted Spanish heritage, but because they were born in this hemisphere, they were ranked below those Spaniards born in Europe. Creoles throughout Latin America sought freedom from the grip of the Spanish monarchy from the mid- to late eighteenth century. The Virgin of Guadalupe was a useful emblem in rallying their cause. And yet, upon obtaining independence in 1821, a similar caste system was perpetuated. Freedom was only for the criollos. Ranking below them were the mestizos—Spaniard mixed with Indian. Guadalupe again became the rallying emblem of the mestizo in the Mexican Revolution a century later. Now she truly represented those of dark skin like hers. Mexico was a nation of mestizos and Indians in rebellion against the elite class. Guadalupe's image restores Indian heritage and cultural philosophy. Thus Niggli saw this as an important aspect of the Mexican story.

Contemporary cultural analysis demonstrates that the propagation of Guadalupe's symbol is a much more complicated issue than that of religious motivation. As noted by Rebolledo (1995), metaphysical concepts of death and resurrection were interpreted through the supreme Náhuatl female deity, Coatlicue, who consumed, cleaned, and purified negative energy from a site within a hill or cave. She is both goddess and monster, thus the hill of "Guadalupe's" appearance (as one facet of the multidimensional goddess) is cited as the "hill of death" in Niggli's novel. But she is connected to nature, where she is transformed and provides caves that shelter, as well as fertile soil and water that secure life for her subjects (Rebolledo 50). In native Mesoamerican thought, caves represent a spiritual center; they were sacred gathering places before temples were built. Some rooms inside temples, constructed later on, emulated caves, with their interior rooms, corridors, and basements.

A temple on the Tepeyac hill, dedicated to the goddess Tonantzín (which means mother-figure), had been demolished by the Spaniards. While Niggli does not cite any goddess names, she interprets in English the Indian terms of affection and respect as "my lady," and "my child" (also using the Náhuatl word *xocoyote* for "dear one") when the Virgin and Juan Diego are in conversation. Toward the end of her novel, Niggli's principal character Martín recalls a storyteller's account that on the day a rose grew on a cactus, the hill would be freed of its curse of death.[3] He is the first to spot such a rose, on a cactus at the edge of the hill. Later the Juan Diego character receives a bouquet of roses from the Virgin. He places these in his cloak to transport them to the Bishop's Palace; the roses paint or stamp the Virgin's image on his tilma, providing miraculous proof that Juan Diego has spoken with her.

Niggli's creation demonstrates that she conducted substantial research, but she also likely based her story on popular accounts from the early twentieth century. Guadalupe is a cultural phenomenon in Mexico; she was, after all, the inspiration and victor of the Revolution. Mexican scholarship on the original Náhuatl version of this account surged shortly after the Revolution. During a stint in exile as a result of the *Cristero* religious conflicts in Mexico in the 1920s, Jesuit historian Mariano Cuevas visited the New York Public Library and came upon a manuscript in Spanish (which had belonged to the Jesuits), expounding the Guadalupe tradition and stated to be a translation from the Náhuatl source. After the Jesuits' expulsion from New Spain in 1767, that document had passed to a Fernando Ramírez, whose secretary had made the translation into Spanish. When Cuevas returned to Mexico City, he found the original text in Náhuatl in the Biblioteca Nacional de México, in a volume of sermons for saints' days, *Santoral en mexicano* (Poole 40). This original is called *Inin huey tlamahuiçoltzin* ("This is the great miracle"), a phrase that is very similar to the title Niggli selected.[4]

Cuevas published an extensive essay on his research in 1924, and a book titled *Album histórico Guadalupano del IV centenario* in 1930. He surmised that the document he had located was a copy of an earlier account, but that does not seem as likely to contemporary scholars, since the *Inin huey tlamahuiçoltzin* dates from the eighteenth century; it is instead considered a particular Jesuit sermon to enhance devotion to Guadalupe. While there is significant similarity between the account found by Cuevas and Laso de la Vega's *Huey tlamahuiçoltica*, the sermon does not claim divine favoritism toward the Indians (Poole 43). The process of study and comparison of accounts, however, opened dialogue in the new society and created a basis for foundational Mexican thought.

Thus Niggli proves to be, as usual, the consummate cultural historian. This novel joins her constant theme of mestizo/Mexican heritage. Toward the end of *A Miracle for Mexico*, her mestizo character is called "the first of a new race," and when the clock strikes midnight (while various characters continue contemplating the portrait of the Virgin on Juan Diego's tilma), the narrative states that "there was no time at all between that midnight and the midnight of September 15, 1810," when the priest Hidalgo raised the banner of Guadalupe in the cry for independence.

Mexican linguist Primo Feliciano Velázquez published *La aparición de Santa María de Guadalupe* in 1931, and noted Náhuatl scholar Ángel María Garibay surveyed and analyzed, to a considerable extent, sources in journal articles and in a series of books published in 1945, *Temas guadalupanos*, and in his *Historia de la literatura Náhuatl* in 1961. It should be noted that his extensive essay in English on Guadalupe was published in 1967 in the *New Catholic Encyclopedia*, three years *after* Niggli's novel.

In Niggli's "Note to the Reader" in the end pages of *A Miracle for Mexico*, she explains her "logic" in creating dialogue for the characters. Surmising that Juan Diego, a farmer and an older man, would not have learned to speak Spanish in the years since Cortés's arrival, the holy woman must have addressed him in his own language. Niggli says that "all of the poetic images are based on those used in pre-Conquest poetry." Thus, all legends and stories related by characters in this novel arise from her own study of ancient poetry and popular tales. Niggli concludes that it is "a pity that Juan Diego could neither read nor write. Otherwise we might have had his own version."

Niggli's intention in her story of Mexico's "miracle" is more than to relate the wonder of the Virgin's apparition. It is also to describe the social interactions between the castes created during the early colonial years, the value of one people's origin in contrast to that of the new people. Her historical and fictional characters include Spaniards, criollos, mestizos, a few high-ranking native or Indian (Mayab and Aztec) people, and various others who are mulatos and Indians.

Niggli's Version

Among the various historical characters, Niggli inserts a fictional figure as her model "first" mestizo. His role is to serve as a mediator, for the reader, between Spanish and Indian cultures. Martín Aguilar is the progeny of a Spanish officer and a woman of Indian royal class from Veracruz (she is different from the Aztec royalty residing in Mexico City, but Martín wryly states that to the Spaniards all Indians look alike). As a member of high social rank on his father's side, Martín attends school, instructed by Jesuits, and since he has recently become an orphan (and his inheritance is being debated because of his mother's Indian race), he is a ward of Bishop Zumárraga's household. He thus works for the bishop, often summoned to his office to interpret, since Martín is fluent in Náhuatl. During class or in the Bishop's Palace, he is addressed as "Don Martín," due to his Spanish heritage. But on the street he is addressed as "Mestizo Martín," thus signaling his status in the strict Spanish caste system. The Indians are ignored or treated as slaves on the public street. African freedmen are addressed simply as Mulato or Zambo (a mixture of Indian and African). When Martín goes to the personal home of Pedro de Moctezuma (the former emperor's grandson), he is addressed in terms of Indian honor and royalty, his name pronounced with the "tzin" ending common in Náhuatl language, or "Martintzin."

The women characters are strong figures, whether the main character's aunt, a young girl who is his betrothed, the Virgin mother herself, or the classic Mexican figure la Malinche—who is not called by that nickname, and is depicted as an intelligent, thoughtful being. When Martín visits Juan Jaramillo's home for an important meeting, Martín quickly becomes a subject of interest to Jaramillo's wife. She is introduced as "the famous Doña Marina," and arrives dressed in a gown of Moorish silk and floating veils woven in Algiers. She addresses him in Náhuatl, later changing to a child-version code of Náhuatl when some of her dialogue is understood by the Spaniards. In this chapter, Jaramillo states that he and Marina have not been able to bear children, which is surprising because Mexican cultural lore asserts that she did. Marina is declared to be from Tabasco, a state on the gulf coast bordering the Yucatán peninsula, Martín's maternal family's place of origin.[5] Described as possessing understanding superior to that of the Spaniards around her, Marina already perceives the path Martín will follow. Due to his "investigation" of the apparition of the Lady on Tepeyac, assigned by the bishop, Martín will facilitate Juan Diego's acceptance and the unveiling of the Lady's image. The last line of the novel states: "By the Grace of Guadalupe, here was, indeed, a world where the Mestizos could stand tall."

Niggli created a believable sixteenth-century society that is seldom represented in novels. The young main character is betrothed or promised in marriage, a tradition that must be upheld unless the young woman herself relinquishes him from the promise. During his soul-searching process, his interviews of others, and his travels as the bishop's employee, Martín is careful never to do anything that would bring shame to her or to himself. He is shown to be most respectful of those who are older, addressing them as "Grandfather" (Indian tradition for elders), "Lady" or "Damsel." The novel shows that Martín and his betrothed are treated like adults in Spanish society, while in Indian communities he is treated lovingly as a child. His actions and his resolve, however, are those of a young man forced to make decisions and protect others as he embarks on his mission.

Niggli's fictional Martín is a logical character, as historical records state that after Juan Diego's second visit to the Bishop's Palace, the bishop sent one of his employees to follow Juan Diego and investigate him. But it is because of this thirteen-year-old character that Niggli's novel was unfortunately labeled a "juvenile" by her publisher, the New York Graphic Society, which was launching a new line of children's books at that time. This tag unwittingly diminished Niggli's record, as her book would forever be relegated to the children's section in libraries, and to this date her third novel goes unrecognized.

Even the very favorable reviews called attention to the fact that it should not be cited as a children's book. The *Chapel Hill Weekly* (April 26) states: "Although recommended for a teenage market, Josefina Niggli has not written 'down' in *A Miracle for Mexico*. This story should make fascinating reading for any person interested in Mexican history," and, "the Aztec names and some of the complicated political and religious history may be a bit difficult for young readers." The headline for a review in the *Catholic Herald Citizen* of Milwaukee, Wisconsin, states, "Intended for Youth, *A Miracle for Mexico* Draws Interest of Oldsters," and *The Rocky Mountain Telegram* (May 10) says it is "announced as a book for teenagers but will be even more interesting and attractive to adults who want to know more about Mexican history and culture." *The Dallas Morning News* (April 5) called it "a book for older boys and girls, a book that may very well be read by their elders, a book that does for the miracle of Guadalupe what has never been done before."

The Chapel Hill Weekly found the Martín character an effective "interpreter between the two races," and a "young devil's advocate as it befalls him to investigate the background of Juan Diego and the scenes of the miraculous appearance of the Blessed Virgin in an effort to decide if the miracle is a true one."

Lauding it as a "historical novel," the *New York Times Book Review* on July 12, 1964, remarked on the novel's excellent preparation, and its unsuitability for juveniles: "Martín is a royally drawn character, and the visitation which inspires him is skillfully developed as both miracle and cultural landmark important to an understanding of modern Mexico. Throughout, there is the natural imagery of Spanish Catholicism, Aztecan and Mayan cultures. But with its profuse detail, numerous characters and mysterious happenings, the unraveling of the story demands more persistence than many young readers will be able to sustain."

Political history in Niggli's novel is well depicted, exploring the tension of the first decade following Cortés's conquest of Mexico City and his drive for immediate expansion. Cortés was amassing great power and became the envy of other conquerors. As rumors and facts reached the royal court in Spain, and the Catholic Church raised concern over the conquerors' treatment of the indigenous population, Spanish King Carlos V sought to replace Cortés's rule in Mexico City and sent his lawyer, Nuño Guzmán de Beltrán, to head the new government and put a stop to anarchy that was growing in New Spain. Unfortunately, he further aggravated the situation upon his arrival in late 1528, unleashing even greater chaos and cruelty (see Verástique). Guzmán ransacked Indian temples searching for treasure, issued orders to sell all Indians into slavery, and exacted heavy tribute payments from local villages. He was just as ruthless with his fellow countrymen, confiscating *encomiendas* granted by Cortés, and inciting the Church leaders with his disregard for their authority and for his abuse of Indians. He was excommunicated from the Church in 1529, and asked to report to authorities in Mexico City. Instead, he proceeded to conquer Michoacán and build an army to improve his range of power, while continuing to commit atrocities. Bishop Zumárraga began building a case against Nuño Guzmán.

While Niggli does not relate this information, she captures the era accurately by creating a character called Guzmán the Cruel, who is intensely feared by the Indians, and whom Bishop Zumárraga wishes to stop. They hear of his exploits in the West and know he is on his way back to Mexico City. But by the end of the novel, his procession arrives at the moment when the Virgin's miraculous apparition is being substantiated, thus changing the course of history.

A Miracle for Mexico is an excellent mix of suspense and cultural history, and like *Step Down, Elder Brother*, constitutes some of Niggli's finest writing on Mexico. While the latter depicted northern Mexico caught in the crux between economic growth and the political strategizing of the post-Revolution, *A Miracle for Mexico* relates the making of one of Mexico's most important cultural images. Had this novel been published in the 1980s, no publisher would have labeled it "juvenile literature." Niggli's use of a mestizo boy as principal character is not that different from contemporary novels by Chicana or Latina women writers. Sandra Benítez's recent novel *The Weight of All Things* (2000) relates the story of the Salvadoran government's repression and persecution of its own people through a nine-year-old boy whose mother is killed during the funeral service for Archbishop Romero. Graciela Limón covers similar Salvadoran history, alternating the voice of a little girl, now a grown woman, with that of her son, a teenage boy preparing for the priesthood, in her novel *In Search of Bernabé* (1993). Sandra Cisneros's acclaimed first novel, *House on Mango Street* (1984), uses a girl to tell the story of a neighborhood, a culture, and a people. Chicana novelists Helena María Viramontes, Estela Portillo-Trambley, and Alicia Gaspar de Alba, as well as Chicano Luis Alberto Urrea, each have novels with child characters whose observations help them assess the events around them.

As in the novels cited above, Martín Aguilar represents an ethnic minority where those who are not of mixed race in their society often control their fate. This character awaits his inheritance, is promised in marriage to a *criolla*, dresses in Western attire, and gazes at the house that belonged to his father with longing. Even as he is grateful for the stories told by his Indian mother's sister and by a wise man on the street, he often corrects those around him who make statements he knows are considered "heresy" and "pagan" by the new, imposed Christianity. As the prototypical first *mestizo*, he is torn between the two worlds that are in the process of educating him. When asked what is his place in this society, he replies: "Half of both and half of neither . . . I am Mestizo, there is no place for me." In Niggli's 1980 interview with Paula Shirley, she calls herself a "half-way child," referring to those who are of both Mexico and the United States.

But by the end of the novel, Martín acknowledges that he must choose his own path, and not allow it to be chosen by those in power in his society. Thus the year 1531—a time of transition—is merged into the era of transition toward independence for the mestizo citizen. As the novel's review in the *Rocky Mountain Telegram* stated, "The Indians were in virtual slavery since they were not regarded by the ruling Spaniards as having souls. It was time for a miracle." And in the *Chapel Hill Weekly*: "To the Spaniards and Creoles in the New World, it is the fear of losing their heritage, of becoming little more than poverty-stricken wards of the state; to the Indians, it is the fear of even greater slavery than they have endured in the past. To the intelligentsia on both sides, it is the slow recognition that without the ready availability of the Indian slave labor, little can be torn from this strange new country in the way of wealth."

Niggli demonstrates that Indian thought was still prevalent, despite strong prohibitions. This is factually accurate, for during the first one hundred years, Indian and Spanish practices were continued side-by-side. By the next century, however, a greater influx of Spaniards tightened rules and prohibitions against Indian practices and freedoms. The preservation of Indian thought, and resistance to Western tradition, is of great cultural importance to the formation of a Mexican ethos. It is also significant that Martín is thirteen years old, for it means (now, in 1531) that he was born in 1518, shortly after Spanish arrival and before the conquest of Tenochtitlán in 1521. Niggli selected his age with impressive forethought. Her novel is as political as it is historical.

Niggli's third novel brings her writing career full circle, back to depicting the mestizo and Indian heritage that created Mexican philosophy and identity. Her first novel represented the Mexican peasant and his folklore (as in her comedies), the second explored the awakening of mestizo national heritage as a result of the success of the Revolution, and her third novel focuses on the instrument of its origin. No novel with this content had ever been published in English.

Despite the fact that she had not published for nearly twenty years, *A Miracle for Mexico* received numerous, very positive reviews. Carleton

Beals and other reviewers contacted by Niggli's publisher wrote letters commending both the fictional portrayal and the historical focus. She was pleased herself, evident in a Christmas letter addressed to Paul Green on December 18, 1964, where Niggli responds to his questions about her historical research for the text, and then mentions her work on a new historical pageant:

> Thanks so much for your nice letter about MIRACLE [*sic*]. I do hope you get to read the ending as I'm right proud of it. I know that it was a lot of fun to read. As for the history, that was a dictionary of dates, a map of Mexico in 1536, the documents on the Miracle, and all the rest was memory. After all, I've been specializing in Mexico for a lot of years.
>
> Right now I'm hard at work on LIGHTNING FROM THE EAST [*sic*], the play for the Texas State Historical Theatre at the San Jose Mission in San Antonio. It will run for about 4 weeks, beginning the middle of June. If you're in Canyon City then, I hope you get a chance to go down to see it. I know that I'm anxious to see your Canyon City job. I'll be in S.A. during rehearsals the early part of June, and even if your play hasn't opened, perhaps they'd let me see some rehearsals. I hear you're going to use a lot of the light and sound techniques you saw in Spain. I've got a gimmick in LIGHTNING that I'm real proud of . . . through a modern narrator (visible) the mission itself . . . or rather herself . . . that Queen of missions . . . tells the story. The main pay-off: no need to worry about language: Spanish, English, Indian, as the Mission remembers in English!
>
> Went to see you the last time I was at the Hill (October) but you and Elizabeth were probably off traveling someplace. Hope I have better luck in April. Much love to you both, from Mamma and me, Jo.

Active as ever with projects, traveling abroad, and spreading her time between Texas, North Carolina, and New York, Niggli again explored new horizons. At the time of the novel's release, the Western Carolinian school newspaper (February 28, 1964) stated that Niggli was headed to New York to spend the month of March "attending the

American Mime Theatre, [which is] comparatively new in the United States." The article said she would then go to England to do research for a new text on period styles in acting—"a subject which has never been written on in the U.S."—for the Holt, Rinehart Publishing Company. This research was likely to update and create her revised edition of *New Pointers on Playwriting*, to be published in 1967. In late July, she was home again; a special-events column in the *New York Times* states that Niggli is to be interviewed on radio station WYNC on the topic of the American Indian. She may have made contacts with members of the Cherokee Reservation, and had done research on Indians in Texas and California.

A Final Play

Early the following year, 1965, Niggli completed *Lightning from the East* and traveled to San Antonio in June. On the 25th she wrote to Paul Green (in Florida) from Texas, remarking on the coincidence that his *Sword and the Cross* play and hers have nearly the same opening date. She then describes two opening receptions she attended:

> One for a beer brawl party to celebrate the 100th anniversary of a local newspaper, and the other to the general public last night. Thanks to your very good suggestions I built my play to a good climax and it went very well indeed. The action swirls across three stages and has everything in it, from an Indian war dance to a procession of mourning women. I'm very proud of Little Bill [her student Shawn Smith who went on to a teaching career in theater] as he did a wonderful job of directing. Most of the comments I've heard is that it's the best play they've ever produced at the Mission.

On June 13, 1965, the *San Antonio Express-News* announced that the upcoming premiere, dramatizing "the exciting era in San Antonio's history when Mexicans were struggling for independence against the Spanish troops," would be directed by a member of the Carolina Playmakers. This period (1810–1821) is in fact seldom, if ever, depicted in U.S. cultural performances—especially in Texas, where Mexican history is only considered in terms of Santa Anna and the Alamo in 1836. Running over several weeks, Niggli's summer play was preceded by a "fiesta" each evening, a strolling event on the grounds of the San José Mission in San Antonio, with the attraction of a Mexican market and booths to purchase food and drink.

The San José Mission is the largest of the four missions in San Antonio (of which the Alamo is one), and is located south of town, not far from the Mission cemetery where Niggli is buried. While "Lightning from the East" is a phrase that conjures a biblical verse, Matthew 24:27, that the second coming of Christ would be as sudden as lightning and emerging out of dark clouds, Niggli appropriates the analogy to capture the sudden moment of opportunity for Mexico to wrest itself free from Spain (when Napoleon invaded Spanish soil). This historical moment is also captured in Niggli's early play *The Cry of Dolores*. The "East" is also the direction from which the Europeans arrived who had forever changed the Americas.

Lightning from the East opened on June 24, and was well received in several articles in the San Antonio newspapers. It is called both a historical pageant and a drama in various references. An article on Sunday, June 20 in the *San Antonio Light* states that the play involves suspense, drama, and excitement, with a cast drawn from Washington, D.C., New York, and North Carolina. Niggli is cited as a graduate of Incarnate Word, with plays performed in Europe and in Latin America. The article also states that her novel *A Miracle for Mexico* has received wide acclaim. The *Express-News* on June 20 calls it a "bestselling book," adding that she is an internationally recognized playwright. A photograph from the play, which ran in the *Light* on July 4, shows a group of women talking and laughing while washing clothes at the river's edge.

Once the play had run its course, Niggli returned to Cullowhee—and on July 19, she left "for my dear London to stay until September 8" [in a letter to Green on June 25]. "Next summer, if they decide not to repeat my play down here, I'll stay at home for a change, as I hope to go around the world year after next. But that's a long way ahead!"

While continuing to make travel plans, Niggli was probably not able to take that trip because of her mother's frailty and age. The following year at Christmas time, she wrote to Paul Green that they had spent August in Florida, and that she finally saw his play. Then she says: "Did a one-act playwriting text for the Writer this Fall and the editorial report is very warm. This started me writing, so I've got 290 pages on a new novel . . . historical . . . set in Mexico in 1876. I think I've got a wonderful heroine ["Pola" of *Beat the Drum Slowly*].

"Mamma, outside of having a flu bug, is doing just fine, although she grows very frail with the years."

Her Mother's Death

Niggli's mother would only live one more year. She died on January 15, 1968, at the age of eighty-five. Josefina buried her in San Antonio alongside her grandmother and her father and other Niggli relatives. She had updated her will in 1967.

The Application for Probate filed after Goldie's death lists bank accounts in the towns of Waynesville and Clyde (near Cullowhee) with about $7,000, as well as real estate in Texas and North Carolina valued at $33,000, and the Wachovia trust account with $206,000. It also refers to a trust created by Josefina in August of 1955 with Wachovia Bank and Trust, successor to the Fidelity Bank in Durham, North Carolina. The witnesses to Goldie's will are three women residing in Sylva, the town nearest Cullowhee (where Josefina first resided upon obtaining work at WCU).

Josefina's will, filed two years before her death, in 1981, was quite different from her mother's. There were no remaining relatives to provide for; she left the bulk of her personal estate to a foundation at Western Carolina University.

Her mother's 1967 will, however, relates interesting information. It was attached to the deed arranging the sale (years earlier) of the King William St. house in San Antonio, but filed in the County of Jackson (where Cullowhee is located) in North Carolina. Should Josefina have predeceased her, it made disposition for the dispersal of Josefina's personal items as follows (it is logical that Josefina herself wrote this):

- All property in her office at WCU to the college theater;
- Her books, color slides, and filing cabinets to the college library;
- Her sewing machine and sewing equipment to the college's Department of Home Economics;

- Her office furniture and equipment in her library and office in her private residence to the college newspaper;
- Her automobiles to Mrs. Fredericka P. Cook [a friend of the Morgan family in Missouri who often resided with Josefina in Cullowhee];
- Her daughter's jewelry and furs to Miss Dorothy Rehn [Josefina's first cousin];
- The property and house located on Cemetery Road in Cullowhee and its contents "other than my daughter's personal papers and manuscripts," as well as the property and house located at 130 Carson Street in San Antonio, "provided that Miss Dolly Niggli [Josefina's aunt, Fritz's youngest sibling] be allowed to occupy the house rent-free during her lifetime," to Rehn and Miss Helen Hackleman [another first cousin];
- Her daughter's personal papers and manuscripts to be burned unread;
- The cash in her daughter's account at Chase Manhattan Bank in Berkeley Square, London, all future royalties, and a property located at 708 Desert Hill Ways in Sun City, Florida, to Mrs. Mary Smallwood Wayte [one of her closest friends in Cullowhee].

Mary Wayte became a close friend after Josefina moved to western North Carolina. Apparently as early as the 1960s, Josefina felt so close to her as to bequeath her future royalties. When her own will was drawn up a couple of years before her death, Josefina was suffering and ill; she may not have thought clearly about the disposition of her goods, but she did request that Mary Wayte handle her estate upon her death. By 1980 Goldie had died, no one close to her was left in San Antonio, her friends were getting older, and Josefina decided simply to have the college foundation receive the bulk of her estate as well as future royalties. Wayte commented to John Igo that Josefina had wanted to change her will but did not have time or the health to do so. Wayte is also now deceased.

The London bank account was opened in the early 1950s when Josefina resided in London. It may have been easier for her to receive and maintain her English royalties in London following the war, because of difficulty trading the British pound in the post-world-war era.

Culminations

New Pointers on Playwriting was published in 1967, and according to an article in the *Western Carolinian* student newspaper in March 1971, it was the text Niggli used for her Dramatic Structure course at WCU. The student reporter mentions it is "advertised monthly in *The Writer* [magazine], on the inside back cover under the heading, 'Important Books for Writers.'" The writer (W. Wat Hopkins) touts Niggli's achievements, and includes three photos of her in different poses as she talks about her career. She is called "An exciting teacher" in the headline, and the article is flattering and tender in its portrayal of a teacher who instills confidence in her students. The reporter quotes another student: "One young writer, speaking about Miss Niggli may have summed it all up. He said, 'I feel like, since I started writing, that I'm looking for something; I don't know what, just something. And I feel like she has looked for it, too, and has found it.'"

Four years after the book's reissue, and three years after her mother's death, the photos show an overweight woman in a checkered shirt and slacks. Niggli would struggle with diabetes and health problems for the next several years.

In the student newspaper article, Niggli is credited with founding the Department of Speech and Theatre Arts, as well as the program in Professional Writing. But it does not mention what she had just achieved. In a letter to the Greens in June 1969, Niggli declares that her effort has "paid off," and her university "now has a full-fledged Department of Theatre Arts." She proposes to introduce the new chairman the following week when she visits "the Hill." Three days later, she sends a new letter with specific dates for visits and brags about "our budding radio-TV program," indicating that she has successfully established a program similar to that of UNC-Chapel Hill.

The fiftieth anniversary of the Carolina Playmakers was held in 1968, coordinated by Samuel Selden, who had just retired as head of the Dramatic Art department at the University of California, Los Angeles. The special event was celebrated throughout the 1968–69 season, also launching a pledge drive to build a new theater. Six thousand Playmaker alumni were invited, and the season's program included plays by Green and Niggli. Times had changed, however. In the fall of 1968, Niggli's play *Tooth or Shave* did not move the audience to laughter as in a previous era; in fact, a student critic called the festivities featuring former Playmakers a "disaster" (Spearman 151). Green's play *Sing All a Green Willow* (a satiric folk fantasy) was staged for the culminating event in March 1969 and called "nothing more than a bloodless ghost of a glorious past" by the *Chapel Hill Weekly.*

In a newspaper interview in 1978, when asked her impression of recent playwrights, Niggli said: "They speak for a generation that is not mine . . . I'm like so many of the old actors. That's why they love to do dinner theater, because they're old plays that have a beginning, a middle and an end.'" (Wolcott). Niggli's preference for the standard formula of Western tradition made her averse to avant-garde or radical innovations in the theater during the late twentieth century. But Niggli's style and her plays, as noted by this journalist, "go on and on, produced all over the English-speaking world and translated into other languages."

From the early 1970s, Niggli began cutting down on her teaching load because of her own failing health. In the 1969 letter to the Greens, she laments, and jokes, that they have not seen each other in so long that introductions will be in order. Then she states, "I've lost so much weight that most of the time I have to tell people who I am anyway." In December 1972, she tells the Greens she "almost traded in my shoes for wings this Fall," indicating she almost died. She mentions a student visiting her in the hospital. Niggli suffered advanced heart disease during the final ten years of her life.

Retirement

At age sixty-five, Niggli retired from Western Carolina University. She had enjoyed a long trajectory in a full-time academic post, as she had desired. She would continue to reside in her home in Cullowhee, only steps from the university, with friends visiting frequently. Sharing her household were longtime companions Tuffy and DeeDee, Yorkshire terriers, who were joined shortly after her retirement by a puppy she named Zorro. Niggli had always enjoyed cooking; she now took to collecting cookbooks. No other hobbies are cited. Niggli's principal enjoyment had always been spending time with friends.

The year following her retirement, 1976, Niggli's first book, the anthology of five one-act plays, was reissued by Arno Press. Two years later, she was honored as "WCU's First Lady of Theatre," with a campus ceremony and a six-day run of a student's play in the first annual Josefina Niggli Theatre Production, according to the *Asheville Citizen-Times* (March 10). It was early 1978; she was feted and celebrated with speeches and various tributes, and presented with an album filled with letters from those who could not be present.

Later that spring she traveled to Texas, where Niggli was also honored in her other "home" town of San Antonio. She was presented with the Arts and Letters Award by the Friends of the San Antonio Public Library. In a photograph that appeared in the San Antonio *Express-News* in May 1978 (photograph now lost, according to archivists), Niggli is handed her "certificate of honor." She looks much older than her sixty-seven years, with unkempt hair and large round-frame glasses. The annual Friends of the Library award is granted for outstanding accomplishments in the arts. It was launched in 1972, making Josefina the seventh recipient. (In 1996, Sandra Cisneros was one of two recipients.) Frank Rosengren, Jr. (whose parents owned the bookstore where Niggli worked in the 1940s) and John Igo (a former English professor at San Antonio College) attended the ceremony, as well as a few of the nuns from Incarnate Word College.

The program for the ceremony states that Niggli is the most often produced writer of one-act plays in the United States, and that her first book has become an American classic. It also indicates that friends accompanied her to San Antonio from North Carolina, and that she was the house guest of her cousin, Mrs. Dick Sherill (aka Dorothy Rehn).

As the festivities ended, Niggli made a gift to the Public Library of her elaborate and heavily sequined Mexican skirt, which she had worn in *Soldadera*, and in which she posed for the photograph in the book. This treasure was unfortunately, and intentionally, destroyed during the early 1990s when a library director decided to prune the library's holdings. John Igo laments his being unaware and unable to rescue it in time, but he did save copies of several of Niggli's books and a handwritten journal, which are now held in the special Niggli collection at the University of Incarnate Word's Mabee Library. The San Antonio Public Library's Texana Collection has only a manila envelope of information on her, which contains six items: three obituary notices, the program for the Friends of the Library's Arts and Letters Award ceremony; a photocopy of an early biographical entry on her, and most of a long article published in 1939 in the *San Antonio Express-News*.

About a year later, in April 1979, Niggli was again in San Antonio and decided to visit her childhood home. She met Julia Cauthorn, an influential member of the San Antonio arts community who lived next door at 217 King William Street, in the house where Niggli had once finished writing her first novel. Cauthorn recorded a short remembrance Niggli related to her, and left the typed copy with the Daughters of the Republic of Texas at the Alamo in San Antonio (see chapter 3). Cauthorn may have been seeking a noteworthy anecdote for the King William district, only declared a historic neighborhood in 1967.

After 1979 there is no other mention of Niggli in San Antonio. Her failing health may have prevented further trips.

End of an Era

Niggli died on Saturday, December 17, 1983 at her home in Cullowhee, following a lengthy, debilitating illness caused in part by diabetes. She had friends taking care of her to the end, including Barbara Eberly, a younger professor at Western Carolina, who years ago mounted an excellent website on Niggli.

Her death certificate indicates her as a "writer," born in Mexico, and "never married." Mary Wayte is named as the informant of the death. Her will drawn up on July 31, 1981 (where the signature of "Josefina Niggli" is somewhat jerky) states that all property not specifically assigned in the will, including the Wachovia Bank trust and any which she might become entitled to after execution of the will, was bequeathed to the Niggli Fund of the Development Foundation of WCU.

A few exceptions: her funds in a Sylva bank and credit union were bequeathed to the Catholic Center for Students at Cullowhee; her collection of cookbooks to the university library; her desk and typewriter to an individual, William Paulk; and her other books to Joe Walker of the WCU Drama Department. All of her "pictures, either on walls or in collections" were assigned to a dear friend and art professor at WCU named Duane Oliver, a microwave oven to Barbara Eberly, a convection oven to Nancy White McIntosh (the executrix). A freezer and the sum of $5,000 were left to Wanda Watson; another freezer and her three dogs to Mary Wayte.

According to Wayte's letter to John Igo (in the Incarnate Word collection) in San Antonio dated February 20, 1984 (in a package with items from Niggli's home), Niggli had wanted to change her will:

In this same mail I'm mailing you one copy of Mexican Village in Spanish. It's the only one I found at the house. It seemed more appropriate to have the Spanish copy in S.A. than in the library here. I've also included a notebook with material that apparently she wrote with the idea of perhaps using it sometime. Further in the notebook are notes in shorthand. The University has taken the notebook containing her lecture materials. I'm not sure whether they took any other notes. I recall that she sent or took to you notes, etc. of her writings for your collection in the library at S.A. At least one if not two people have been working on Josefina's works—one on her one-act plays and one on her books as being a person or American writer who wrote well about Mexico.

Slowly we are trying to get the items of her will taken care of, and then the lawyer and executrix will have to have an auction of the contents of her home in order to meet obligations, all because of the wording of her 1981 will that she wanted to change but never did. I miss Josefina more each day but cannot grieve for her as she had suffered enough over the past two years and died quietly in her home.

The *Asheville Citizen* paid her homage in an obituary, and stated that she "was largely responsible for the development of a major curriculum in dramatic arts" at the university. She was said to be a member of St. Mary's Catholic Church.

Paula Shirley wrote Niggli's obituary for the scholarly journal *Hispania*, noting that Niggli "frequently manifested her feelings of being a 'halfway child,' one caught between two worlds," and how *A Miracle for Mexico* describes "another 'halfway child,' a mestizo boy," as well as the half-American, half-Mexican character Bob Webster of her first novel. She also notes that while other playwrights explored American folk ways in the groundbreaking early days of this theatrical form, Niggli was unique in concentrating on Mexican folk or peasant lives.

The obituary in the *San Antonio Light* states that a graveside service was held at the Mission Burial Park at 3 p.m. on December 20. She was laid to rest alongside her family, not far from the site where her last play, *Lightning from the East*, was produced. This local newspaper says "her most prolific writing was during the 1930s and 40s," but fails to mention the final play or her novel from the 1960s, or her great devotion to a true representation of Mexican culture.

An obituary in the *North San Antonio Times* on December 22 (probably written by John Igo) states that the world-renowned playwright and novelist "had three homes: San Antonio, Hidalgo, Mexico and wherever she was teaching at the time." The article cited her last public visit to San Antonio for the Arts and Letters Award in 1978: "At the close of the ceremonies, she donated to the Theatre Archive the sequined skirt she had worn in her play "La Generala" [*sic*], her first big role with the Carolina Playmakers." The writer had apparently confused "soldadera" with "generala," making Niggli's character a general. Although an error, it is a fitting tribute.

In June of the following year, the board of trustees at Western Carolina University voted to name the university's Little Theatre "the Niggli Theatre" to honor their professor emeritus. This action included the following commentary:

"Josefina Niggli was one of the truly remarkable persons in the life of Western Carolina University. She served on the faculty for nearly 18 years, and there are few teachers whose impact on students has been as profound as hers. She was a celebrated author and playwright, and her reputation brought recognition not only for her, personally, but for the university as well. . . .

"Professor Emeritus Niggli remained an active supporter of the WCU Theatre program in her retirement years. Her former students and colleagues were frequent visitors, and she shared generously with them until her health failed."

Josefina Niggli, *Presente.*

Beat the Drum Slowly
(selections from unpublished novel, ca. 1950s or 1960s)
Part II (folder 53, MSS 85–13.1)

The sky was still black in the predawn of Monday, February 14, when Ramón Burdet, clad in an English riding suit with gleaming brown boots, ran down the side steps of the Burdet house to the horse he had ordered saddled. In the distance the lights of Botón de Ancla shimmered in the cold desert air. There was a legend on the silver train roads that a man lost in the mountains could always guide himself to safety by those lights.

The cluster of ranch buildings made a small town of their own. But at this early hour even the chapel was dark when he galloped past it. Thirty minutes later he was in the streets of Botón de Ancla, hunting for his name-twin.

He was riding out this early for two reasons. He loved the pre-dawn, for he was a child of the night, preferring the soft circles of lamplight to the brilliant glare of the sun. Also, this was the best time to find Ramón the Dark alone, for the tall young man was very popular with the sporting young gentlemen of the town, and he was usually surrounded by a circle of admirers.

As usual, even at four-thirty in the morning, the streets were filled with traffic. Heavily loaded freight wagons lumbered along, carrying imported goods to the great warehouses. Mule-train guards thronged the streets, staring with avid curiosity into the windows of the exclusive shops, as fine as any in Mexico City. Brothels, famed on the frontier for their gilt furniture and red velvet drawing rooms, and the select Chinese gambling establishments were already releasing their fashionable customers into the major side-streets, while the lesser brothels and opium parlors on the back streets were, as always, doing a constantly changing flow of business.

Under the loud hum of pedestrians, small street bands on the corners clashed their brass melodies with the gay dance tunes of saloon orchestras. There was a smell of cheap perfume, the acid tang of excrescence, and to that was added the fragrance which is characteristic of every town. If Mexico City smelt like a woman freshly powdered after her bath, if Monterrey had the dusty odor of silver stacked in bank vaults, Botón de Ancla had the carnation scent of a whore at a Sunday picnic.

Ramón Burdet loved the perfume and the noise and the traffic. Here every child knew him. Laughing women, arms entwined with their escorts, waved at him from passing carriages. Mule-train guards stared wide-eyed at him, later boasting of how they had seen the young Burdet. This was his world. He had hated the streets of Paris where he was merely an anonymous figure in the crowd. He had always hated anonymity, and this was one of the reasons why he had returned from school in Switzerland, preferring to have private tutors imported to Botón de Ancla.

Now he had reached the corner of the Alardín bank. The windows were covered with heavy steel shutters. Two private guards, guns on their shoulders, stood in front of the nail-studded door. Their sergeant, lounging on a window ledge, sprang to attention and saluted as the young Burdet rode by. He responded with a wave of his hands, more interested in the display of saddles in the shop next door, a shop so famous for its leather work that young gentlemen from as far away as San Luis Potosí sent there to have their saddles made. Then he passed the street's only two-story building that housed the Burdet ranch offices, the ground-floor filled with fine woolens from London, dresses from Paris, shoes from Spain, bonnets from Italy. There were perfume shops, and jewelry stores, with windows protected by steel bars; wine shops, and Spanish groceries selling condiments from all over the world. There was even a hairdressing establishment much patronized by young dandies. Other streets, with small shops of cheap materials and celluloid jewelry, belonged to the lower classes, but this was the Avenue San Fernando where muleteers, factory workers and servant girls could wander at four in the morning, but by nine were supposed to return to their own section of town. After that, it belonged to the aristocracy, when the crowds thinned to a procession of silk-hatted men and Creole ladies, while the lumbering freight wagons were replaced by deep-slung victorias and satin lined carriages perfumed like jewel boxes. At present, the wooden sidewalks were packed with Chinese farmers in blue cotton, with cues dangling from their round hats; Turkish merchants, some of them wearing the fez, on their way to open their shops for the farmers' trade; men in overalls and canvas caps from the Rocamuno glass factory changing shifts; and cowboys in skin-tight leather trousers from all the neighboring ranches. The shawled women were either lower-class wives or cooks from the great houses trotting toward the open air market where the Avenue dead-ended.

Ramón passed them all, waving his hand now and then to a ranch hand or a childhood companion. At the market, with the stands of fresh vegetables and fruits covered by purple netting to protect them from flies, and the open air restaurant tables, he paused to look around for the tall figure of his name-twin, clad in his accustomed black with no gold or silver ornamentation to relieve even the black felt sombrero. Not seeing this, and knowing someone would answer, Ramón Burdet called out "Has anyone seen Ramón the Dark?" from long practice pitching his voice to a shrill tone that cut through both speech and the dance music of the market orchestra.

A fat woman, bent over a brasier on which sat a huge pot of brown beans, waved a wooden spoon at him. "The news is that he left town last night."

This information upset the young Burdet. His name-twin had lately acquired this habit of slipping out of town without first asking permission. Since, he said, he was no longer officially attached to the ranch, he saw no reason to ask Burdet permission for anything. This, in the Fair Ramón's opinion, was ridiculous. A name-twin should have only one loyalty: his master. Being dismissed from the ranch did not change that relationship in the slightest.

Ramón the Dark's secret life was a constant source of irritation to the young Burdet. It had not been there in the old, good days of childhood when little Pola had been an annoyance to the Fair Ramón, and the most wonderful toy ever invented to the Dark One. She followed Ramón the Dark everywhere on her unsteady colt's legs, interfering with such manly sports as cave-exploring in the nearby mountains, and fishing on the banks of the river that smelt like wet sateen. During their games Pola never acted correctly. Instead of being properly grateful at being saved by the brave Spanish captain from the wicked English pirate, she would struggle free from Ramón the Fair and run back, smiling, to Ramón the Dark. He would pet her and feed her the jellied candies she loved which he saved up all his money to buy from Mareos Farías, the trader of Woman's Goods, while Ramón the Fair, sputtering with anger, would yell that this was no way for pirate and captive to behave.

Then came the morning when they said farewell to Pola. It seemed she was being taken by doña Brígida to a place called Paris. After that, Ramón the Dark began his long retreat into his solitary world. . . .

Part II (folder 54, MSS 85–13.1)

. . . The maid, an avid reader of the more lurid adventure tales, said, "All Mexican gentlemen are dark."

A slight frown pulled Pola's wing-like brows together. This was not the usual exclamation of awe with which her schoolmates greeted her announcement. Indeed, this was a bit of information unknown to her since the only Mexican gentleman she had seen in eleven years was the two brief glimpses of her father, a short, stocky man with gray streaked hair and side whiskers. She said wonderingly, "Is that true? I didn't know . . ."

"But Mademoiselle is Mexican . . ."

I haven't been home since I was seven, Pola thought, eleven years ago. To her eighteen years, the gap was over half her life an eternity of time.

She shut her eyes and tried to remember the days of childhood. There was a range of mountains shimmering blue in the distance. There was a town of squat, gaily colored adobe buildings, and a plaza on which orange trees bloomed. She could remember the spicy scent of the orange leaves when her nurse crushed them in her fingers as they rode round and round the plaza in a small pony cart after Sunday mass. There was a vague recollection of a house with green tiled halls, and a garden filled with roses over which a woman leaned, a very tall woman with a cloud of dark hair. The face was hidden in the mist of years, but she must, of course, have been dear Mamá who died less than three months after Pola and her aunt sailed for France.

But the most vivid memory was of an iron gate wide enough to admit a carriage, and a tall dark boy pressed against a tree, crying while the carriage took her away from him. . . .

[new fragment]

He had asked to marry her. How kind he must be. How wonderful to have such a man for a husband. She drew a deep breath, straightened her shoulders, and went down the stairs to meet the tall dark boy who had grown into a tall, dark man.

The formal drawing room was another background for doña Brígida's black-and-silver elegance. Instead of topaz, this one was the dark green of malachite. The walls were papered in green brocade sparked by gold medallions, and covered by the small gold-framed paintings of German forests that were so popular. The greenish marble fireplace was outlined by gilded ropes, and the tall, floor-length windows were set in heavy green drapes looped with golden cords. Rosewood furniture was upholstered in the same brocade as the walls, relieved by gilded statues of discreetly draped youths and maidens holding gold-branched candelabras. The entire effect was a lusterless jewel set in gold against which doña Brígida's silver hair shone with moonlight beauty.

Pola hated the room. It was gloomy to her, and the entrance to the glass-domed conservatory filled with tropical plants reminded her too vividly of the St. George episode. She was glad to advance toward the fireplace with downcast eyes.

First she saw her suitor's glossy, patent leather shoes with the lavender spats that were so fashionable this season. Then the gray trousers, and the closely buttoned black frock coat revealing a stiff collar circled by a narrow cravat held in place by a stickpin set with a carnelian engraved with an ornate script letter "B." Finally she saw his narrow shoulders and his long, narrow head with the fleshy nose, the large blue eyes, and the silky beard that outlined his jaw (like Toinette's policeman, she thought dazedly). And she saw his hair. Sun, filtering through the lace glass-curtains, dusted it with gold. She said, unbelievingly, "But you are blond."

He laughed and came to her. As he kissed her hand, he spoke in French in a pleasant, clear tenor. "In Botón de Ancla I am called Ramón the Fair." His blue eyes were smiling at her. She knew she was staring and hastily lowered her lids.

"Eh," he protested, "Look at me. I want to see if your eyes are really that clear green or only brown with green lights in them." He spoiled this romantic statement by adding, "I had heard your mother's Portuguese blood was strong in you. It's true. You have Portuguese eyes."

He sounded like Sister Marie Carmel correcting the logic in one's composition. Resentfully, she pulled her hand free and moved toward the round center table of gilded wood with a marble top. This was a very strange proposal, she thought, playing with a black wooden box inlaid with mother-of-pearl that contained candy. They were the very sweet jellied kind dusted with sugar that she loved, but now, for the first time in her life, she did not want one. This, she thought drearily, was possibly what Sister Marie Carmel meant when she said, "One day, without warning, you will grow up." Not wanting the candy seemed to be the division line between childhood and the world of adults. Very silly. Everything was very silly.

She moved past the table and sat in the bustle chair, automatically giving a small flip to her bustle so that it would settle correctly into the groove provided for it. The blond young man was talking, but his voice seemed separated from her by vast space. She tried to listen, yet heard nothing because of the confusion in her mind.

This—little blond man with the golden beard was the playmate of her childhood? This blond man who was not tall—only a little taller than herself—was the one who had wept when they parted as children? This short man with yellow hair and blue eyes—it made no sense at all! Who, then, was the tall, dark boy of memory? Did he exist? Was he merely a dream image? Had she read the scene in a book, liked it, and made it a part of her own past? Perhaps in the real Botón de Ancla there was not even a tree nor a carriage gate. Sister Marie Carmel had often warned the girls of such romantic dangers.

By an effort of will, she refocused her eyes and saw the real Ramón outlined against the green wallpaper. Its scrolls were no more golden than the head that he had tilted to one side as though he were waiting for her to speak.

She was horrified. He had finished his proposal and she had not heard a single syllable! In this important moment, the climax of her life, the culmination of her training years: of learning to walk, to dress, to play two sentimental tunes on the Italian harp and three on the piano, his proposal had slid past her while she thought of dream images from the past! . . .

A Miracle for Mexico
Sunday: 11:00 a.m. (one chapter, pp. 92–103)

The house covered the block that separated the Augustinian convent from the Grand Plaza. Unlike the other Conquerors, Jaramillo had not taken on the plumage of a newly created hidalgo, refusing even the identifying "de" of a gentleman to separate his first and last names. He came from a family of merchants, and, with his Conquest loot to aid him, he was now one of the most powerful merchants in the New World.

The boys, led by a cautious Martín, fastened the two horses and the white mule to the post at the warehouse entrance. Inside the large, thick-walled room, they saw ceiling-high stacks of bales containing silks and velvets, ribbons and laces. The air was fragrant with imported spices and the scent of coffee beans brought from the Orient. Clerks on high stools at tilt-top desks were making out inventories for traveling merchant customers, and at each end of the room small Sunday auctions were in progress for vendors who sold their goods to the Indian villages.

As the boys advanced, Martín was surprised to see the Spanish Secretary storming at two Indian porters. "But you must have seen him. He had to pass this warehouse—I repeat, this warehouse—to reach his own village."

The blank Indian stares made him bounce his clenched fists in the air. "He couldn't have disappeared—impossible—the road is straight and wide . . . you saw him, wicked creatures."

Martín, with a half-bow of excuse to his companions, quickly went to the Secretary's side. "They can't speak Spanish," he explained soothingly. "What happened, good Secretary?"

"Your Indian farmer—what a dance he has led me—a dance, I tell you." He mopped his pale forehead with his loose sleeve. "I lost him," he admitted miserably.

Martín bit down on his lips to keep from smiling. Using rapid

Nahuatl, he discovered that Juan Diego, already famous for daring to invade the Bishop's private study, had indeed trotted past the warehouse that morning, but he may have gone into the Augustinian convent for all they knew.

When the Spanish Secretary heard this, he clapped his hands over his ears. "I went there. They never heard of the creature. No one has heard of him. He's a myth—I repeat—he is not human. He's a myth. And the Audience Patio filled with Spanish gentlemen . . . Dr. Blás does not understand protocol—he will let anyone in to see the Bishop regardless of rank—and me, running after myths!"

"It is easy," Martín said gently, "to lose an Indian in a crowd of Indians."

"Not that Indian!" The Spanish Secretary waved his bony finger under Martín's nose. "I'd know him if he sat on the tongue of Grandfather Devil himself. I was on a horse, he was on foot. We reach a hill, and zut! He disappears!"

This was no longer amusing. Martín asked sharply, "The Hill of Death?"

"Hill of Death . . . Hill of Life . . . how know I the names of hills? He was in front of me, then"—he whistled through his teeth—"he was not in front of me. I tell you the Devil snatched him up, and me running here—there—forward—back—trying to find him! And my poor Spanish gentlemen . . . aye, what a scandal! Dr. Blás will admit a penniless adventurer ahead of a great mine owner. I know that blue-robed Friar. He knows Latin. Good. He knows mathematics. Very good. He knows philosophy. Astoundingly good. But proper respect for protocol? Magnificently bad! Ha!" He folded his arms in total disgust.

Martín proceeded to frown. "You are right, señor Secretary. You are truly needed in the Audience Patio. Tell the good Friar that I kiss his hands and feet and will myself seek for Juan Diego."

"As you should have done in the first place!" The thin little man glared at the Indian porters. "Only Nahuatl, indeed! They should be forced to learn a Christian tongue."

He darted toward a nearby entrance, almost bumping into the artist, Damián. He did not bother to bow, for in the book of protocol artists came below stableboys.

Damián gave him sidewalk room, then entered the warehouse. He was careful to keep a wall of bales between himself and the boys, but listened intently to Alonso's question as Martín returned to his companions who had been watching the scene with curiosity. "Why was the Spanish Secretary sent to follow an Indian?"

Martín said loftily, "The business of the Bishop is not our concern," but secretly he was worried. If Juan Diego disappeared at the Hill of Death, perhaps the Blessed Virgin had snatched him up, and he was safe beyond any earthly help. But if the kidnappers were paid by Guzmán the Cruel, he was not safe at all, poor creature.

But this was no time, he decided, to worry over the fate of Juan Diego. He followed his companions through the small door that connected the warehouse with the house proper.

Unlike the stone fortresses the other Conquerors had built, Jaramillo's resembled his old home in far off Córdoba, once the home of Caliphs. In Moorish tradition, the small patio was protected by an awning of split bamboo. The rooms were all very large, with wide sitting ledges of stone jutting out from the plastered walls. Huge piles of down-filled cushions were piled on the floor. Near each pile, set like jewels on thick silken rugs, were delicately carved tables holding brass trays. In the same Moorish tradition, Juan Jaramillo wore a long white gown covered with a striped, wide-sleeved robe. Beside him, on a lower cushion, sat the famous doña Marina. Ten years had ripened her. Her gown of Moorish silk, with floating veils woven in Algiers, seemed to fit her soft brown skin and slanted eyes.

Near them, stern in Spanish doublet with a breastplate of etched gold, stood the one man who outshone the dark intensity of Hernán Cortés himself. There were many Conquerors with fair hair. There were many more with blue eyes. But Pedro de Alvarado, shining even in the darkest shadow, had the added gift of personal beauty. His skin was as clear as a woman's. His beard extended the delicate molding of his cheekbones to a golden point. And his height, making him nearly as tall as Xavier, gave him the broad-shouldered, narrow-hipped insolence of strength. Many Indians still thought he was their fabled Fair God, who had brought them the gift of fire. Alvarado had indeed brought them fire, but his was the fire of torture and pain. Of all the Conquerors, he was the most hated and feared.

Seeing the boys, he held up his long arm. "So! It pleases you to arrive at last."

Young Jorge hurried forward to kiss his father's hand. "Don Martín was late, honored sir."

"Do not blame others for your own fault."

With cold precision, Alvarado bowed his head to Martín. "Señor, your servant."

"Señor, kissing your hands and feet," Martín responded automatically. In spite of what the Bishop had told him, he still found it difficult to respect this man.

Now that the formal greetings were over, Martín turned to the formal Jaramillo. "To you, Señor, I bring the blessings of the Friar Bishop and the hope that you can supply new laces for the altar's tablecloth."

Jaramillo's hand moved in a graceful arc from his breast to his forehead. "Inform His Excellency my house will be honored to make a gift of the lace for the holy days of Christmas."

The two other boys had already kissed doña Marina's hand. Martín went to her now, but she took his hand instead, and pulled him down to her. Her soft lips brushed each of his cheeks, and she laughed softly as she spoke to him in Nahuatl. "How fares your mother's family?"

"Well, lady."

"Does your aunt know this village Indian who was given audience by the Friar Bishop?"

Knowing the Indian love for gossip, he was not surprised by the question. "His uncle, Bernardino, suffers from a serious illness. My foster father, Xavier the herbman, attends him. In that way she knows him."

"So." The slanted eyes, common to the people of her native Tabasco, looked at him curiously, as though she knew he was evading a true answer; but she merely bowed her head when Jaramillo said testily that there was no time in these stolen moments for village gossip.

As Martín straightened to face the others, Jorge said, "Honored father, we have left the real news for you to tell."

Alvarado nodded. He began pacing the room, his square-toed velvet slippers making no noise on the thick rugs. "It is in my mind that everyone present knows that Guzmán the Cruel approaches the City. He is traveling like a king," he added bitterly, "stopping at each major village to exact homage and tribute."

Jaramillo was scandalized. He tossed off a small cup of hot coffee before he said, "It is revolution against the King's own command."

"Not so!" Alvarado answered. "The King's command exiles him from this City, yes, but there is no mention of the country around us. We can be encircled, cut off from all supplies . . ."

"A siege!" cried Alonso de Avila. "Is that what is in his mind?"

Doña Marina spoke softly to Martín in Nahuatl. "A siege can stop food from entering, true. But it can also stop messages. And sometimes the message is more important, Martintzín."

This calm statement brought silence to the room. Everyone present could understand Nahuatl, although the two men could not speak it as fluently as the boys.

Jaramillo leaned toward the nearby table and poured himself another cup of coffee with a steady hand. "Has there been a message, don Martín?"

The boy flushed, and moved into the room's deeper shadows. "Why ask me this question?"

"I know my wife's method of indirect statement, don Martín."

And so now, Martín thought, they suspect I have a deeper knowledge than themselves. He glanced sideways at doña Marina. To Spanish eyes, she would be merely a beautiful woman, lounging on heaped cushions. To Martín's eyes, trained to Indian cunning, there were betraying signs in the slight curve of the lips, in the way her lashes fluttered a bit too fast. Her spies have told her, he thought, of my visit to don Pedro de Moctezuma this morning, but does she know what was said there? Don Pedro would never tell her himself. He hates her for helping Cortés capture Tenochtitlan. Yet she is a clever woman. It is possible she has a spy inside his house. Stubbornness choked Martín. She might know that he had chosen the Spanish road this morning, but that did not mean he would betray the plans of Pedro Moctezuma.

He said harshly, "The Conqueror Alvarado promised me a message about my sainted father. That is the only message that interests me."

The three adults were silent, their controlled expressions showing neither disappointment nor anger.

In the silence, an Indian servant glided into the room, knelt by doña Marina and murmured something to her. She nodded and rose in the easy single movement of a woman trained from childhood to dance the difficult patterns of religious ceremonies.

"Forgive me," she murmured in accented Spanish. "There is a problem in the warehouse with some of the Indian vendors." As she passed Martín, she spoke again in Nahuatl, but this was a different kind of speech. Children of all countries learn to twist and reshape words into a private code of their own. In English it is called "pig-latin," in Spanish, "the *effe*." It has value only to those who grow up in the language. It was this speech doña Marina was using now. "These Spaniards know an important message has reached the Cruel One. They suspect you know what it is. I love them, but they have no interest in the fate of Indians. You must decide what to tell them."

After she left, Jaramillo, curious as an Arab, burst out, "What was she saying to you?"

Martín glazed his eyes with Indian blankness. "She was warning me that the message you have may not be about my father at all."

This aroused Alvarado's quick anger, as Martín knew it would. "Your father discovered the shell of our danger when he was trying to make you his legal heir. The Spanish courtiers smashed through to the heart of it. Aye, it is fine scheming, worthy of Foreign Favorites, for the King loves the plan. Naturally he loves it." He paused, his hands linked behind him, his head bowed. Martín had a sudden image of his standing just this way when he realized that no torture would ever tear the truth of hidden treasure from Cuauhtémoc.

Jaramillo sighed as he put down his empty cup. "My dear wife and I have wept for lack of children. Now, I am glad. My only heirs are my brother's children, true Spaniards born on Spanish soil."

Alonso de Avila, quicker to grasp hidden meanings than the others, cried out, "You mean it involves our inheritance?"

Alvarado half nodded. "There is a document ready for the King's signature. It says that a Conqueror's son may not inherit his father's lands. It says that when we die—we who won all this New World for the Crown—our holdings will revert to the Crown."

"You really mean," Alonso whispered, "that no Creole child can inherit his father's wealth?"

"No Creole child," agreed Alvarado, "here, or in Cuba, or the Islands."

Martín heard the words but they seemed far away, like a thin echo on a hilltop. "But men who fought the Infidels can pass their holdings to their sons."

"True. A field of sand with a castle on a rock are of no value to the Crown," murmured Jaramillo. "But silver mines and forests of ebony and fields of pearl-oysters? Ah, the Crown is very practical. When need arises, it can strike a harder bargain than any merchant I know."

Alonso de Avila gave a low cry of anguish. "My father is ill. He has the chest sickness, and every morning I pray that his soul will find an easy entrance to Glory. Are you saying that when he dies, the Royal Audience will turn me, my mother, and my sister from our house? Is that what you are saying?"

"Respected father," Jorge moaned, "please do not die. I am not clever like Martín. I could not serve as a page in the Bishop's Palace."

Martín thought to himself that they finally understood, these Creoles, what it meant to be without substance. Once they had smiled as at a little joke when he prayed to receive his father's inheritance. Now they were not smiling.

Jaramillo was saying, "Does our sacrifice of war count for nothing with the King?"

"At the moment," a strange voice answered, "the King is interested only in planting the flag of Spain in Holy Jerusalem."

Martín looked across the room and saw that the newcomer was the artist, Damián.

Behind him stood doña Marina. This must be the person she had gone outside to meet. What strange circles were here, interlocked? And who was Damián? What was he? Artist, mountebank juggler, or still a servant of the King? If this last were true, then what he was saying was important.

"To Charles the colonies are only treasure houses to help that dream come true. Added lands mean added funds. What else does the King need to understand?"

"He should understand," Alvarado said, glaring at the artist, "that we are three thousand miles from Spain. A message of what happens here may take a year to reach him. Guzmán taught us that arithmetic. And by the end of a year perhaps his royal wish will have no value."

Martín caught his breath. These were indiscreet words to speak to the King's servant. Damián, however, merely smiled, teetering back and forth on his toes, his gay clothes brilliant in the slanting sun as Alvarado's golden breastplate.

Doña Marina sighed. Taking Martín's hand, she led him to her throne of soft cushions and pulled him down beside her. In the soft child-code Nahuatl, she murmured small endearments to him. "Relax, my poor darling. They have put too much on you this day."

"I am a man," he flared at her.

She smiled with the woman wisdom of doña Beatrice. "So the Spaniards say. But we know you will not really be a man until you are twenty-one. Even our sweet last Emperor was a nineteen-year-old child when he commanded the arrow flights of Aztec warriors. He was too young for such responsibility, and you are younger still." She reached for a plate of sweets on a nearby table. "Take a jelly candy. The red ones, rolled in powdered sugar, are very good."

Her voice was so much like his aunt's that he obeyed automatically. She was right. The tart sweetness melted on his tongue, and the sugar took away his tired despair.

He looked up to see Damián standing in front of him.

"This morning," the artist said smoothly, "you refused to lead the Moctezuma Indians in revolt against the Spaniards. How say you now, don Martín?"

The boy looked into the dark eyes that were no longer filled with the humility of artist rank. "It is in my mind," Martín said slowly, "that you are a very dangerous man."

The sapphire eyes turned colder than don Pedro de Alvarado's. "So the King said when he ordered me to this barbarian world with the two great gentlemen. Do you think with the mind of a king, Martín de Aguilar?"

"Since your spies told you of my meeting with don Pedro de Moctezuma, they must have told you I chose to remain a Spaniard . . ."

"Oh, they told me." Damián bent and picked up a jelly candy. For a moment he held it toward the sunlight. "Very clear, of excellent Turkish manufacture, Merchant Jaramillo . . . Yes, they told me. One moment you are all afire for Spain. The next you flame for Indian wrongs. What are you, don Martín, Spanish or Indian? Spanish or Indian?" Damián repeated the question parrot fashion.

Martín, not wanting to face the question, thrust his own question at Damián. "And what are you, señor Artist? What are our Creole problems to a born Spaniard?"

Damián's face was suddenly drawn and old. It was as though a mask dropped, and the real face was revealed, a face tired of the world's problems. Then the mask slid back in place. He minced across the room and pulled aside transparent draperies that covered a wall mirror of beaten silver. Turning this way and that, adjusting his curls and smoothing his mustaches, he looked more like a cat than a man. "An artist, I, born in a street studio in Madrid. From the gutters I watched the great lords ride past, and I swore that someday . . ." He shrugged gracefully. "I joined a group of players, and we traveled as far as Italy. There I was found by my dear master Leonardo da Vinci. He wanted an errand boy; I wanted his knowledge. He taught me how I could be more important than any great gentleman. So I went back to Spain. I became the King's jester."

He whirled and went up on his toes in the age-old attitude of Harlequin. Like that mysterious sprite, Damián seemed, for a moment, a creature not quite human. Then his heels touched the tiled floor, and he was once again a man.

"Even the Foreign Favorites sought my good will, for a jester is a privileged creature, and Charles loved my snakelike mind. It is so much like his. That's why he sent me to guard the Spanish lords. Without me to guide them, they would never have trapped Guzmán. When they left, I was still the giver of orders, even to Hernán Cortés, the richest man in the world!"

He stepped away from the mirror, and with one hand on an imaginary great sword, the other pretending to twirl a two-foot mustache, turned into the comic figure of the Braggart Soldier. "The gutter child becomes the secret lord of a New World. Am I not very grand, Don Martín?"

The boy, more sensitive to mood than the Creoles, recognized beneath the posturing a spirit as lonely as his own. He asked slowly, "Is it true what you say? Are you really our secret lord?"

Everyone in the room was very quiet. Then Damián changed from Braggart Soldier to Harlequin in Despair. He sank to the floor, his legs crossed, his upturned palm folded above his drooping head. "Let us say it is a lovely dream."

"Pah!" snorted Alvarado. "A mountebank!"

"No, no, no!" Damián protested. "Sometimes a mountebank. Forever an artist. And always a schemer. My snakelike brain tells me now that this new law, if it is passed, will destroy you. If it is passed. Now there's the secret phrase."

"You mean the King may not sign it?" Alonso de Avila demanded.

Damián's shoulders rose in a high shrug. "How events go here will decide his signature. If Guzmán wins, you can say farewell to your inheritance."

In his lightning way, he turned quite human and very serious. "Hear my true words. If a Creole child cannot inherit, then New Spain will become nothing more than a passageway for Spanish adventurers, who will stay a few years, gather a sackful of wealth, and return to Spain to marry Spanish women and rear Spanish children."

Don Pedro de Alvarado caught the meaning now. He said, appalled, "But this is far worse . . . it isn't just we few who will be affected. Why, all our cities will disappear! There will be only forts to hold back the Indians."

"Precisely." Damián unrolled like a stiff ribbon. As though fatigued with so much speech, he trotted over to doña Marina and crouched within easy reach of the plate of Moorish jellies.

The three boys sank on the wall ledge like three dolls whose stuffing had run out. Jaramillo crossed to Alvarado, and the two spoke in whispers. Only doña Marina seemed at ease, reclining on the cushions, her head supported by her hand. She was staring at Martín as though he held the answer to a problem she wanted solved.

Alvarado broke the tension by coming to Martín. The boy rose, and as he looked up into the Conqueror's eyes, he decided that all enmity must be banished. What use for private quarrels when a whole world lay about them in ruins? He said heavily, "Your servant, my Captain."

The Spaniard grunted in response. "What do you know of a rumor among the Indian porters that a new land richer with gold than Mexico has been discovered to the south?"

Before Martín could answer, Damián drawled, "Everything. Don Martín knows everything in the Indian world, everything in the Spanish world. I told you this morning, señor Captain, he was the man for us."

Martín's eyes moved from the blond bearded face of the artist to the blond bearded face of Alvarado. What strange plot had they been hatching between them? Love of gold, he knew, brought strange types together as companions, but an artist and the Mayor of Mexico City? It seemed incredible. And even more incredible was the phrase "man for us." It sounded too much like the refrain heard in the Moctezuma interview this morning. Now, as then, anger bubbled in Martín. "I am not your man! I am Mestizo. To you I am little better than an Indian until you need me."

Pedro de Alvarado, usually curt with everyone, was oddly gentle now. "We need each other, boy. Creole or Mestizo, there is no difference if the King signs the new law. We have no alternative. We must seize Mexico for ourselves." He looked at Jaramillo, who nodded.

Martín caught his breath, then whirled on Damián. "Oh, very clever, mountebank. Now you can report pure treason to Charles."

"I? I report such a thing?" Damián flung out one arm, almost as though he were pleading. "I gave up that favoritism when I elected to stay here instead of returning with the great lords."

"And why would you want to stay here?" Jorge wanted to know. Damián stood stroking his chin. He was giving his entire attention to his answer. Finally he said, "It is the geography, I think. In Spain you travel a mountain road until you turn a sharp corner of stone and find a village filled with perhaps honest folk, but usually brigands. In Mexico, you stand on a mountain ledge and see beyond you waves of mountain peaks, like a great sea frozen in stone. A blue mist softens the view and finally the mist turns into the sky. Sky and mist and frozen sea, like a landscape on the canvas of my master Leonardo, only this is a landscape on the canvas of God." He looked at all of them. "Yes, there is no doubt of it. Geography has turned me from a man of the world into a man of Mexico. I am an artist. My talent gives me the power to recognize the mysterious handiwork of our true Lord. Would you deny me citizenship, don Mestizo Martín?"

Martín, looking at him, saw that he was quite serious. For the first time it occurred to him that there might be men who stayed in Mexico for other reasons than gold, men who found an inner kinship with this wild new land. He mutely shook his head, even as Jaramillo, far more Moorish than Spanish, having no interest in why a man wanted to be a Mexican, waved his hand toward Alvarado. "I won't see all that I have built, that we have built—destroyed. If what you said was true, Damián, that a new land has been discovered in the south—"

"It is true. Ask don Martín."

The boy did not move, but continued to look at Damián, still trying to find the secret twists in the artist. Damián, as though reading his mind, said harshly, "Yes, I have a spy in don Pedro Moctezuma's house. Do you think Indian slaves are so loyal there is not one to betray his master? I have a spy there and so has Guzmán the Cruel, I can tell you."

"Ahhh!" Martín released his breath on a thread of sound. What he had feared was true then, and there was no point now in trying to keep the Moctezuma secrets. He told them of the treasure house of Perú, and of Pizarro's murder of the Emperor Atahualpa.

Pedro de Alvarado twisted the news in his soldier's brain. "How long do you think Guzmán has known this?"

"Some time," Martín admitted. "He murdered the Master Runner Cipriano to keep it his private secret. My foster father knows—"

"He can be silenced. Who else?"

Martín flushed angrily, yet behind the anger was awe that he was no longer afraid of any of these men. He had not, he realized, been afraid since he had claimed the protection of the Virgin. "My foster father is a man of honor! He is not an animal to be killed for barking."

Doña Marina murmured, "Our brave Captain meant only that Xavier, as an Indian, would understand the need for silence. Who else knows?"

"Don Pedro Moctezuma—"

"Who keeps silent for reasons of his own," Damián drawled. And the two great Friars—"

"Dr. Blás and the Holy Bishop?" Alvarado asked.

Martín nodded. "I had to tell them. It was ordered by"—he hesitated, slid past the name of Juan Diego, and said—"my foster father, Xavier."

"And how did the Holy Bishop receive the news?" Damián wanted to know.

"He wept. He wept like a child."

Doña Marina, still gravely studying Martín, said, "Naturally. He is a very gentle man."

"True," agreed Damián, "but totally lacking in practical experience. Why do kings put duties involving world experience on the shoulders of gentle men?"

"He has the guidance of God!" Martín flared.

"I do not think," Damián said dryly, "that God is concerned with the price of Cadiz oranges."

Jaramillo, thinking with his merchant's brain, said, "If the agents of Guzmán buy up every Indian slave, then he will control the entire slave market. He can ask any price he wants from independent miners, oyster fishers, and caravan merchants. Even if the inheritance law fails to please the King, Guzmán will still control the treasure flow from Mexico. The Foreign Favorites will control the Perú treasure, and the Spanish court-iers, dependent on us, will lose their power. No wonder the Bishop wept. I also weep!"

He flung himself down on the cushions near his wife, and touched her shoulder as though his fingers could suck her quiet strength.

Pedro de Alvarado's face looked very pale against his golden beard. "There is no doubt of it. We must seize control or we have lost every-thing." He moved to Martín's side, towering over the boy. "Hear my words, don Martín. Cortés is no use in this venture. He lives inside the glory shell he has built about himself. Also Pizarro is his cousin-german. We could not convince Cortés in time that his own cousin would betray him. We need a new man to lead us, one whom both Spaniards and Indians will accept."

Martín retreated from him toward the soft woman haven of doña Marina. "You ask me to lead you, me whom Spaniards and Indians alike despise . . ."

Damián murmured, "You turned away from don Pedro Moctezuma because you loved your Spanish blood. You have already committed yourself."

Martín slashed his arm through the air. "I am committed to only one thing: the orders of my Lord Bishop! And this meeting has nothing to do with those orders. I don't want to hear about your plans. I am not interested in Spanish plots . . ."

"Such fury," Damián said, his sapphire eyes fixed on Martín's. "This morning you were all Spanish, this afternoon all Indian. You cannot be both, don Martín, at your pleasant convenience. Your true choice was made this morning. You belong to us here in this room, to everyone in it. Look at us, son of the Hidalgo Aguilar, look at us and see you have no other choice!"

Martín's eyes traveled from Damián's impassioned face to the blank misery of Jorge de Alvarado, to the strangely solemn Alonso de Avila, to the golden beauty of the Conqueror captain, and the Moorish darkness of the merchant Jaramillo. Finally his eyes stopped at the slanted eyes of doña Marina.

She bent forward, her Algerian veils rippling about her. "You ask the impossible, my Spanish lords. Don Martín can say nothing. He is on another errand. A very important errand."

"What can be more important than this?" Damián demanded roughly.

"I think," she murmured, "the finding of a little Indian farmer who has disappeared might be more important."

Martín, too inexperienced to know how to conceal shock from these watching eyes, froze into stillness.

"You see?" she asked Damián in her accented Spanish. "There are secrets, old hawk, among the fluttering doves. Tell us, don Martín, why an Indian farmer gains entrance to the Bishop's private study? Tell us why the Spanish Secretary left his important post to follow him? Tell us why you looked so frightened when you heard that the farmer had disappeared?"

Martín looked very Mayan as he answered coldly, "I suggest that the Lady Marina ask her questions of the Friar Bishop. As for me, I have duties in my aunt's house. My grandfather is dead, and there is need for songs of mourning. Doña Marina, I kiss your hands and feet. Great gentlemen, I salute you and leave you to your planning . . ."

Alvarado said contemptuously, "The son of Aguilar deserts his friends in their hour of need."

"You will find a way. Spaniards always do."

"And the Indians?" Damián asked softly. "Can the Indians find a way when they are enclosed in the Guzmán slave pits?"

Martín sighed, remembering Xavier's maxim: "Indians see the eagle; Spaniards see the nest." He made a special bow to the little man in the gay silken clothes. "Señor don Artist Damián, has it not occurred to you that a public pronouncement of Guzmán's plan to buy all slaves will rouse the adventurers and merchants to such fury that only the Friar Bishop will dare to hold a slave auction? And that every purchaser will have to produce documents to prove his good faith? Guzmán would not be able to buy one crippled slave with the coughing sickness under those circumstances!"

There was no response from the two boys, but Damián's eyes widened at the simplicity of the solution. Doña Marina laughed and clapped her hands. Alvarado and Jaramillo half nodded to each other.

As Martín started for the door, it was Jorge who growled the question. "But you never answered us, don Martín. Is your place with us or with the Indians?"

Martín frowned. "Half of both and half of neither, how can I choose only one? I am Mestizo, don Jorge. There is no place for one like me."

As he left, it puzzled him why doña Marina was smiling at him as though, in her quiet way, she knew a truth he could not yet understand.

CHAPTER FIVE

Conclusions

Niggli's Legacy and Resurgence

In 1980 husband-and-wife scholars from South Carolina contacted Niggli and asked to interview her. Paula Shirley wanted to write an in-depth biographical essay on Niggli for the *Dictionary of Literary Biography Yearbook*. She and her husband Carl, who tagged along and asked as many questions, are both Spanish professors (she also specialized in women's studies, he in theater). They wanted to assess Niggli's contribution to what was now being called Chicano Literature. As a result of this interview, Paula Shirley published a seven-page essay in the dictionary, issued the following year.

In a letter dated February 1981 (in Niggli's WCU manuscripts), Niggli provides Paula Shirley with a sample of her writing and a photo, as requested in follow-up for the publication. She states the following:

> This manuscript page has been copied off, so you don't have to treasure it. If it gets lost it's no loss. I'm sorry it has to be from an, as yet, unpublished book, but all the other manuscripts

are either in the archives at Chapel Hill or at the San Antonio Public Library where they have . . . Lord defend us . . . a "Niggli" collection.

On spring break why don't the two of you come up and spend the night? I'd like to hear about Atlanta.

The footnote indicates Niggli is attaching a "Page from POLA."

During this interview, conducted at her home in Cullowhee that summer, Niggli states that she travels to San Antonio[1] twice a year. She tells the Shirleys that she had recently (two to three years earlier) offered to meet Raymund Paredes in San Antonio—for when he interviewed her for his article on the evolution of Chicano literature, he said he wanted to meet her but "could not afford" to travel such a great distance. Paredes completed his doctorate in 1973 and took a job as assistant professor of English at the University of California in Los Angeles. When he telephoned her, he was living in California, she recalled, but would return to Texas to visit family. Paredes was born and raised in El Paso, but he received his Ph.D. from the University of Texas at Austin, where his mentor was Américo Paredes (not a relative). Three decades later, he is doing much better financially; he left California and holds the post of commissioner of higher education in Texas. Niggli seemed to feel an affinity with him, perhaps because he was the first person to contact her as a fellow Mexican-American or "Chicano" scholar. He became co-editor of the *Heath Anthology of American Literature* (where he cites Niggli's groundbreaking work), the first major collection of American writing to seriously represent its diversity. During his many years at UCLA he served as editor of the scholarly journal *Aztlán*, and now serves on the editorial boards of several journals.

After contact with Paredes and before the Shirleys arrived to interview her, Niggli was pursued by telephone from New York. Dexter Fisher, director of English Programs and of the Association of Departments of English (ADE) of the "MLA" or Modern Language Association (the largest professional organization for literature in the United States), was preparing an innovative text for the era. It became the very first book to focus on the perspective of Third World women writers living and writing in the United States. Published in the same year the Shirleys interviewed Niggli (in fact, Niggli assumes they contacted her as a result of the newly issued book), *The Third Woman: Minority Women Writers of the United States* is a nearly 600-page resource book. This anthology, consisting of stories, poetry, and folklore (no theater), does little critical analysis, but it set a milestone for the rediscovery and understanding of non-mainstream, ethnic women's voices and place in literature. It succeeds in portraying women living between two worlds, in each of which she has little or no power.

Fisher had received degrees at San Diego State University and her Ph.D. at the City University of New York (CUNY), and taught English in San Diego and at Hostos Community College in New York. Thus she was familiar with different regions. As an administrator of the MLA, and with a grant from the National Endowment of the Humanities (NEH), she was developing seminars and conferences to encourage the study and teaching of minority literature. Fisher had previously, in 1977, edited a volume for the MLA titled *Minority Language and Literature: Retrospective and Perspective.*

In her preface to *The Third Woman*, Fisher says the book is "a collective effort to bring together in one place the best of the literature by minority women." The text is divided into four sections or minority groups—American Indian Women Writers, Black Women Writers, Chicana Writers, and Asian American Women Writers—each with about twenty examples. Niggli's "The Street of the Cañon" (from *Mexican Village*) is included in the Chicana section, along with writers who would soon become luminaries in the field: Ana Castillo, Margarita Cota-Cárdenas, Carmen Tafolla, Estela Portillo-Trambley, and Angela de Hoyos. Most had not yet published some of their most important works. Although sources are well documented, and various periodicals as well as books are suggested for additional readings, in Niggli's case (who is represented, along with Fabiola Cabeza de Vaca, as one of the earliest writers) some of her contribution goes unmentioned. The short biographical note preceding her sample indicates that Niggli only has four books published— one collection each of plays and short stories, *A Miracle for Mexico*, and *New Pointers for Playwriting* (although in the bibliography at the end of the Chicana section, *Step Down, Elder Brother* is cited and not *Miracle*). Confusion and misstatements about Niggli's works have done a disservice to her literary legacy. Fisher's book also includes appendices with thoughtful questions and suggestions for topics for additional study.

During the interview with the Shirleys, Niggli took issue with Fisher's remarks in the Introduction, where Niggli's story is called "a reworking of the familiar folktale of the devil disguising himself as a lover to court a pretty and innocent young woman." Fisher says Niggli opens the story with a proverb to signal the presence of "tradition," and further proclaims that "Niggli gently but ironically points out the folly of blind adherence to tradition." Reading this passage aloud elicited a guffaw from Niggli; she explained to the Shirleys that back when she created *Mexican Village*, she thought it would be "fun to have a proverb at the beginning of each story," and that she had purchased a book on Mexican sayings and proverbs in Mexico City. The strategy she then followed was to "drop the book on the floor and wherever it opened, the first one I saw I would use. That's my adherence." Niggli concluded with, "I have no particular interest in *esoteric* writing [her emphasis]. I am interested in the story, I am interested in the people."

Critics since, while crediting Fisher for collecting a record of literature by minority women, have also taken issue with her trite and stereotypical renderings of Chicana representation. Fisher's anthology was remarkable for being one of the earliest to signal and categorize ethnic perspective in women's writing. It was soon overshadowed, however, by better texts, especially the significant *Borderlands/La Frontera: The New Mestiza* (1987) by Gloria Anzaldúa, followed by her anthology *Making Face, Making Soul/Haciendo Caras: Creative and Critical Perspectives by Women of Color* (1990). Paredes and Fisher must be credited, though, with bringing Niggli's work to the forefront in an era that was about to change dramatically in terms of representation of U.S. ethnic literature.

Critical evaluations of her work, which are still lacking, especially in terms of narrative, would not be as likely were it not for dictionaries and anthologies that highlight an author. In 1980, Niggli herself pointed out that her work had not been truly studied. "There are critical evaluations of [*Mexican Village*] but not on the basis of the story, only critical evaluations on the folklore" (Shirley). Even the more recent *A Miracle for Mexico* needs scholarly evaluation. Shortly after the book's release, Niggli was contacted by the president of the Americas Catholic Society, who said her elaboration of the "electrical energy passing from one person to another," and the magic quality of the Virgin's image "was exactly what happened. He wanted to know what book I found that in.

I said, 'Please forgive me, I made it up.'" He seemed dumbfounded, Niggli said. Later she received a book with a full scientific description of the painting, which was similar to her portrayal.

"I believe in miracles," Niggli added." I believe that God never gives a miracle that is outside the comprehension of the people who receive it. In other words, the painting could not be a phony."

Despite not being aware of Dexter Fisher's book, Paula Shirley is concerned with whether Niggli should be considered a Mexican (international) writer or Chicano, as Raymund Paredes has classified her. "You don't write about any Chicano problems. Your work is older, Chicano literature is pretty young," Shirley says. Niggli doesn't agree: "There's a double thing there, I think. You see, when I came along, they would say, you don't really think anyone will read this, do you? You have to have an American hero [prominent], only the villain [could be] a Mexican." Niggli kept to her resolve: "It happened," she was published, widely acclaimed and read, and in the process, "I think it was when I started doing my thing that the door opened for Chicano literature."

Thus Niggli demonstrates a better understanding of issues around the "new" Chicano Movement than her interviewer. In addition to her place in U.S. literature with Mexican themes, the Shirleys were interested in Niggli's place in Mexican letters, in Spanish language. They asked her about possible collaborations with the Spanish department at Western Carolina University, and she responded that in all of her time there, she had never been invited to give a talk or participate in any way in that department. She explained their attitude (probably the propensity for Peninsularists to state that Mexican Spanish is inferior) as "They know Spanish, we don't," when in fact, several of her drama students could converse quite well in Spanish.

From a contemporary gaze, some of Niggli's earlier writings may seem stereotypical or accommodating, in terms of ethnic descriptions. It is important to be aware of the era in which she produced her works, to understand that in her writing she pushed to reveal a cultural philosophy and existence ignored by the United States. She additionally possessed a feminist inclination. Interviews conducted with Niggli never address the feminist edge in her writings, nor ask her about her intentions and goals.

Niggli's artistic contribution is much more extensive than that

reflected in initial scholarship, and for that matter, in her second hometown of San Antonio. Nor is it gleaned and comprehended in its totality
from perusal of her manuscripts at Western Carolina University. For
Mexican culture, her work is as significant as the Casasola photographic
collection, a portrait in words of Mexican cultural history and immediate post-Revolution Mexico. Hers are works created at a time when
little appeared by women writers and nothing on northern Mexico. But
it is just as significant to Chicano culture in the United States. Niggli
is a trailblazer among writers revealing the Mexico of their childhood,
and a significant early twentieth-century novelist and playwright writing in English on Mexican-origin topics, focusing on female as much as
male concerns.

It does seem unusual that Niggli's second and third novels have not
been discussed in contemporary criticism on her works. My impression is that her plays served as the first step for evaluating societal and
cultural issues (as well as indigenous legends) that she then elaborated
further in longer narrative with more complex characters. When considering all three of Niggli's novels, the importance of indigenous roots
in Mexican identity and the foundation of *mestizaje* is plainly evident as
a constant and strong element of her writing. As stated to Maren Elwood
and repeated in the *Western Carolinian* student newspaper, Niggli never
felt she understood "Americans," or the American cultural makeup; she
only understood Mexicans.

Her Overlooked Works

The titles of Niggli's second and third novels may be in part to blame
for lack of knowledge of her contribution in contemporary criticism.
Titles that more clearly reflect the novels' content or themes would
better identify their importance, in the first case for revealing post-
Revolution Mexican society and life in the significant industrial city of
Monterrey, and in the second case for the important cultural symbol of
Guadalupe. These titles, and the unfortunate categorization of her final
novel as juvenile, could explain why these novels never saw new editions, even during the 1980s renaissance of Chicano literature. Another
reason could be her last name, which does not connote Mexican heritage.
Ironically, however, her possession of a non-Spanish-derived surname,

as well as her appearance (European features) and facility for English, may have actually helped Niggli have access to a world that other Mexicans in San Antonio (or other locations) were denied during the early twentieth century.

Landing in just about the most prominent playmaking company in the United States at the time surely helped refine Niggli's talent and launch her professional writing career. She would not have had as great a professional opportunity had she remained in Texas, which was more severely impacted by the Great Depression. Her move to the Carolina Playmakers shaped her playwriting into the specific "folk" genre, and provided the opportunity to seek fellowships, to travel, and to become recognized in New York and California. Her own initiative in seeking further professional-writing training in New York also helped further her opportunities in radio and television writing.

Niggli's decision to remain in the United States as an adult and publish here was probably more instrumental to building a writing career than remaining in Mexico would have been, for women writers found even more obstructions in Mexico in the early and mid-twentieth century. The exception in Spanish is Nellie Campobello, who published a beautiful and scintillating avant-garde novel on the Revolution, *Cartucho* (1931), but she was little recognized. She soon disappeared from public view and died in oblivion. Also complicating publication in Mexico was the fact that 85 percent of the Mexican population was illiterate in the post-Revolution era. Thus, it was fortuitous that Niggli crossed the border and honed her craft in the United States.

By writing in English, Niggli taught the English-speaking world about Mexican cultural heritage; she elaborated on Mexican politics and class struggle in such plays as *The Cry of Dolores*, and more extensively in her novels. Principal male characters defined Mexican history, attempting to reconcile Indian and Spanish heritage, but the female characters revealed the spunk and independent streak of Mexican culture—from an instigator of the Independence struggle, Josefa Ortiz de Domínguez, to the *soldadera* who is not afraid to fight for a cause, to Malinche/Marina who is wiser than the men in her midst, to Sofía who takes a stand against Mexican proper society in *Step Down, Elder Brother.*

Her Mexican-American Peers

Among Chicana writers in the United States in the early twentieth century, none achieved the renown Niggli did. The earliest known U.S. Chicana or Latina writer who published novels is María Amparo Ruíz de Burton, a *Californio* (as the Spanish residents of California were called) born in 1832. Her two books, *Who Would Have Thought It?* (1872), and *The Squatter and the Don* (1885), do not portray the initiative of female figures, and take an anti-Union stance. The second comprises a strong denunciation of the terrible violence and fraud committed on the Californios as the Anglo-Americans stripped them of their land holdings and businesses by means of a newly implanted U.S. legal system. But it is also racist in portraying Californios as equal to the white population, deserving of better treatment because of their European, non-Indian origin.

Ruíz de Burton and María Cristina Mena (born in 1893) grew up in well-to-do families, the latter in Mexico City during the waning years of the Porfirio Díaz dictatorship. Mena was sent to New York City in 1907, where she remained the rest of her life. She also wrote in English, publishing short stories and nonfiction articles between 1913 and 1916, all of which take place in Mexico and involve Mexican high society. Although principally love stories, her female characters—drawn along somewhat stereotypical lines—do appear to resist the inferior social position allotted to women. Years later, as a widow, Mena published five books for children (between 1942 and 1953) that introduce Mexican history and culture. In 1997, her short stories were recovered and published by Arte Público Press. While Ruíz de Burton is notable for criticizing Euro-American injustices against Californios in her novels, Mena is notable as the only writer of non-racist perspective on Mexican culture in New York magazines. Each, however, writes from an aristocratic Mexican point of view, in contrast to the Chicano Movement writers of the 1970s.

Although Niggli's family fared well financially, they were not of the aristocracy (grounded not only in the Porfirian society, but from the earlier colonial elite); thus this perspective is not the orientation from which her narrative speaks. Instead, this perspective is frequently contrasted with that of the mestizo and Indian class. In addition, living on either side of the Texas border gave her an experience more in common with the Chicano.

Jovita González, who was born in Texas in 1904, was an early specialist in Texas folklore (in fact, predating the work of celebrated Chicano scholar Américo Paredes). She did not write about Mexican society in Mexico as Niggli did, but focused on the changing societal pressures on the Mexican in Southwest Texas, tensions that led to the class and race divisions that would mark twentieth-century Texas. González first worked as a high-school teacher, then earned an M.A. at the University of Texas in Austin in the early 1930s. Her thesis was on the social life of three South Texas border counties, work she further pursued with a Rockefeller grant in 1934. She then lived in Corpus Christi, where she and her husband (a grade-school teacher) collaborated on creating two books to teach basic Spanish and struggled against racial prejudice throughout their teaching careers. A large wave of Anglo-Americans from the Midwest, seeking cheap land and exploitable labor, moved into South Texas early in the twentieth century, forever changing the good relations that had existed for many years between "Mexicans" and Anglos. This experience is related in González's novels written in the 1930s and 1940s, *Caballero: An Historical Novel* and *Dew on the Thorn*, which she was not able to publish during her lifetime (these were published with a foreword by José Limón in the mid-1990s). The second novel is a rich portrait of the Olivares family clan and their ranch life in south Texas, focusing on the cultural traditions of Texas Mexicans.

Fabiola Cabeza de Baca Gilbert (born in New Mexico in 1893) wrote a novel that was not published until 1954, *We Fed Them Cactus*, depicting a sense of alienation from mainstream society in terms of both language and culture. She describes the livelihood, social life, and customs of residents of northern New Mexico at the turn of the century, including buffalo hunting, rodeos, and raids by Indians and bandits, but also a domestic life that is of mixed Indian and Spanish traditions. Her novel was reissued in the 1990s with a critical introduction. Another New Mexican, Nina Otero-Warren, published a book of similar tone in 1936, *Old Spain in Our Southwest*, but it has received little attention. The cultural revelations and literary accomplishment of these novels by Chicana writers could be compared to African-American writer Zora

Neale Hurston, who published *Their Eyes Were Watching God* in 1936, and likewise received little critical attention until decades later.

An excellent female playwright who succeeded Niggli is Estela Portillo-Trambley. She emerged during the 1970s Chicano Movement with her play *The Day of the Swallows*, which focuses on the collective will of a culture that denies women voice and any role other than that of submission in marriage. Born in El Paso, Texas, in 1927, Portillo-Trambley was the first Chicana writer to adapt the seventeenth-century nun of colonial Mexico as a model of intellectual aspiration, in her play *Sor Juana*. She published a book of short stories, *Rain of Scorpions*, in 1975, and a novel, *Trini*, written during the 1970s but not published until 1986. This remarkable novel is a coming-of-age story about a *mestiza*, raised in Tarahumara land in northern Mexico, who, after several hardships, crosses the border to live in the United States. The main character traverses borders in both a physical and spiritual sense, trading her worship of Tonantzín for the Virgin Guadalupe in the chapel she seeks in El Paso. Her Indian *self* becomes more and more westernized as she leaves the rural land of Chihuahua for the capital city, and later for the border town, each move necessitated by economic hardship. A unique novel for the study of Chicana identity, its significant content was likely overshadowed by the publication of Sandra Cisneros's *House on Mango Street* two years earlier.

Although women such as González and Cabeza de Baca were writing books, neither was able to publish during the late 1930s and early 1940s when Niggli released her major works. The difficulty for a woman writer to publish in Mexico was matched by the difficulty for Spanish-surnamed women to gain notice in the United States, especially if the content of their novels was on Mexican-American life. It was obviously helpful that Niggli left Texas for the East Coast, and that she was able to maintain an independent life and career. She succeeded as a woman writer.

Niggli likely had easier access to the publishing world because she did not have a Spanish surname, but she carved a path for representation of Mexican culture, and depicted significant characters who were always peasants and mestizos. Her final novel was erroneously categorized as juvenile; had it not been released a full decade before the Chicano Movement, it could have been classified as Chicano literature just as *House on Mango Street* was.

A Niggli Resurgence

Eleven years after Niggli's death, in 1994, *Mexican Village* was reissued by the University of New Mexico Press, with a foreword by prominent Chicana critic María Herrera-Sobek. This activated new interest in Niggli for her place in Mexican-American literature. Four recent doctoral dissertations include some of her work as a part of their commentary, which may elicit future academic publications. Currently, plans are underway for a centennial celebration in 2010—commemorating the year of her birth—in San Antonio. Such an event will help remedy the lack of attention to this native daughter. The University of Texas, San Antonio has begun organizing a special collection of San Antonio authors, which will include Niggli.

Internationally, Niggli's first novel, *Mexican Village*, was translated into German, Italian, an Eastern European language, and at least two Asian languages, soon after its English release. The Spanish translation received attention in the United States for its use as a text in Spanish classes, as well as some attention in Mexico, but Niggli was disappointed with its rendition. In an interesting turn of events, her second novel, *Step Down, Elder Brother*, has now been resurrected in Spanish translation. With the title *Apártate Hermano*, the novel was greatly acclaimed after its highly publicized release in 2004. Niggli was celebrated as a precursor of northern Mexico writers who described Monterrey.

Niggli would surely approve of this version. The translator, David Toscana, was also born in Monterrey. He is a prolific and widely translated novelist himself, and undertook this task because he found her novel fascinating and significant for revealing an era little documented in literature. Unlike the first novel, this one was translated in its entirety. Despite the fact that a translation is seldom lucrative, Toscana dedicated time not only to his translation, but also to identifying support for its publication. A new collection created by the sophisticated Mexican Consejo para la Cultura y las Artes de Nuevo León (CONARTE) served his purpose. Dubbed *Arido Reino*, the collection was announced with great fanfare in late 2002, with especial attention give to *Apártate Hermano*. An article by writer Hugo Valdés, also of Monterrey, calls Niggli's novel an "enviable find" for its portrait of northern Mexican thought, and depiction of a significant era in Monterrey. He calls Niggli the "invisible precursor" of women writers from this region and a "pioneer" of the contemporary novel based in Monterrey.

In May 2003, Toscana participated on a panel convened at the cultural center to unveil the collection. In a report filed for the Mexican broadcast media, he is quoted stating that Niggli's novel hit him strongly from its very first phrase, "Monterrey in February is not a happy place," because only a native could understand its climate so well as to state this. Toscana also found Niggli's representation—he calls it "testimony"—of Monterrey families highly significant, together with her depiction of an era moving rapidly to industrialization. He calls Niggli a great writing talent.

Later that year, a new article in *El Norte* announces *Apártate Hermano*'s imminent release. It is called unique for depicting Monterrey's transformation during the 1940s; for background history of the city's most important periods, such as the French invasion of the nineteenth century and the impact of the Revolution; and for its portrayal of significant Indian legends. At nearly 500 pages (with a foreword by María Herrera-Sobek), *Apártate Hermano* is referred to by the president of CONARTE as the important recovery of a novel "unknown to us for decades."

The following May, the translation was formally released in the Alfonso Reyes Hall of Monterrey's Casa de la Cultura de Nuevo León, with several dignitaries presiding. In a June 1, 2004, article, Niggli is now hailed not only as the precursor of literature by *regiomontana* women, but also as a forerunner of Chicana writers (those who write in English about their Mexican culture and history). This literary event, transpiring across several days, ended in a dramatic tone decrying the lack of attention to Niggli.

On June 4, Daniel de la Fuente wrote that the honorary event served to "exigir la pronta revaloración de una de las autoras más importantes de la historia literaria del país, pero más olvidadas" (implore the need to value/honor one of the most significant and yet most overlooked female authors of Mexico's literary history). One speaker passionately deplored the lack of critical attention to Niggli's novel, and expressed his exultation that it was now fortunately rescued from its forgotten state. Why does this vacuum exist? why have critics and literary scholars not previously analyzed this novel? Hugo Valdés and others are said to have asked during the event. The suggestion is apparent that Niggli's work was over-looked because she was female. Another speaker stated that plans were underway to publish a translation of this very novel in 1997—to commemorate its fiftieth anniversary—but that various factors delayed its release. It was also noted that several details were corrected in the translation (such as the wrong names of historical figures) so as to make the novel more credible and solid.

Thanks to Toscana and an entire literary community, the unveiling of Niggli's Monterrey-based novel twenty years after her death has now restored her to Monterrey and to Mexican letters. Fifty-five years after the release of an abridged version of her first novel in Spanish translation, the translation of *Step Down, Elder Brother* is nearly as excellent as the original. Mexican scholars have already begun to publish readings and studies on it. Niggli has not been forgotten by the city that brought her into the world, nor by the culture that inspired her life's work.

Not only do her plays continue to be performed, she now occupies her rightful place in literature as an innovator, playwright, novelist, and cultural historian, documenting Mexican society and heritage in the northern region and the early twentieth century. Niggli is a forerunner in Mexico as well as in the United States. As new scholars rediscover her, evidenced by six dissertations (five since 1997), her works will also occupy their deserved place in the space of Chicano literature. Many, although not all, biographical dictionaries for U.S. Latino writers include an entry for her, and four different scholarly books currently include chapters on her works.

It is fitting that Niggli's works are now being restored and reviewed in both the English and Spanish language, as she lived her life bilingually, binationally, "half-way" between the two countries of Mexico and the United States. The woman who "could not help writing," has left behind a very unique contribution.

Notes

Notes to Chapter One

1. In 2006 Esquivel published *Malinche: A Novel*, featuring the life story of the woman credited with helping Hernán Cortés as an interpreter during the conquest of Mexico, but with her own alternate view. Niggli's third novel, *A Miracle for Mexico* (1964), also depicts a minor character, Malinche, portrayed as an intelligent and discerning figure.

2. On July 31, 1926, the practice of Catholicism was suspended in the Mexican Republic. Neither mass nor any of the holy sacraments, including baptism and weddings, could be conducted. The government had put into law a growing conflict arising out of the 1917 Constitution's ratification of various articles that denounced the Catholic hierarchy as detrimental to the Church and its followers (and actually originated in the 1857 Constitution). The Church had amassed great wealth and substantial tracts of land, even since colonial days, but it was protected by the elite minority in power. The leaders of the Revolution wanted to eliminate all wealth and political control in the hands of aristocrats, foreigners, and the Church; they did not expect, however, the people's strong objection to making Church practices illegal. The problem was that Church ceremonies were interlocked with the practices of small town life; to prohibit the first made it impossible to carry on their traditions. For an excellent novel on the impact of the Cristero War on a small village, see Elena Garro's *Recollections of Things to Come*.

3. His uncle ran a general-goods store and a bank. These Nigglis had moved to Eagle Pass in the early 1860s, most likely escaping South-sympathizing vigilantes during the Civil War. Many people from Castroville and the Texas Hill Country moved to border cities for protection during the Civil War; they were Union sympathizers, some of whom had been lynched.

4. Specifics on the Niggli family in Eagle Pass, as well as Josefina's father's business activities in Mexico, were provided by Bill Fisher.

5. An entrepreneur born in 1859 in Memphis, Brittingham arrived in Torreón in the late 1880s and is responsible for creating major commerce in the region. His soap company employed many locals for decades, he

launched the cultivation of cotton in this area, and he established a bank. He is considered a founding father in Mexican historical records.

6. During the late 1930s, this publication regularly made mention of Niggli's accomplishments, from the North Carolina playwriting award to the presentation of her plays—for example, when *The Red Velvet Goat* was staged in New York, and when a radio broadcast was made of her Pancho Villa play in 1941, at that time with the title of *Death and Pancho Villa*. In 1951, her play *Sunday Costs Five Pesos* was staged at Incarnate Word, cited in this newspaper.

7. Information found in San Antonio historical records.

Notes to Chapter Two

1. In 1976 the Carolina Playmakers group was reorganized as the Playmakers Repertory Company, a professional, resident theater company serving the Research Triangle Park area of North Carolina. Though still administered by the UNC Department of Dramatic Art, it is now subject to the standards of professional acting associations.

2. For this magazine, she spells her name "Josephine." Among English-only speakers in a region of the U.S. denoted the Old South, Niggli must have felt she needed to identify in this manner. Later on, her North Carolina friends would always call her "Jo." However, from the very first play written for the Carolina Playmakers, she spells her name as it was pronounced in San Antonio, "Josephina."

3. After winning some and losing other battles, by spring of 1811, Hidalgo and Allende were traveling north to join another large uprising in what is now the city of San Antonio, Texas. They were ambushed by a traitor in their midst, however, and delivered to the Spanish authorities in Coahuila. In July they were marched over hot desert sands to the city of Chihuahua and executed. Allende was only thirty-one. They were then beheaded and their heads hung in the public square to warn other rebels not to follow in their steps (none of this is in Niggli's play). It did not stop the rebels, though, and by 1821 Mexico had finally struggled free. Because of this painful beginning to a new nation, each year on the evening of September 15, thousands of people throng to the Zócalo, or main public square, in Mexico City to hear the president of Mexico lead the yell from the balcony of the government palace. The shout is "Viva México," with a response, and the president waves the flag after ringing the bells. Similar celebrations are held in all major cities of Mexico, and even in the U.S. in populous Mexican communities. Hidalgo is forever remembered as the "father" of the struggle for Mexican independence, and Allende's name was added to the town where he was born, San Miguel de Allende in the mountains of Guanajuato.

4. Soldaderas, or soldier women, have received little tribute in Mexican society. The few prominent creative works depicting soldaderas are written by women: In Elena Poniatowska's novel *Hasta no verte, Jesúsa mío* (1969; *Here's to You, Jesusa*, 2001), a main character accompanies her father, becomes the sixteen-year-old wife of a soldier, then a widow and soldier-woman herself, and is denied her widow's pension by the new government. Ángeles Mastretta's novel *Mal de amores* (1996; *Lovesick*, 1998) presented a woman riding the trains during the Revolution, and helping heal the sick and wounded. This character is an educated woman who practiced medicine and learned curandera skills. Poniatowska has also published an essay accompanying numerous photographs (from the historic Casasola collection) of these valiant women in her book *Las Soldaderas* (1999).

5. See discussion on the Casasola photographs in chapter 3.

6. A biographical note in the 1937 issue of *One Act Play Magazine* states that Niggli is a "native of Mexico," that she has written plays for the Carolina Playhouse, and that she "plans on her return to Mexico to establish a native Folk Theatre, utilizing her own repertory [which may have been her plan when she worked with Usigli in Mexico City]. The increasing tide of American visitors will have a better understanding of the Mexican people by seeing her plays." Niggli's goal after completing her master's studies was obviously to return to Texas and/or the family home in northern Mexico.

7. Niggli once joked to San Antonio friend John Igo that she could practically live on the royalties from this play, relating that frequently in her mail delivery she would find several envelopes, each with the five-dollar royalty payment for a performance.

8. In the United States, this would be a situation comedy serial, or *sit-com*.

9. Contemporary telenovelas employ similar storylines. For example, in Televisa's *Apuesta por un amor* (2004), a rich landowner controls a small town and the countryside community near the city of Mérida. All of the villagers (peons) must work for him, and he owns the only market. A newcomer with newly acquired money arrives, defies the long-term *hacendado* or plantation owner (who states he has history and tradition on his side), and will not be run out by him. Eventually the newcomer (who has won an hacienda on a bet) creates a cannery and food-packing business, hires the peons as employees, and creates a collective farm where villagers supply the products. They are more than content to leave the ruthless hacendado and enjoy these opportunities. Naturally, there is also a love story. Both the hacendado's daughters fall in love with the newcomer. Indian lore and custom is portrayed through a female witch doctor or curandera, but there is also a male curandero, who rights evil she unleashes. There are Indians who live in the jungle nearby, and at

some point an "Ixtabai" figure appears, confusing the newcomer and causing problems for him.

10. Niggli and Usigli (with similar six-letter last names) were possibly more than close friends. They met either through the Larraldes or on the East Coast, but they moved in the same circles. His well-known play on Maximilian's short reign in Mexico, *Corona de sombra* (1943), appears to be dedicated to Niggli. The first publication of the play (in book form) states: "a Josette, con todo." When Cuadernos Americanos published the play separately in 1947, the dedication was changed to "A Josette, R." The dedication of the English language edition, published in London in 1946, is "to Josephine, with my everything."

11. A play featuring the revolutionary general of northern Mexico would appear to be influenced by northern-Mexico writer Nellie Campobello, whose novel *Cartucho* was published in 1931. However, it does not seem likely that Niggli read Campobello's book (which paints Villa in a much more positive light), as she never mentions her, nor was *Cartucho* widely available. It was even greatly ignored by critics. Novels in that era were usually first serialized in newspapers, the foremost example is Mariano Azuela's *Los de abajo*, collected into a book in 1916. Called the *first* Mexican novel of the Revolution, it did not even see popular circulation until a new release in 1927.

12. *One Act Play Magazine* was a cutting-edge publication for drama in the 1930s. Niggli's manuscript collection at Western Carolina University contains no copies of this important early record of her plays, but each of the three issues is found in the Niggli collection at the University of the Incarnate Word in San Antonio, Texas.

13. This has been identified from a copy of the play in the Niggli collection at WCU, as well as in Betty Smith's manuscripts at the University of North Carolina, Chapel Hill.

14. It is unsure whether an award actually existed in this case, since research shows that Betty Smith and Niggli at times made up information for each other, such as awards.

15. As with her play *Soldadera*, Niggli chooses her dates carefully. *Soldadera* is set in the mountains near Saltillo in 1914. By that year, President Madero had been killed, and the revolutionary leaders had ousted Huerta (who killed Madero) and were fighting each other for command of the nation.

16. Niggli cleverly employs the surname of a rebel leader from Morelos, Genovevo de la O, who controlled the Mexican region west and south of Cuernavaca before and during the Madero era. The troops he controlled were a separate army; he did not defer to Zapata or any other leaders.

17. It should be noted that Niggli's published plays are not always quickly located, for the library cataloging system, at least in the past, only

classifies an anthology by the editor's name, and seldom indicates the names of each playwright.

18. Another Alexander Street Press database, *Twentieth Century North American Drama*, does not include an entry for Niggli.

19. This comment is in the biographical note accompanying an article titled "Betrothal in Hidalgo," published in *Senior Scholastic* (April 1946). The article is an excerpt from *Mexican Village*, and describes the traditional walk around the plaza that publicly commits a couple to marriage.

20. Letters referenced here to Green are found in the Paul Green Papers in the Southern Historical Collection, Manuscripts Department, Wilson Library at the University of North Carolina, Chapel Hill.

Notes to Chapter Three

1. Green did a lecture series in New England in early 1943, then returned to Los Angeles. He traveled to Chapel Hill in late 1943 and then to L.A. again in May 1944 and back to Chapel Hill by December. In May 1945 he again returned to Los Angeles for a year.

2. Located in the Betty Smith Papers (box 5, folder 97) in the Southern Historical Collection at the Wilson Library of the University of North Carolina, Chapel Hill.

3. The one-page transcription of this interview is held in archives maintained by the San Antonio women's organization Daughters of the Republic of Texas at the Alamo.

4. I personally remember the same village this novel depicts, as my parents moved there in the 1960s, while my father worked at a foundry in Monterrey. We rented a country home in the open terrain around the village, where other homes were scattered. At about 5 p.m. each day, I would stroll out to await "Daddy's" arrival, swinging on the gate and watching the cows head home at feeding time. Soon the dust of the dirt road would clear to reveal his Volkswagen bug. Niggli's characters walk into the village to find a beer in the evening, when people relax and stroll around the main plaza, but the daytime was busy with shopping activities. As a child, I liked being dispatched, when my mother was elsewhere, to buy fresh tortillas at a shop in the main plaza area. While I waited for a kilo of fresh tortillas to roll off the conveyor belt, be weighed and packaged in thick brown paper, the attendant would sprinkle salt on a hot tortilla, roll it and hand it to me to eat.

5. Coincidentally, a note on the release of the English translation of his book *The Land of the Pheasant and the Deer* appears in the same annotated bibliography (two entries above hers) published by *The English Journal* in 1942, where Niggli's *Mexican Folks Plays* is cited.

6. The eminent scholar of Mexican indigenous heritage Miguel León Portilla estimates there are eighteen different books of the Chilam Balam (these two words mean "sayings," or writings, of the high-level "priest-scribes" or wise men), of which only three have been meticulously studied. Chumayel denotes a village or people; each of the other books relates the accounts of other groups, such as the Maní.

7. The era following the decade of armed struggle of the Revolution and settling in of the new government is called the *Maximato*, the period of the *jefe máximo*, men who applied tight control over restoring the economy. There was a need to find jobs for the many people who fled to the capital for safety, or arrived there after fighting during many years, having nothing left. The Cristero War erupted against rigid new laws outlawing the Catholic Church, ordered by the new government in order to put an end to the Church's centuries of power, but which backfired. Lázaro Cárdenas's presidency, from 1934 to 1940, was the first stable presidential term and launched the drive for progress that Niggli's Vázquez de Anda family seems to benefit from. Between 1935 and 1940, the GNP grew by 27 percent; manufacturing production increased 53 percent during this presidential term, more than twice that of the total economy. Mexico had become an active state directly involved in the production and creation of infrastructure.

8. These photographs can be appreciated in books published recently by Elena Poniatowska (1999), David Elliott (1986), and Pete Hamill (2003).

9. The Casasola Archive includes more than 480,000 negatives for photographs taken by Casasola, his brother and son, and various employees between 1892 and 1972. Contemporary researchers have found the work of more than 480 photographers in the Casasola Archive. The entire collection was acquired for purposes of historic preservation by the Mexican government in 1976, and is maintained by the National Institute of Anthropology and History (INAH). The extensive archive is organized by series, themes, dates, encompassing historical record, economic activity, entertainment and sports, ceremonies, courtroom activity and jails, factories, and social mobilizations. A smaller collection of additional Casasola negatives and photographs (2,481, mostly portraits) is housed at the University of Texas at El Paso, of which a large amount are available on a database. A member of the Casasola family had an office in El Paso in the early twentieth century called "Casasola, Home of Fine Portraits."

10. This could possibly be Aureliano Urrutia, a cabinet minister under Huerta who supposedly cut out the tongues of political opponents. After Huerta went into exile, Urrutia moved to San Antonio and built a large house there—in fact, across the street from Incarnate Word College.

11. In 1980, Niggli uses the term "Chicanos," but it was not a term that would have been used in the early 1950s.

Notes to Chapter Four

1. His book titled *Child Photography, the Modern Way* was published in 1949 in Baltimore by the *Camera*. A child psychologist turned photographer, Schneider's photos of babies graced the ad campaigns of Gerber, Campbell's, Johnson & Johnson, Nestle's and other companies during the 1940s and 1950s. In this book he described his creative techniques, such as identifying the baby's own fascination with something, like a blanket, the mother's face, a trinket, or a sound, to then capture its reaction in the very moment.

2. The book included several full-color scenes of childlike characters by the populist Mexican artist Alejandro Rangel Hidalgo, which contributed to the idea that it was a book for children. This painter was well known in the mid-century; his depictions were frequently available in Mexico as postcards in tourist gift shops, and still hang as framed décor in many prominent city hotel rooms.

3. Niggli aptly notes that oral history continued to be propagated in the colonial era, outside or alongside official history.

4. During the colonial era, Náhuatl was referred to as *Mexican*. In the present era, the words "Virgin of Guadalupe" would have figured in a title for such a story, but in Niggli's era "the miracle" was the working reference and link to the original title in Náhuatl.

5. Niggli, as did most educated Mexicans, and because of her interest in cultural history, likely read the early chronicle by Bernal Díaz del Castillo, *La verdadera historia de la conquista de la Nueva España*, which describes Doña Marina's work as interpreter for the Cortés party, as well as her marriage to the *hidalgo* Juan Jaramillo. Niggli does not state in this novel that she was first Hernán Cortés's concubine. Marina (or Malinche/Malinalli) was not from Tabasco, however. Díaz del Castillo's chronicle explains that she was sold to people from Tabasco and had mastered their language, as well as others, by the time she was given to Cortés.

Note to Chapter Five

1. John Igo has said that when he served as her "chauffeur" on her trips to San Antonio during the 1950s and 1960s, she would often ask him to drop her off at the Mexican market downtown. He would then find parking and come to look for her. She never bought anything, she just liked "smelling" the goods, which conjured memories of Monterrey. He often found her standing in the leather-goods section, "just standing there, taking in the smell" of products made from genuine leather.

Niggli's Works

Poetry

Entries marked "unverified" are listed in a job application that Niggli prepared in the 1950s, but have not been independently confirmed. Many of the other works listed on the application that have been confirmed appeared under different names and/or in different years.

"The Texas Child." *Main Avenue Huisache* (San Antonio Main Avenue High School newspaper) 30: 2 (October 1, 1925): 2.

"A Tourist in a Mexican Town." *The Echo: The Rocky Mountain Magazine* (Denver) 6: 2 (April 1928): 11.

"Mexican Serenade" and "Goat Herder's Song." *Young Pegasus: Poems of Children* (San Antonio: The Carnegie Library) (Spring 1928): 27.

"The Pathway." *The Logos Yearbook* (1928), 2.

Chapbook *Mexican Silhouettes*. Privately printed in Mexico (December 1928, first sent as a Christmas greeting); revised edition with five previous and six new poems. San Antonio: Silhouette Press, 1931.

"In Just That Hour," and " L'Envoy." Incarnate Word's *The Logos Yearbook* (1929): 154, 156.

"Portrait of a Mexican Idler" and "Goat Herder's Song." First- and second-place awards, Catholic Young Poets Contest. In *This Light: An Anthology of Catholic College Verse*. Brooklyn, NY: The Literary Society of St. Joseph's College Alumnae, (1930), 26–27.

"Mexico, My Beloved." *Mexican Life: Mexico's Monthly Review* (Mexico City) 8: 10 (October 1931): 12.

"Philosophy." *The Embryo: A Book of Verse* (Akron) 4: 2 (October–November 1931).

"Discontent." *Mexican Life: Mexico's Monthly Review* (Mexico City) 8: 11 (November 1931): 10.

"The Mexican Idler." Second prize, Young Poet's Contest. *Interludes: A Magazine of Poetry and Prose* (Baltimore) 8: 3–4 (Christmas 1931–32): 54.

"False Blue." *Mexican Life: Mexico's Monthly Review* (Mexico City) 8: 12 (December 1931): 20.

"Secret Places," "Vain Advice," and "Ambition." *Popular Poetry* (1931)
    [unverified].
"Sonnet from the Spanish." *Poetry* (1931) [unverified].
"Prayer for a Soldier." *Girl's Companion* (1932). Republished in unknown
    anthology in 1949.
"Victorian Shawl." *Embryo* (Niggli said "1932" but it is not found in that year)
    [unverified].
"Portrait of a Victorian Lady." *L'Alouette* (1932) [unverified].
"Three Chants to the Sun." *Mexican Life: Mexico's Monthly Review* (Mexico
    City) 10: 9 (September 1933): 15.
"Goat Herder's Song." *Mexican Life: Mexico's Monthly Review* (Mexico City) 11:
    7 (July 1934).
"Mexican Lullaby." *Real Mexico* (December 1934) [unverified].
"Doña Perfecta." *Mexican Life: Mexico's Monthly Review* (Mexico City) 11: 10
    (October 1934): 18.
"Space of Earth." *American Poetry Journal* (1935) [unverified].
"Mexico, My Beloved." *North American Review* 240 (December 1935): 433.
"Washington at Valley Forge." *Thomas Cook* (1935) [unverified].
"Chapel Hill." The Carolina Play-Book (Chapel Hill) 9:2 (June 1936): 49.
"A Prologue for *The Drunkard*" The Carolina Play-Book (Chapel Hill) 9:3
    (Sept 1936): 65.
"False Blue" and "Three Chants to the Sun." *Hecho en Tejas*. Albuquerque:
    University of New Mexico Press, 2007 [last stanza of each poem omitted].

Short Stories

"The Sacrifice." *The Logos Yearbook* (1928): 67–69.
"Kate Buys a Dress." *The Bright Scrawl of the Junior League of San Antonio* 4: 2
    (November 1930): 5.
"A Matter of Fourteen Hens." *Mexican Life: Mexico's Monthly Review* (Mexico
    City) 10: 3 (March 1933): 15–16, 57–59.
"The White Shawl." *Mexican Life* 10: 6 (June 1933): 15–16, 57–62.
"Slippers for the Bride." *Mexican Life* 12: 2 (February 1935): 12–15, 43.
"This Bull Ate Nutmeg." *Mexican Life* 12.5 (May 1935): 13–14, 55–62.
"Dust of Mexico." *Mexican Life* 12: 7 (July 1935).
"Saint's Day." WCU manuscript collection.
"Betrothal in Hidalgo." *Senior Scholastic* 48: 11 (April 14, 1946): 25–26, 36.
"Salt in the Air." *Collier's* 120 (11 October 1947): 14–15, 88–89. Same story
    released in *Argosy* (UK) 9: 8 (1948): 59–64.
"A Visitor for Domínguez." '*47, the Magazine of the Year* (August 1947): 122–28.
"Call Them Dreams." *PAX* (San Antonio) 3: 1–2 (Winter 1985–1986): 98–102.
"The Runaway." Unpublished. Posted on *Latino Literature* database, 2006.

"The One Room Inn." Unpublished. Posted on *Latino Literature* database,
    2006.
"The Grace of Guadalupe." (WCU archives). Posted on *Latino Literature* data-
    base, 2006.
"Night of Champagne." (WCU archives). Posted on *Latino Literature* database,
    2006.

Nonfiction Articles

"To the Editor." Letter published in "Between Curtains" section of *Theatre Arts
    Monthly* 19: 6 (June 1935): 469.
"Log of the Show-Bus: The Carolina Playmakers' Thirty-Third Tour." *The
    Carolina Play-Book* 8: 4 (December 1935).
"A Note on Mexican Pronunciation." *The Carolina Play-Book* 9:1 (March 1936);
    and later as Afterword in *Mexican Folk Plays* (with "Spanish" substituted
    for "Mexican").
"Proportion in Writing." *The Writer: The Oldest Magazine for Literary Workers*
    66: 1 (January 1953): 300–301.

Plays

Sorella. First produced in San Antonio, November 18, 1932. Never published;
    script cannot be located.
Tooth or Shave. First produced November 13, 1935. Published in *The Carolina
    Play-Book* in 1936, and in Niggli's anthology *Mexican Folk Plays* 1938.
    Script published by Samuel French, ca. 1939.
The Cry of Dolores. First produced April 25, 1936. Never published (possibly in
    part recreated in *Lightning from the East*, produced in San Antonio
    in 1964).
The Fair God (three-act play). First produced December 3, 1936. Never pub-
    lished in its entirety; an excerpt from final scene in *The Carolina Play-
    Book* 9:4 (December 1936).
Soldadera. First produced February 27, 1936. Published in *The Best One-Act
    Plays of 1937*, ed. Margaret Mayorga, pp. 25–71. New York: Dodd, Mead &
    Company, 1938. Also in Niggli's anthology *Mexican Folk Plays*, and script
    published by Samuel French, ca. 1939.
Azteca. First produced April 25, 1936. Published in Niggli's anthology *Mexican
    Folk Plays*, 1938.
The Red Velvet Goat. First produced April 25, 1936. Published in *One Act
    Play Magazine* 1:3 (July 1937) 250–70; Niggli's anthology *Mexican Folk
    Plays* (1938); *American Folk Plays*, ed. F. H. Koch (D. Appleton-Century
    Company, 1939, 247–75); and in *International Folk Plays* (as a "Mexican"
    play), ed. Samuel Selden, 139–222 (Chapel Hill: University of North
    Carolina Press, 1949). Script published by Samuel French, ca. 1939.

Sunday Costs Five Pesos. First produced April 25, 1936. Published in *One Act Play Magazine* 1:9 (January 1938) 786–820; Niggli's anthology *Mexican Folk Plays* (1938); also appeared in *Best One Act Plays of 1938*; *Invitation to Drama: One Act Plays for Secondary Schools*, ed. Andrew A. Orr (1956; London: Edward Arnold/Macmillan, 1962); *15 International One-Act Plays*, ed. John and Mollie Gassner (New York: Washington Square Press, 1969); and in Américo Paredes, *Mexican American Authors* (Boston: Houghton Mifflin, 1972). Script published by Samuel French, ca. 1939.

Singing Valley (three-act play). First produced July 15, 1936. Niggli's master's thesis, 378.756 Dramatic Arts N686s, University of North Carolina Special Collections. Excerpt from Act II published in *The Carolina Play-Book* 9:4 (December 1936). Published in revised form in *Adventures in Playmaking: Four Plays by Carolina Playmakers*, ed. John W. Parker. Chapel Hill: University of North Carolina Press, 1968, 5–71.

This is Villa! First produced in 1938. Published in *The Best One-Act Plays of 1938*, ed. Margaret Mayorga. New York: Dodd, Mead & Company, 1939; and in *One-Act Play Magazine* 2:7 (January 1939): 611–38.

This Bull Ate Nutmeg. In *Contemporary One-Act Plays*, ed. William Kozlenko (New York: Charles Scribner, 1938), 115–44; and in *Plays without Footlights*, ed. Esther E. Galbraith (New York: Harcourt, Brace, 1945).

Miracle at Blaise. Published in *25 Non-Royalty One-Act Plays for All-Girl Casts*, ed. Betty Smith, 1–21. New York: Greenberg, 1942; and Samuel French, 1946.

The Faces of Deka (under pseudonym Michael Morgan). Published in *25 Non-Royalty One-Act Plays for All-Girl Casts*, ed. Betty Smith, 270–90. New York: Greenberg, 1942.

Crime in Granada (radio play). Fifth play in series "Men in Action" by the Carolina Playmakers of the Air, directed by Earl Wynn (7 February 1942). WCU Special Collections.

The Ring of General Macías. Published in *Twenty Prize-Winning Non-Royalty One-Act Plays*, ed. Betty Smith. New York: Greenburg, 1943; more recently in *Close-up: A Collection of Short Plays*, ed. Sylvia Z. Brodkin. New York: Globe Book Company, 1970 (acknowledging permission from Samuel French); and in a series of Glencoe/McGraw-Hill study texts.

"Bitter Olives: A Comedy in Three Acts." Apparently unproduced and unpublished play. A partial script (complete first two acts and portion of third) is found in folder 381 of the Betty Smith papers (#3837) of the Southern Historical Collection, Manuscripts Department, Wilson Library, the University of North Carolina at Chapel Hill. The script is undated, but has Niggli's 221 King William address in San Antonio on title page.

Sombrero. Screenplay with Norman Foster. Metro-Goldwyn-Mayer, released 1953.

Sunday Costs Five Pesos. Opera. Premiere of Charles Haubiel's version of the
  folk play, with a libretto by Josefina Niggli. Charlotte Opera Association,
  Charlotte, N.C., September 1950.
Serenata. Musical play. Produced with Paul Green for Santa Barbara Old
  Spanish Days Fiesta, California, August 1953 (according to program,
  Niggli wrote the lyrics).
Lightning from the East. Produced for San Jose Mission Fiesta event in San
  Antonio, Texas, 1965 (directed by WCU student Shawn Smith). Never
  published; script cannot be located.

Books

Mexican Folk Plays (anthology of five plays: *Tooth or Shave, Soldadera, The
  Red Velvet Goat, Azteca,* and *Sunday Costs Five Pesos*). Chapel Hill:
  University of North Carolina Press, 1938. Reprinted, Arno, 1976.
Mexican Village. Chapel Hill: University of North Carolina Press, 1945. Also
  released by Sampson, Low, Marston & Co (UK), ca. 1946. Reissued by
  University of New Mexico Press in 1994, with Introduction by María
  Herrera-Sobek.
Pointers on Playwriting. Boston: The Writer, 1945.
Pointers on Radio Writing. Boston: The Writer, 1946.
Step Down, Elder Brother (Book-of-the-Month Club selection). New York:
  Rinehart, 1947. Also released by Sampson Low, Marston & Co. (UK) in
  1949.
Un pueblo mexicano. Trans. Justina Ruíz-de-Conde. New York: Norton, 1949.
A Miracle for Mexico. New York: New York Graphic Society, 1964.
New Pointers on Playwriting (revised and enlarged edition of earlier book).
  Boston: The Writer, 1967.
Apártate Hermano. Trans. David Toscana. Preface by Maria Herrera-Sobek,
  Monterrey: Consejo para la Cultura y las Artes de Nuevo León, Consejo
  Nacional para la Cultura y las Artes, 2003.

Unpublished Novel Fragments:

Beat the Drum Slowly. One hundred and fifty pages of unfinished manuscript
  in WCU Niggli collection.
Farewell, Mama Carlotta. New York Times note in 1949 states that Rinehart
  will soon publish, but no records found.
Green Grow the Rushes. 270 pages of incomplete manuscript in WCU Niggli
  collection, and posted on *Latino Literature* database.

Bibliography

Short items about Niggli appear in various issues of the Incarnate Word student newspaper (with a lot of alumni news). San Antonio, TX: *The Logos* 1: 1 (1935); 1: 4 (1936); 1: 8 (1936); 2: 4 (1937); 4: 4 (1937); 4: 1 (1938); 4: 6 (1939); 6: 6 (1941); 6: 7 (1941); 7: 7 (1942); 9: 1 (1943); 11: 2 (1945); 11: 5 (1945); 13: 5 (1948); 16: 8 (1951).

No author. "Chapel Hill Woman's New Book Gets Much Praise Nationally." *Greensboro Daily News* (14 October 1945).

No author. "People Who Read and Write" (column). *New York Times* (21 December 1947): BR10.

No author. "Books, Authors" (about novel *Farewell, Mama Carlotta* about to be released). *New York Times* (30 August 1949): 25.

No author. "Josephine Niggli Will Be Feted at Dinner by A.A.U.W. Board." *Greensboro Daily News* (13 March 1949).

No author. "Other Historical Activities" section. *American Historical Review* 55: 2 (January 1950): 465–66.

No author. *Memoria del primer congreso de historiadores de México y los Estados Unidos celebrado en la ciudad de Monterrey, Nuevo León, México del 4 al 9 de septiembre de 1949*/Proceedings of the First Congress of Historians from Mexico and the United States Assembled in Monterrey, Nuevo Leon, Mexico, September 4–9, 1949. México: Editorial Cultura, T.G.S.A. (Comisión de Historia/Editorial Cultura), 1950.

No author. "Santa Barbara Prepares for Old Spanish Fiesta." *Los Angeles Times* (9 August 1953).

No author. "Bells to Open Old Spanish Days Fiesta." *Los Angeles Times* (16 August 1953).

No author. "Fourth Annual North Carolina Writers' Conference." *Greensboro Daily News* (15 July 1954).

No author. "Pot Pourri: Teaching Job in Britain." *San Antonio Express* (c.1955).

No author. "Writer's Conference Planned." *Asheville Citizen-Times* (11 May 1958).

No author. "'Four Times One Equals Fun' on Bill in Burbank." *Los Angeles Times* (19 July 1974).

No author. "WCU's First Lady of Theatre Honored in Campus Ceremony."
    Asheville Citizen-Times (10 March 1978).

No author. "Josefina Niggli." Obituary. *North San Antonio Times* (22 December
    1983).

No author. "Josephina Niggli Authored Many Works about Mexico." Obituary.
    San Antonio Light (20 December 1983).

No author. "Josefina Niggli Dies at 73; Poet, Novelist, Educator." *Asheville
    Citizen-Times* (19 December 1983).

No author. "Josephina Niggli." *Latino Literature.* Alexandria, VA: Alexander
    Street Press, 2005. Found under search for authors. Database [PL023738].

Adams, Mildred. "People of Nuevo León." Review of *Mexican Village* by
    Josephina Niggli. *New York Times* (16 December 1945).

———. "Social Evolution in Monterrey." Review of *Step Down, Elder Brother*
    by Josephina Niggli. *New York Times* (8 February 1948).

Aguilar Camín, Héctor, and Lorenzo Meyer. *In the Shadow of the Mexican
    Revolution.* Trans. Luis Alberto Fierro. Austin: University of Texas Press,
    1993.

Anzaldúa, Gloria. *Borderlands/La Frontera: The New Mestiza.* 1987; New York:
    Consortium, 1999.

———. *Making Face, Making Soul/Haciendo Caras: Creative and Critical
    Perspectives by Women of Color.* San Francisco: Aunt Lute Press, 1990.

Armitage, R. H. Review of *Un pueblo mexicano. Hispania* 33: 1 (February
    1950): 84–85.

Arrizón, Alicia. "Soldaderas and the Staging of the Mexican Revolution." *TDR:
    The Drama Review: A Journal of Performance Studies* 42: 1 (157) (Spring
    1998): 90–112.

———. *Latina Performance: Traversing the Stage.* Bloomington: University of
    Indiana Press, 1999.

Asturias, Miguel Ángel. *Leyendas de Guatemala.* 1930; Madrid: Alianza
    Editorial, 1981.

Beardsley, William A. Review of *Un pueblo mexicano,* translator Justina Ruíz-
    de-Conde. *Modern Language Journal* 34: 4 (April 1950): 329–30.

Benítez, Sandra. *The Weight of All Things.* New York: Hyperion, 2000.

Benson, Nettie Lee. "Book Reviews and Notices." *Hispanic American Historical
    Review* 32: 1 (February 1952): 89–91.

Brady, Agnes Marie. "Materials for Teaching Spanish in Elementary and
    Junior High Schools." *Hispania* 42: 3 (September 1959): 385–405.

Brenner, Anita. *The Wind That Swept Mexico: The History of the Mexican
    Revolution, 1910–1942.* Austin: University of Texas Press, 1971.

Brodkin, Sylvia Z., and Elizabeth Pearson, eds. *Close-up: A Collection of Short
    Plays.* New York: Globe Book Company, 1970.

Cabeza de Baca Gilbert, Fabiola. *We Fed Them Cactus.* Albuquerque:

University of New Mexico Press, 1954. Reprinted with Introduction by
   Tey Diana Rebolledo, 1994.
Campobello, Nellie. *Cartucho: Tales of the Struggle in Northern Mexico.* Trans.
   Doris Meyer. Austin: University of Texas Pan American Series, 1988.
Cantrell White, Anne. "Babies Are Babies Pictorially Speaking—Even Crown
   Princes." *Greensboro Daily News* (5 February 1955).
———. "Historian, Novelist, Editor Are Booked for Historical Luncheon."
   Greensboro Daily News (8 January 1955).
Cantú, Norma Elia. *Canícula: Snapshots of a Girlhood en la Frontera.*
   Albuquerque: University of New Mexico Press, 1995.
Carrera, Magali M. *Imagining Identity in New Spain: Race, Lineage, and the
   Colonial Body in Portraiture and Casta Paintings.* Austin: University of
   Texas Press, 2003.
Cauthorn, Julia. No title. Transcript of interview with Niggli recorded on
   April 30, 1979. Held in archives by the Daughters of the Republic of Texas
   at the Alamo in San Antonio, Texas.
Chevigny, Bell Gale. "The Transformation of Privilege in the Work of Elena
   Poniatowska." *Latin American Literary Review* 13: 26 (July–December
   1985).
Cisneros, Sandra. *Caramelo.* New York: Vintage/Random House, 2002.
Claiborne, Jack. "'Hollywood Has Spoiled Me,' Says Chapel Hill's Josephina
   Niggli." *Raleigh News and Observer* (29 March 1953).
———. "N.C. Authoress Says Hollywood 'Spoiled' Her. Josephina Niggli's Book
   Is Filmed; She's Got Lowdown on Movie-Land." *Winston Salem Journal-
   Sentinel* (29 March 1953).
Cook, Helen Fetter. "Two One-Act Operas Get Enthusiastic Reception."
   Charlotte Observer (7 November 1950).
Cranford, Lois. "Josephine Niggli's Book Soon to Be on Screen." *Greensboro
   Daily News* (25 August 1946).
De la Fuente, Daniel. "Llevarán de gira su reino literario." *El Norte* (Mexico),
   sección *Vida* (5 July 2004).
———. "Discuten el vacío en torno a Niggli." *El Norte* (Mexico), sección *Vida*
   (4 June 2004).
———. "Reviven narrativa de pionera." *El Norte* (Mexico), sección *Vida* (1 June
   2004).
———. "Rescatan visión de Josefina Niggli." *El Norte* (Mexico), sección *Vida*
   (29 September 2003).
Díaz del Castillo, Bernal. *La verdadera historia de la conquista de la Nueva
   España.* 3rd ed. México: Editorial Porrúa, 1964.
Deschin, Jacob. "Children's Portraits: A Top Man in the Field Tells His
   Techniques." *New York Times* (30 October 1955).
———. "Children's Pictures: Book by a Psychologist Offers Advice on Posing."
   New York Times (20 March 1949).

Dobie, J. Frank. *Guide to Life and Literature of the Southwest.* Austin:
    University of Texas Press, 1943.
Domincovich, Harry. "Latin American Literature for the English Classroom."
    The English Journal 31: 8 (October 1942): 594.
Elliott, David, ed. *Tierra y Libertad! Photographs of Mexico, 1890–1935, from
    the Casasola Archive.* New York: St. Martin's Press, 1986.
Ernst, Robert, and George Stumpf. *Deadly Affrays: The Violent Deaths of the
    U.S. Marshals.* Avon, IN: ScarletMask Enterprises, 2005.
Fisher, Dexter, ed. *The Third Woman: Minority Women Writers of the United
    States.* Boston: Houghton Mifflin, 1980.
Fitterer, Gary P. "Part Three: F. Thumm, Der Revolverheld von Deutschland."
    NOLA 15: 2 (April–June 1991).
Freeman Lee, Amy. "Playmaker of Mexico." *San Antonio Express-News* (4 June
    1939).
Fuentes, Carlos. *La nueva novela hispanoamericana.* 1969; México: Joaquín
    Mortíz, 1980.
Galbraith, Esther E., ed. *Plays without Footlights.* New York: Harcourt, Brace,
    1945.
Garro, Elena. *Recollections of Things to Come.* Austin: University of Texas
    Press, 1986.
Gassner, John, and Mollie Gassner, compilers. *15 International One-Act Plays.*
    Introduction by Morris Sweetkind. New York: Washington Square Press,
    1969.
Gillin, John. Review of *Mexican Village. Social Forces* 24: 4 (May 1946): 476–77.
Glusker, Susannah Joel. *Anita Brenner: A Mind of Her Own.* Austin: University
    of Texas Press, 1998.
González, Jovita. *Caballero: An Historical Novel.* Ed. José E. Limón and María
    Cotera. College Station: Texas A&M University Press, 1996.
———. *Dew on the Thorn.* Ed. José E. Limón. Houston: Arte Público Press,
    1997.
Guerrero, Vicente. "Breves." *El Norte* (Mexico), sección *Vida* (29 May 2004).
Hamill, Pete. Introduction. *Mexico: The Revolution and Beyond, Photographs
    by Agustín Víctor Casasola, 1900–1940.* New York: Aperture Foundation,
    in cooperation with Conaculta-INAH (Mexico City), 2003.
Hopkins, W. Wat. "Josephina Niggli—an Exciting Teacher." *The Western
    Carolinian* (4 March 1971): 3.
Hoyle, Bernadette. "Josephina Niggli Going to England." *Raleigh News and
    Observer* (3 July 1955).
Jason, Rick. *Scrapbooks of My Mind: A Hollywood Autobiography by Rick
    Jason.* Argoe Publishing, 2000. Maintained on website http://www.scrap-
    booksofmymind.com/
Jones, Willis Knapp. "Shop-Talk: Latin America through Drama in English: A
    Bibliography." *Hispania* 28: 2 (May 1945): 223.

Kean, Claude. Review of *Mexican Village*. *The Americas* 2: 4 (April 1946): 534–35.

Kelly, Edith L. Review of *Step Down, Elder Brother*. *The Americas* 5: 3 (Jan 1949): 367–69.

Keresztesi, Rita. "Romancing the Borderlands: Josefina Niggli's *Mexican Village*." In *Doubled Plots, Romance and History*, ed. Susan Strehle and Mary Paniccia Carden. Jackson: University Press of Mississippi, 2003.

Koch, Frederick H. *American Folk Plays*. New York: D. Appleton-Century Company, 1939.

Kozlenko, William, ed. *Contemporary One-Act Plays*. New York: Charles Scribner, 1938.

Leh, Carol. "Hollywood's Version of Niggli Story." *Durham Morning Herald* (15 February 1953).

———. "In Mexico: Chapel Hill Writer Assists with Filming of Her Book." *Raleigh News and Observer* (15 February 1953).

———. "'Village' to Become a Film." *Raleigh News and Observer* (12 January 1952).

Linhard, Tabea Alexa. "Adelita's Act of Counter-Writing." *Dressing Up for War: Transformations of Gender and Genre in the Discourse and Literature of War*. New York: Rodopi, 2001.

Locklair, Wink. "Miss Niggli Going to England and Ireland on Fellowship from Rockefeller Foundation." *Chapel Hill Weekly* (25 August 1950).

———. "Writing on Schedule." *Durham Morning Herald* (10 September 1950).

Martinez, Elizabeth Coonrod. "Resistance, Revolution and Recuperation: The Literary Production of the *Mestizo*/Mexican-American/Chicano." In *A Companion to U.S. Latino Literature*, ed. Carlota Caulfield and Darien Davis, 12–36. Suffolk, UK: Tamesis/Boydell & Brewer, 2007.

———. Introduction. *Lilus Kikus and Other Stories by Elena Poniatowska*. Albuquerque: University of New Mexico Press, 2005.

———. "The Cultural Significance of Maya Themes in U.S. Latino/Chicano Literature." *Community College Humanities Review* 22: 1, special issue on the Maya (Fall 2001): 114–30.

Martinez, Julio A. *Chicano Scholars and Writers: A Bio-Bibliographical Directory*. Metuchen, NJ: Scarecrow Press, 1979.

Marshall, Douglas. Personal interview conducted on October 10, 2006.

Mastretta, Ángeles. *Tear This Heart Out*. Trans. Margaret Sayers Peden. New York: Riverhead Trade, 1998.

Mayorga, Margaret, ed. *The Best One-Act Plays of 1937*. New York: Dodd, Mead & Company, 1938.

———. ed. *The Best One-Act Plays of 1938*. New York: Dodd, Mead & Company, 1939.

McFee, William. "The Reviews: Josephina Niggli's Outstanding Novel." *New York Sun* (22 January 1948).

Mena, María Cristina. *The Collected Stories of María Cristina Mena.* Ed. Amy
    Doherty. Houston: Arte Público Press, 1997.

Merlin, Milton. "Conflict of Old and New in Mexico Portrayed." Review of
    Step Down, Elder Brother by Josephina Niggli. *Los Angeles Times* (22
    February 1948).

Michael, James E. Review of *International Folk Plays* (1949), ed. Samuel
    Selden. *Educational Theatre Journal* 2: 3 (October 1950): 266–67.

Moraga, Cherríe. *The Hungry Woman: A Mexican Medea*, and *Heart of the
    Earth: A Popul Vuh Story* (two plays). Albuquerque: West End Press, 2001.

Orr, Andrew A., ed. *Invitation to Drama: One Act Plays for Secondary Schools.*
    London: Edward Arnold/Macmillan, 1956.

Padilla, Yolanda. "Reading the Folk: Revolution and Genre in Josephina
    Niggli's *Mexican Village*." Unpublished selection from dissertation found
    on author's Internet site at University of Chicago: uchicago.edu/~aypadill/
    padilla-diss-abstract.pdf

Paredes, Américo, and Raymund Paredes. *Mexican American Authors.* Boston:
    Houghton Mifflin, 1972.

Paredes, Raymund A. "The Evolution of Chicano Literature." *MELUS* 5: 2
    (Summer 1978): 71–110 (88–91 for Niggli).

———. "Teaching Chicano Literature: An Historical Approach." *The Heath
    Anthology of American Literature,* 2d ed. Online at: http://www.george-
    town.edu/tamlit/essays/chicano.html

———. "West View: Up from Obscurity: Voices of Mexican-American
    Literature." *Los Angeles Times* (9 November 1980): M3.

Parker, John W, ed. *Adventures in Playmaking: Four Plays by Carolina
    Playmakers.* Chapel Hill: University of North Carolina Press, 1968.

Parker, William C. "Door Locked on Josephina Niggli Forced Her to Write
    First Story." *Raleigh News and Observer* (29 February 1948).

Peacock, Bill. "Miss Niggli Finds Writing for Movies Is Difficult." *Greensboro
    Daily News* (12 February 1952).

Poniatowska, Elena. *Las soldaderas.* Mexico: Ediciones Era/Conaculta-INAH,
    1999.

———. *Here's to You, Jesusa.* New York: Farrar, Straus & Giroux, 2001.

Poole, Stafford. *Our Lady of Guadalupe: The Origins and Sources of a Mexican
    National Symbol, 1531–1797.* Tucson: University of Arizona Press, 1995.

Poore, Charles. "Books of the Times." Review of *Step Down, Elder Brother* by
    Josephina Niggli. *New York Times* (31 January 1948).

Portillo-Trambley, Estela. *Trini.* Binghamton, NY: Bilingual Press, 1986.

———. *Sor Juana and Other Plays.* Ypsilanti, MI: Bilingual Press, 1983.

———. *Rain of Scorpions.* Berkeley, CA: Tonatiuh International, 1975.

Prescott, Orville. "Books of the Times." Review of *Mexican Village* by Josephina Niggli. *New York Times* (16 October 1945).

Pryor, Thomas M. "Metro Schedules 'Mexican Village.'" *New York Times* (2 September 1952).

Rebolledo, Tey Diana. *Women Singing in the Snow: A Cultural Analysis of Chicana Literature.* Tucson: University of Arizona Press, 1995.

Rey, Agapito. Review of *Mexican Village. Journal of American Folklore* 60: 237 (July 1947): 326–27.

Rothwell, John. "Focus on 'Sombrero' below the Border." *New York Times* (18 September 1952).

Salazar Parr, Carmen, and Genevieve M. Ramírez. "The Female Hero in Chicano Literature." In *Beyond Stereotypes: The Critical Analysis of Chicana Literature,* ed. María Herrera-Sobek. Binghamton, NY: Bilingual Press, 1985.

Schallert, Edwin. "The Best Pictures Earn Praise—But Rest Make Money." *Los Angeles Times* (16 August 1953).

Schneider, Josef. *Child Photography, the Modern Way.* Baltimore, MD: The Camera, Inc., 1949.

Selden, Samuel, ed. *International Folk Plays.* Chapel Hill: University of North Carolina Press, 1949.

Shirley, Paula, and Carl Shirley. Personal interview conducted with Niggli at her home in Cullowhee, on June 29, 1980 (recording).

———. "Josefina Niggli." In *Dictionary of Literary Biography Yearbook 1980,* ed. Karen L. Rood, Jean W. Ross, and Richard Zeigfeld, 279–86. Detroit: Gale, 1981.

———. "Death of Mexican Novelist." *Hispania* 67: 4 (December 1983): 655.

Smith, Betty, ed. *25 Non-Royalty One-Act Plays for All-Girl Casts.* New York: Greenberg, 1942.

———, ed. *Twenty Prize-Winning Non-Royalty One-Act Plays.* New York: Greenberg, 1943.

Smith, Cecil. "Throngs Greeted at Santa Barbara." *Los Angeles Times* (20 August 1953).

Spearman, Walter, with the assistance of Samuel Selden. *The Carolina Playmakers: The First Fifty Years.* Chapel Hill: University of North Carolina Press, 1970.

Terry, C. V. "Curtain Going Up." *New York Times* (4 November 1945).

Valdés, Hugo. "Josephina Niggli: La precursora invisible." *El Norte* (Mexico), sección *Vida* (23 November 2002).

Verástique, Bernardino. *Michoacán and Eden: Vasco de Quiroga and the Evangelization of Western Mexico.* Austin: University of Texas Press, 2000.

Wolcott, Mary Ellen. "Josefina Niggli: Pages from a Creative Career." *Asheville Citizen-Times* (19 March 1978).

Doctoral Dissertations with considerable reference to Niggli's works

Bost, Suzanne Michelle. "Mulattas and Mestizas: Mixed Identity in Women's Writing of the Americas, 1850–1996 (Creoles)." Vanderbilt University, 0242. DAI 58, no. 08A (1997).

Lópes, Shirley. "Remembering the Brave Women: Chicana Literature on the Texas-Mexico Border, 1900–1950." University of Iowa (65: 4). DAI 3129320, ISSN: 0419–4209 (2004).

Nieves, Ervin. "Beyond Darwinism: Chicana/o Literature and Modern Scientific Literary Analysis: A Biographical, Historical, and Interdisciplinary Reappraisal of the Literary Works of Josefina Niggli and Oscar Zeta Acosta." University of Iowa. DAI, no. 3158008 (2005).

Padilla, Yolanda. "Indian Mexico: The Changing Face of Indigeneity in Mexican American Literature, 1910–1984 (María Cristina Mena, Josephina Niggli, Arturo Islas)." DAI, Section A (65: 10) 2005 April, 3809. University of Chicago. DA 3149349 (2004).

Treat, Rita Keresztesi. "Strangers at Home: Ethnic Modernism between the World Wars." University of California, Santa Cruz, 0036. DAI 61, no. 07A (1999).

Velasquez Treviño, Gloria Louise. "Cultural Ambivalence in Early Chicana Prose Fiction (Mexican-American)." Stanford University, 0212. DAI 46, no. 08A (1985).

Index